KNIGHTLEY, Phillip

# AN AFFAIR
# OF STATE

# AN AFFAIR OF STATE

## THE PROFUMO CASE
## AND THE
## FRAMING OF STEPHEN WARD

*Phillip Knightley*
*and*
*Caroline Kennedy*

JONATHAN CAPE
THIRTY-TWO BEDFORD SQUARE
LONDON

For Elisar, Mayumi, Jasmine, Aliya, Marisa and Kim —
and for Stephen Ward

First published 1987
Copyright © 1987 by Phillip Knightley and Caroline Kennedy

Jonathan Cape Ltd, 32 Bedford Square, London WC1B 3EL

British Library Cataloguing in Publication Data

Knightley, Phillip
An affair of state: the Profumo case and
the framing of Stephen Ward
1. Profumo, John D.   2. Ward, Stephen
3. Great Britain—Politics and government—1945–
I. Title   II. Kennedy, Caroline
941.085'6'0924   DA591.P7
ISBN 0-224-02347-0

Printed in Great Britain by
Mackays of Chatham Ltd

# CONTENTS

Introduction   xi

Acknowledgments   xvi

1 Scandal in High Places   1

2 The Crusading Osteopath   11

3 Ward Cracks the Social Scene   19

4 A Magnet for Girls   25

5 A Rising Star in the Tory Party   33

6 The Waif and the Crooked Businessman   37

7 Delightful Days at Cliveden   46

8 The Promiscuous Showgirl   53

9 Living Together   58

10 The Artist and the Royals   61

11 Enter Ivanov, Soviet Spy   67

12 Mandy and Christine Run Riot   78

13 Astor's Summer Swimming Party   84

14 Playing International Politics   90

15 Wigg Seeks Revenge   93

16 The FBI and the London Call Girl   97

17 The New York Caper   100

18 Cooling the Cuban Missile Crisis   105

19 Problems with Profumo   113

20 A Knife Fight in Soho   117

21 A Shooting in Marylebone   121

22 Ward Stops the Presses   129

23 The Police Show Interest   138

24 The Scandal Begins to Break   144

25 The Boil is Lanced   148

26 The Move to Silence Ward   161

27 Cooking a Case   168

vi                          CONTENTS

28  Ward Fights Back                         177
29  Profumo Confesses                        181
30  The Government Endangered                189
31  Save John F. Kennedy                     197
32  Ward's Faith in Justice                  208
33  The Trial of the Century                 212
34  A Spirited Defence                       228
35  An Unprecedented Intervention            236
36  The Need for a Sacrifice                 241
37  To Disappoint the Vultures               244
38  Mystery, Whitewash and Retribution       248
    Select Bibliography                      261
    Index                                    263

# ILLUSTRATIONS

PLATES

*Between pages 76–7*

1 Stephen Ward in Kirksville, Missouri, 1937
2 Ward's marriage to Patricia Baines, 1949
3 Eunice Bailey
4 Ward with Kim and Kay Kendall and Freda Fairchild Ferrier
5 Ward with Maureen Swanson and Arthur Ferrier
6 John Lewis
7 Frederic Mullally
8 Joy Lewis and Suzanne Mullally
9 Cliveden
10 Nancy Astor, with her son and grandson
11 Douglas Fairbanks, Jnr and his wife and daughter at her coming-out party, 1957
12 Ward's cottage at Cliveden
13 Vickie Martin
14 Margaret Brown
15 John Profumo
16 Profumo with his wife, Valerie Hobson
17 An engagement portrait
18 Christine Keeler, Murray's Club showgirl
19 Her family home at Wraysbury
20 Mandy Rice-Davies
21 Peter Rachman and his wife, Audrey
22 One of Rachman's properties
23 Yevgeny Ivanov, with his wife, Maya
24 Ivanov, as sketched by Ward
25 Sir Colin Coote, editor of the *Daily Telegraph*
26 Sir Roger Hollis, Director-General of MI5
27 Oleg Penkovsky
28 President Kennedy with Nikita Khrushchev

29 Bronwen Pugh
30 Lord Astor
31 The swimming pool at Cliveden
32 Hod Dibben marries Mariella Novotny
33 Mariella arrives at a New York court
34 Harry Alan Towers
35 Dr Teddy Sugden
36 John Profumo as a Privy Councillor
37 Lucky Gordon
38 Christine Keeler
39 Nubar Gulbenkian, his wife, and John Profumo
40 Paul Getty with Madame Mary Tessiers
41 Ward's consulting rooms in Devonshire Street

*Between pages 172–3*

42 Ward after his release on bail
43 Michael Eddowes
44 William Shepherd, MP
45 Sir Godfrey Nicholson, MP
46 Ward's flat, scene of the shooting
47 Paul Mann and Christine Keeler
48 Lucky Gordon being ejected from the Old Bailey
49 Harold Wilson
50 George Wigg
51 Lord Hailsham with Sir William Haley, editor of *The Times*
52 Profumo and his wife at the races
53 Harold Macmillan with President Kennedy
54 Macmillan out grouse-shooting
55 William Rees-Davies, QC
56 Robin Drury with the Keeler tape
57 Mandy apprehended at Heathrow
58 Profumo after his resignation
59 Lucky Gordon with his lawyer
60 Rudolph Fenton
61 Christine Keeler and Paula Hamilton-Marshall
62 Lucky Gordon and John Hamilton-Marshall
63 The policemen
64 Ward leaves the Magistrate's Court for Brixton Prison
65 Mervyn Griffith-Jones
66 Mr Justice Marshall
67 Lord Chief Justice Parker
68 James Burge

69 Stephen Ward
70 Christine Keeler
71 The Duke of Edinburgh sits for Vasco Lazzolo
72 Noel Howard-Jones
73 Vickie Barrett and Brenda O'Neil
74 Ronna Ricardo
75 Two anonymous prosecution witnesses
76 Christine Keeler and Paula Hamilton-Marshall
77 Crowds waiting for the verdict
78 Ward is carried unconscious to hospital
79 An official bulletin
80 Crowds outside the hospital
81 At Mortlake Crematorium
82 Lord Denning with his files

Cartoon by Trog in *Private Eye, page 192*.

You sad Andronici, have done with woes!
Give sentence on this execrable wretch
That hath been breeder of these dire events.
Set him breast-deep in earth, and famish him,
There let him stand and rave and cry for food.
If anyone relieves or pities him,
For the offence he dies.

TITUS ANDRONICUS
William Shakespeare

# INTRODUCTION

It was in the attic of an old English farmhouse, on a lovely autumn evening in September 1984, that this book had its beginnings. Two years earlier Caroline Kennedy, doing some research for a television film, had arrived at this same house to interview the owner. As they talked she found out he was an old friend of her late brother-in-law, Dominick Elwes.

Later in the day the discussion turned to Elwes's friendship with Dr Stephen Ward, the society osteopath, who had committed suicide at the height of the Profumo scandal in 1963. Elwes, her host said, had stood bail for Stephen Ward, had worked with him on a proposed television programme about his life and had produced a film entitled, *The Christine Keeler Story*. In a trunk in his attic, he explained, he had tape recordings and scripts which Elwes had given him years ago. Would she be interested in taking a look some time? Caroline Kennedy was intrigued. Like nearly everyone else she remembered the Profumo scandal but only faintly remembered Ward.

So, on her return visit that autumn evening, after riffling through the contents of the trunk, she returned home with a box full of old letters, voluminous pages of handwritten and typed filmscript and reels of tape. She immediately transferred the tapes on to cassettes and, through the scratchy quality of the 1960s' recordings, emerged Ward's compelling voice:

This whole business developed so gradually that the increasing horror of my situation did not become apparent to me for some time. Everyone is lying to grind his own axe. Every witness who does not give the answer the police want is tampered with. Every person who goes abroad has fled. Every person who speaks for me does so from fear. Every motive I had is twisted. All I have left between me and destruction is a handful of firm friends, the integrity of the judge and the 12 men on the jury. God alone knows what will happen. I know that one day the truth will eventually come out. And the truth is very simple: I loved people – of all types – and I don't think that there are very many people the worse for having known me. This is the whole story . . .

Caroline Kennedy listened to Ward with absolute fascination. 'Only a week earlier I'd heard Lord Denning on TV saying that Ward was the most evil man he had ever met. Ward hardly sounded like an evil man to me. He was rational, intelligent, persuasive. I knew as little about Ward as the next person but I began to wonder. Had we got him wrong? I decided to try to find out.'

In many ways it was an ideal time to take another look at Ward and the Profumo affair. Enough time had passed for the passions and divisions it had aroused to quieten. Many of those involved were still alive and perhaps ready now to reveal matters that at the time had been concealed.

Until I joined her in the spring of 1985, Caroline Kennedy had worked alone, becoming more and more involved in Ward's life, often travelling hundreds of miles in a day in the hope of finding one elusive fragment, or to check one significant anecdote. But the information she had gathered about Ward's relationship with the British Security Service, MI5, made her realise that she would need the help of someone more experienced in this field. My one doubt about the project – that it would be unfair to turn the spotlight on Profumo yet again – yielded to her argument that the story would concentrate on Ward, not Profumo.

The quest for the truth took us all over Britain, to the United States and to Europe. In the end, the raw research broke down into four major areas: Ward's own tape-recorded words; interviews with some 80 of his friends and enemies; a folio of FBI documents obtained under the American Freedom of Information Act; and our own interpretation and analysis of all this new information.

Ward's tape recordings were more extensive than we at first realised. In them he spoke frankly of his early life, his first sexual experiences, his student days in the United States, his wartime service in Britain and India, his early struggles in a London just coming out of its post-war gloom, his ambition, and his steady climb to success both as an osteopath and as an artist. We get his story of his recruitment into MI5, his version of his relationship with Christine Keeler and Mandy Rice-Davies and his account of his close friendship with Lord Astor. Finally we hear Ward's devastatingly accurate assessment of why he was framed.

The interviews proved the most difficult part of the research. At first those people who had known Ward were wary. We had to assure them that we had no preconceived view and were determined to produce a rounded picture of an obviously very complex character. Slowly doors opened. In the end we knew the versions of every major participant in the drama who is still alive (except Profumo). Many had never spoken before.

Ward's friends and enemies, including Lucky Gordon, Lord Denning, Ward's lawyers, FBI informers, the CIA officer in charge of the case in London, nearly every member of the Astor family, Douglas Fairbanks Jnr, various MPs involved in the affair, and, most important, those members of the police team handling the Ward case, agreed to tell their stories. Most spoke directly to us; one or two, for personal reasons, preferred intermediaries.

Two policemen in particular, conscience-stricken over what had happened, spoke for the record of what the police were told to do, how they did it, and how they felt when Ward killed himself. MI5 officers, now retired, revealed exactly how the service recruited Ward, what it wanted him to do, how he did it, and how it was decided to dump him when the service's links with him threatened to become too embarrassing. One officer says that MI5 should have revealed Ward's role – 'if we had he might be alive today' – but it was decided to cover up.

An American who had close links at that time with the United States Embassy held back a vital piece of information until he had read the first draft of the manuscript. Then he gave evidence that the Prime Minister, Harold Macmillan, had been told of Profumo's involvement with Christine Keeler two months before Profumo made his statement to the House of Commons denying any impropriety. This gave the political part of the affair an entirely new significance.

It will be impossible for anyone ever to duplicate this research because several of the major characters have since died, and others, for various reasons, have retreated into silence again. Sir David Tudor-Price, who as a junior barrister was the defence number two in the Ward trial, braved the Lord Chancellor's ire by agreeing to an on-the-record interview in which he was highly critical of the way the legal establishment had handled the case. He died suddenly only a few months after his elevation to the High Court.

Although we knew that we risked an action against us for contempt of court, we were able to locate and interview one of the Ward jurors who told, on the promise of anonymity, what had gone on in the jury room. He revealed why the jury had decided to convict Ward, even though the jurors were very impressed by him. We found and interviewed a senior civil servant who attended a meeting of Ward's friends at which it was decided that no one would give evidence on Ward's behalf. We persuaded Astor's brother, David, to tell us why Astor himself had decided to abandon Ward.

Because a lot of people were now prepared to talk, we were able to identify some of those participants who had mysteriously escaped publicity at the trial. Mandy Rice-Davies's lover, the 'Indian doctor', who was not even called as a witness, turns out to have been Dr Emil Savundra, later to be notorious because of the Fire Auto and Marine insurance case which cost Britain's motorists hundreds of thousands of pounds. Christine's lover, 'Charles', also avoided the spotlight because Christine swore on oath that she could not remember his surname. We discovered that he was the millionaire businessman Charles Clore.

The role of Dr Teddy Sugden, the well-known society abortionist of the period, took some unravelling but we eventually established his relationship with Christine Keeler and Stephen Ward. The part that the famous Murray's Club, with its beautiful 'showgirls', played in the affair puzzled us until some of the club's former employees and some of its distinguished former members explained it all.

After many hours in the FBI library in Washington, we finally obtained an FBI secret file. This consisted of about 800 heavily-censored pages headed 'Profumo-Keeler, Russian Intelligence' and, later, 'Operation Bowtie'. This material enabled us to learn the reason for the panic in the United States over the Profumo affair, to explain why the head of the FBI, J. Edgar Hoover, was so obsessed with it, and why the Kennedy family was so worried.

New information about the way Ward's trial was conducted and new interpretation of the part played by Lord Justice Parker and the Court of Criminal Appeal made it crystal clear that the British legal establishment did everything in its power to make certain that Ward would be convicted. This is a serious charge to make, so to give it weight we interviewed some of the leading jurists of the period who gave us, for the first time, their opinion of what was done to Ward. One, a High Court Judge, was unable to talk about the case, even so many years later, without bitterness and anger, while Lord Goodman had no hesitation in describing Ward as 'the historic victim of an historic injustice', likening him to 'a British Dreyfus'.

When we got down to interpreting the research material, the motives of the major characters began to emerge with frightening clarity. We learnt why George Wigg was out to get Profumo; why John Lewis, Labour MP, was determined to ruin Ward; why the police set out to frame Lucky Gordon; why Christine Keeler and

Mandy Rice-Davies told the stories they did; and why the legal establishment put its weight behind the move to send Ward away for a long time.

We were able to see what part Ward and the Russian GRU officer, Yevgeny Ivanov, played during the Cuban missile crisis when the super powers took the world to the brink of atomic war. What at the time was considered to be one of Ward's fantasies turned out to have been true. This added a whole new dimension to Ward's life and the espionage section of the book became a major one.

In the course of our interviews, we learnt how the principal characters have come to terms with that traumatic period of their lives, how they have coped — or have failed to cope — with what the scandal did to them. Some have achieved fame and fortune; others have gone under with scarcely a ripple. Some have difficulty even recalling what occurred; others relive it day by day. One continues to live in the same area and to follow the same profession. Another went into exile abroad, disgusted that in Britain Ward could have been treated in the way that he was.

When we pulled all these threads together we found that we had an entirely new account of the Profumo affair. It is a story of sexual compulsion, political malice, jealousy, envy and hate. It is a story of friendship, loyalty, honour, betrayal, and the forces of the State bent upon the destruction of one abandoned individual, the only one to leave the scene with dignity. In the end it is our hope that this book says something for Stephen Ward: it may not be too late for the truth.

*London, January 1987*                          PHILIP KNIGHTLEY AND
                                                CAROLINE KENNEDY

# ACKNOWLEDGMENTS

Our thanks go to John Bennett and Georgina Yates at the Metropolitan Police Press Office for their help in locating retired police officers, to the staff at Canford School, Dorset for looking up old school records, and to Tricia Chamberlain for transcribing hours of tapes. We are obliged to Mr Wayle at the City of Westminster Coroner's Court for kindly producing the autopsy documents, the Federal Bureau of Investigation Library in Washington, DC for their declassified information, and librarian David Fletcher at the Tank Museum of the Royal Armoured Corps and the Royal Tank Regiment in Bovington for looking up Stephen Ward's army records.

We would also like to express our appreciation to Peter Harris of the *Washington Post* for arranging the use of their library, to David Warner and Jan Faull from ITN Film Library and the staff of the BBC Television Film and Archives Library for searching for relevant film clips. Thanks, too, to seven former students of the Kirksville College of Osteopathy and Surgery, Missouri for sharing their memories, among them, Dr Burnham Brooke, Dr Ron Hargrett, Dr William McClurg, Dr John Montgomery, and, in particular, Emily Kenney Jackson, who graciously lent her photographs, scrapbook and a copy of the College Yearbook, the *Osteoblast*, in which Dr Stephen Ward was singled out in appreciation by the Class of January 1938 for 'his inspirational Graduation address'.

We are grateful to Pat Knopf and Tom Stewart of Atheneum Publishers, New York for their immediate interest, to Chris Jones, the Medical Director of A. H. Robins Ltd, for his explanation about the early medical trials and applications of Doxapram and to the secretary of Nashtam Abbey for information regarding the exorcisms by Dom Robert Petitpierre at Cliveden. Thanks also to the relevant staff at the Newspaper Library, Colindale, the British Library, the Public Affairs Office in Washington, DC, the John F. Kennedy Memorial Library, the Public Record Office, London, Andy Roth at Parliamentary Profiles, and the various photo libraries for their help.

Personal interviews proved an incalculably rich source of anecdotes, impressions and information. To all those who agreed to share their memories, named or anonymous, our thanks. Of the former we must mention: Mrs Bronwen Astor, the Hon. David Astor, Lady Philippa Astor, Dr Samuel and Dr Dorothy Ball, Alexandra Wilson Chambers and family, Warwick Charlton, Lord Denning, Horace 'Hod' Dibben, Peter Earle, Michael Eddowes, Douglas Fairbanks Jnr. KBE, Freda Fairchild Ferrier, Jan Forman, Lucky Gordon, Logan Gourlay, PC Derek Ingram, John Kennedy, Ludovic Kennedy, Leila Lazzolo, Hugh Leggatt, Tom Mangold, Beecher Moore, Harry Myers, R. Barry O'Brien, Jon Pertwee, Michael Pertwee, Jocelyn Proby, Mandy Rice-Davies, Archibald B. Roosevelt Jnr, Annie Ross, William Shepherd, Dr Ellis Stungo, Feliks Topolski, Harry Alan Towers, Claus Von Bulow, Nigel West and others too numerous to credit here but who, by willingly giving up their time to assist us, made our task that much easier.

A special thanks for their invaluable recollections, support and tolerance goes to the following: Thomas Corbally for his constant encouragement and for trusting us with his knowledge of the American activities, to Harry Cox, former chief Librarian of Mirror Group Newspapers, for expertly coping with requests for all the press cuttings of the period, to retired police officers Arthur Eustace and Mike Glasse and to the anonymous juror who all agreed the time had finally come to talk publicly. Thanks too to Lord Goodman for devoting time to reading the manuscript on behalf of John Profumo, to Noel Howard-Jones for his unfaltering loyalty to Stephen Ward and for reliving the years 1960–3 for us, and to Yvonne Knightley for her expert typing skills.

Thanks are also due to Frederic Mullally, Jeff Selznick and Margaret Brown Styne for their very detailed impressions of Stephen Ward between 1945 and 1961 and for being determined to set the record straight, to James Burge and the late Sir David Tudor-Price for their invaluable recollections of the trial, to Tim Vigors for Stephen Ward's family background and to our editor, Jill Sutcliffe, and designer, Ian Craig, for their respective skills.

This list cannot possibly be complete without extending our gratitude to David Ya!lop for his belief in the early development and research of the book, for his close personal interest in the subject and, above all, for his inspired introduction to Tom Maschler, whose immediate and continuing enthusiasm for the project intoxicated all around him and made it all seem so easy. Finally, we owe an enormous debt of gratitude to John Zieger, whose previous friendship with Stephen Ward and whose work commitments never once clouded his ability to tackle an endless barrage of legal questions, queries and problems without bias, pre-judgment or complaint. To all these and many more we extend our thanks.

The authors and publishers would like to thank the following for permission to reproduce illustrations: BBC Hulton Picture Library (Plates, nos 5, 16, 31, 39, 40, 50, 57, 61, 64, 65, 66, 70, 75, 77, 78, 79); Camera Press (nos 17, 20, 24, 27, 71, 82); Robert Hunt Library (nos 46, 51, 56, 62); Photosource (nos 6, 7, 9, 10, 12, 14, 15, 22, 26, 29, 30, 32, 34, 37, 41, 48, 52, 60, 68, 69, 73, 74, 80, 81); Popperfoto (nos 2, 11, 18, 19, 21, 23, 28, 33, 36, 42, 49, 59, 72, 76); Press Association (nos 43, 67); S & G Press Agency (nos 8, 35, 45, 55); Topham Picture Library (nos 3, 13, 25, 38, 44, 53, 58), and Trog and *Private Eye* for the cartoon on page 192. Other pictures are from private sources (Plates, nos 1, 4, 63). They also thank the *News of the World* and *Woman's World* for permission to quote from articles and reports.

PK and CK

'This is a political revenge trial. Someone had to be sacrificed and that someone was me.' – Stephen Ward to a journalist at the Old Bailey, 1963.

'Society created him, used him, ruthlessly destroyed him, and then closed ranks around his body.' – Kenneth Tynan in a television interview after Ward's death.

# 1 | *Scandal in High Places*

Friday, 28 June 1963 was one of those steamy, London summer days. There had been showers of rain followed by bursts of sunshine since early morning, so by 10.30 a.m., Marylebone Magistrate's Court, once a public baths, was like a sauna. For although the tiny and distinctly seedy No. 2 courtroom was designed to accommodate 30–40 people, 120 were now crammed into the public gallery, the press area, and the lawyers' benches.

Despite the discomfort, the lack of windows, and the depressing atmosphere, no one showed any sign of wanting to surrender his place to the hundreds still waiting outside. They had all come to see – some to take part in – the beginning of what promised to be one of the trials of the century, that of Dr Stephen Ward, 50, a London society osteopath. Ward was charged with a variety of violations of the Sexual Offences Act of 1956, including brothel-keeping, procuring, living on the earnings of prostitutes, and abortion offences, all – in the archaic language of English law – 'against the peace of our sovereign lady The Queen, her crown and dignity'.

Marylebone Court, covering as it does the fashionable area of London's West End, was well accustomed to hearing such charges. They usually rated a column or two in the local weekly newspaper, but seldom made the national press. In a city like London, which drew young people from all over the world seeking to advance a career, find a fortune, meet the opposite sex, or simply enjoy themselves, pimps, prostitutes, brothel keepers, and abortionists flourished. True, prostitutes no longer lined Park Lane as they had done in the 1950s, the 1959 Street Offences Act having banished them from the streets. They now operated from flats and rooms, and providing they did so discreetly, the law left them and their pimps largely alone. In the year before Ward's trial, for example, the authorities had successfully prosecuted 160 men for pimping, dealing with them all in the lower courts and in most cases imposing only a fine.

It was already abundantly clear, however, that Ward's case was going to be very different. To begin with, Ward was famous and well-connected. He moved in London society on three different levels. First there were people who had come to him because of his remarkable skill as an osteopath. A graduate of the Kirksville College of Osteopathy and Surgery, Missouri, USA, Ward had a full American medical degree and was entitled to practise in the United States in all areas of medicine. His sympathies lay with osteopathy, the art of treating diseases by removing structural derangements of the body, especially of the spine, by manipulation. Ward had 'healing hands' and had quickly attracted to him a list of patients from all over the world. They were often rich, prominent, and talented. Over the years he had treated prime ministers, ambassadors, royalty, politicians, film stars, authors, international businessmen, sportsmen and academics.

He treated Winston Churchill and his son, Randolph, Sir Anthony Eden, Hugh Gaitskell, Nancy, Lady Astor and her son, Lord Astor, Averell Harriman, Paul Getty, Nubar Gulbenkian, Joseph Kennedy, Elizabeth Taylor and Mike Todd, Danny Kaye, Robert Taylor, Mary Martin, Douglas Fairbanks Jnr, Frank Sinatra and Ava Gardner, the Maharajahs of Jaipur, Cooch Behar, and Baroda, King Peter of Yugoslavia, Prince Christian of Hanover, Jack Hylton, Sir Alan Herbert, Sir Malcolm Sargent, Sir Thomas Beecham and Lord Rothermere. His patients spanned all walks of life, from the British carpet king, Cyril Lord, to the Indian political leader, Mahatma Gandhi. They all found relief from pain and discomfort at Ward's hands.

Then there was Ward's other gift, as a portrait artist. Working in pencil and crayon he could produce striking likenesses of people's faces – not shallow, amateur sketches, but portraits of power and insight. (One – of Christine Keeler – now hangs in the National Portrait Gallery.) He often sketched his patients, and, equally, people he sketched often then came to him for treatment. Apart from those already mentioned above, Ward sketched Prince Philip, Princess Margaret, the Duchess of Kent, Princess Marina, the Duke and Duchess of Gloucester, Harold Macmillan, Sir Hartley Shawcross, Archbishop Makarios, John Betjeman, Henry Moore, Peter Sellers, Sophia Loren, Jack Hawkins, Terry-Thomas, Kenneth More and many, many others.

Finally, there was the Ward of London society, high and low. He was a guest at many tables, welcome at any party, a regular at first nights, gallery openings, new and old nightspots, bars, popular pubs, exclusive clubs, dives and seedy cafés. London life in all its variety fascinated him. He lunched at the Thursday club with Prince Philip, Baron Nahum, David Milford Haven, Feliks Topolski, and Lord

Boothby. He was a guest at Sarah Churchill's wedding, at Sir Alan Herbert's party to celebrate the 100th Oxford-Cambridge boat race, and at Lord Astor's dinner parties at Cliveden, the magnificent family seat on the Thames an hour's drive from London. He played bridge with Sir Colin Coote, editor of the *Daily Telegraph*. He went to art exhibitions with the actress Maureen Swanson. He helped Mike Todd and Elizabeth Taylor celebrate the London première of *South Pacific*. He was a guest at the coming-out party which Douglas Fairbanks Jnr gave for his daughter, Daphne, at Cliveden. Among the other 500 guests were the Queen, Prince Philip, Princess Margaret, Princess Marina and the Duke of Kent, Princess Alexandra, Prince Aly Khan, the Duke and Duchess of Bedford, Jack Heinz (of 57 varieties), Stavros Niarchos, Prince and Princess Frederick of Prussia, and the Cuban, Spanish and Austrian ambassadors. And whether it was a society party like this, an opening night at Leicester Square with floodlights, the popping of flashbulbs, and a red carpet, or a basement café in a back street of Notting Hill with a West Indian steel band and the air thick with the leafy smell of marijuana, Ward was always with one of London's prettiest girls, sometimes with two or three.

But not now. He arrived at the court, tall, slim, handsome, but humiliatingly handcuffed to a warder from the prison where he had spent the previous three weeks. He stood in the carved wooden dock before the magistrate, Mr Leo Gradwell, and listened impassively as the clerk read out the list of charges. If the reporters who jammed the press box had expected to see a broken man, then Ward disappointed them. They agreed later that as Ward faced the full might of British justice he looked quietly confident.


Two months earlier, on Thursday, 14 March 1963, another trial directly linked to that of Stephen Ward had started sensationally. This was the arraignment at the Old Bailey of a West Indian called Johnny Edgecombe, also known as 'Johnny Shit' because he was a part-time pusher of marijuana.

The police case was that Edgecombe had driven to Dr Stephen Ward's flat in Wimpole Mews, Marylebone, where Edgecombe's girlfriend, a beautiful 20-year-old model called Christine Keeler, and Mandy Rice-Davies, 18, an unemployed actress, were both Ward's house guests. Believing that Keeler had returned to an old love, another West Indian called Lucky Gordon, Edgecombe had demanded to see her. When she had refused to let him in, police said, Edgecombe, in a fit of jealous rage, had opened fire at the windows with a handgun, narrowly missing the two girls. The tabloid press had looked forward to the trial with some eagerness. It had all the elements for a front page splash – jealous black lover, West End society doctor, two attractive girls and gunplay. But the press was disappointed. The principal prosecution witness, Christine Keeler herself, failed to turn up at the trial. She had, said an embarrassed prosecuting counsel, simply disappeared.

Eight days later the House of Commons was packed to hear Her Majesty's Secretary of State for War, John Profumo, fifth baron of the late United Kingdom of Italy, OBE (military), Privy Councillor, a Conservative MP many thought had the makings of a future Prime Minister, make a personal statement to Parliament.

It was not just the fact that a personal statement is such a rarely used parliamentary convention which had caused such interest. MPs hoped that they might learn what had happened to Christine Keeler, 'the missing model', and whether there was any truth in the rumours that had been engrossing London for the past six months.

The previous evening, a senior Labour MP, George Wigg, had brought the main rumour into the open. At its simplest and crudest, this had it that Profumo, a married man, had been having an affair with Christine Keeler. But Keeler had also been sharing her bed with, among others, the assistant naval attaché at the Soviet Embassy, Yevgeny Ivanov.

The rumour had even made its way into print. In the August 1962 issue of *Queen*, the magazine's associate editor, Robin Douglas-Home, a nephew of the then Foreign Secretary, Lord Home, had written an article headed, 'Sentences I'd Like to Hear the End Of'. The idea was that a series of short, incomplete sentences would enable Douglas-Home to pass on to his readers some of London's choicest gossip by innuendo rather than by direct accusation. One of the incomplete sentences read: 'Called in MI5 because every time the chauffeur-driven Zis drew up at her *front* door, out of the *back* door into a chauffeur-driven Humber slipped . . .'

The narrow London and County circle that read *Queen* drew the conclusions it was meant to: a chauffeur-driven Russian car meant a Soviet diplomat; a chauffeur-driven Humber meant a British government official; the use of 'MI5' suggested that the combination would interest the British Security Service. It did not take Fleet Street long to put names to the parties. But no newspaper published a thing. It reeked of libel.

The Edgecombe trial might just have provided a way out. Anything Christine Keeler said in the witness box could be printed in newspapers without risk as a fair and accurate contemporary report of the court proceedings. What would Keeler say? Was it just possible that if asked why Edgecombe should want to shoot her, she would reply, 'Because he was jealous that I was having an affair with Jack Profumo'? Viewed in this light, Christine Keeler's disappearance took on a sinister aspect.

Wigg wanted to flush all this into the open, emphasising that if the rumours were true and a call girl was sharing her favours with the Secretary of State for War and a Russian assistant naval attaché, then there was an important security aspect to be considered. He was able to bring up the matter by using the privilege of the House of Commons — no MP can be sued for libel over anything he says in Parliament. Wigg named names, and he challenged the Government to deny the rumours. His call was taken up by another Labour MP, Mrs Barbara Castle. She went even further than Wigg. She said that although the press was pursuing the question of where Christine Keeler had gone — 'the missing call girl, the vanished witness' — it could be that there was a public interest behind it all.

'My hon. and learned Friend, the Member for Northampton [Reginald Paget] said that if it is just a case of a Minister having been found with a pretty girl, good luck to him,' Mrs Castle said. 'But what if there is something else of much greater importance? What if it is the question of the perversion of justice at stake? If accusations are made that there are people in high places who do know [Keeler's whereabouts] and who are not informing the police, is it not a matter of public interest?'

The Government had wanted to squash the stories about Profumo and Keeler for some time. Now that these also included allegations that Profumo, and perhaps others 'in high places', had had a hand in Keeler's disappearance to prevent her from giving evidence at a criminal trial, it decided that this was the moment to act. Overnight a statement was prepared and barely twelve hours after Wigg had brought up the matter, Profumo, tall, balding, elegant but weary-eyed, was on his feet before a hushed House.

I understand that in the debate on the Consolidated Fund Bill last night, under the protection of Parliamentary privilege, the hon. Gentlemen, the Members for Dudley [Wigg] and for Coventry East [Richard Crossman] and the hon. Lady, the Member for Blackburn [Barbara Castle], opposite, spoke of rumours connecting a Minister with a Miss Keeler, and a recent trial at the Central Criminal Court. It was alleged that people in high places might have been responsible for concealing information concerning the disappearance of a witness and the perversion of justice.

I understand that my name has been connected with the
rumours about the disappearance of Miss Keeler. I would like to
take this opportunity of making a personal statement about these
matters. I last saw Miss Keeler in December 1961 and I have not
seen her since. I have no idea where she is now. Any suggestion
that I was in any way connected with or responsible for her
absence from a trial at the Old Bailey is wholly and completely
untrue. My wife and I first met Miss Keeler at a house party in July
1961 at Cliveden. Among a number of people there was Dr.
Stephen Ward, whom we already knew slightly, and a Mr. Ivanov,
who was an attaché at the Russian Embassy. The only other
occasion that my wife or I met Mr. Ivanov was for a moment at the
official reception for Major Gagarin at the Soviet Embassy. My
wife and I had a standing invitation to visit Dr. Ward. Between July
and December 1961 I met Miss Keeler on about half a dozen
occasions when I called to see him and his friends. Miss Keeler and
I were on friendly terms. There was no impropriety whatsoever in
my acquaintanceship with Miss Keeler. Mr. Speaker, I have made
this personal statement because of what was said in the House last
evening by the three hon. Members, and which, of course, was
protected by privilege. I shall not hesitate to issue writs for libel
and slander if scandalous allegations are made or repeated outside
the House.

British newspapers are inhibited in their reporting of the news by
fierce libel laws, strict rules about contempt of court (they can
publish nothing which might prejudice a fair trial), and by their own
chicken-hearted approach to the problems that these laws present. So
the ordinary reader with no access to the inside knowledge and gossip
of Fleet Street and the House of Commons, found that the press
coverage of the Ward case, the Edgecombe case, the Commons
debate, and Profumo's personal statement raised more questions than
it answered.

There was no explanation of the role of Christine Keeler or her
actress friend, Mandy Rice-Davies, and no indication of what they
were doing living in the flat of the bachelor osteopath, Dr Stephen
Ward. It was hard to understand where the mysterious Russian,
Ivanov, fitted into the picture or why Profumo had mentioned him in
his statement. And if Profumo's relationship with Keeler was as
innocent as he had said, why was it necessary for him to make a
statement at all? No one appeared to know why Keeler had vanished
on the eve of Edgecombe's trial or where she might have gone.

Almost every day there were new developments in the affair that made it even more murky. Christine Keeler turned up in Spain, expressing surprise that anyone was looking for her. Yes, she said, Profumo's account of their relationship was correct. But soon afterwards, Profumo issued writs for libel against two European newspapers. No British paper would repeat what they had printed from fear of a similar action. Out of the blue, Lucky Gordon, Keeler's other West Indian lover, was arrested and charged with wounding her in a West End street. Two days later Mandy Rice-Davies was taken off a plane at London Airport when she was about to leave for Majorca and was placed under arrest.

The British reader was desperately trying to make sense of these disparate yet somehow linked events when, on 5 June, John Profumo suddenly resigned and admitted to the Prime Minister that he had lied in his personal statement to the House of Commons. Christine Keeler *had* been his mistress. This made headlines all over the world, but there was more sensation to come.

Lucky Gordon's trial for wounding Christine Keeler began on the very day of Profumo's resignation and Gordon, conducting his own defence, claimed that the policeman who had arrested him had at first said that he was making inquiries about 'Dr Stephen Ward procuring young girls for high society'. Ward appeared on television to deny this and claimed that early on he had revealed everything, including the Profumo-Keeler affair, to MI5. On 6 June Gordon was sentenced to three years in jail for assaulting Christine Keeler. Two days later Ward was arrested and charged with living on the earnings of prostitution.

No wonder the British public was both excited and frustrated. A Minister of the Crown had had an affair with a call girl who had been shot at by one West Indian and then assaulted by another. A society osteopath friendly with a Russian diplomat had told MI5 about the affair. The Minister had lied about it to the House of Commons and had then recanted and resigned. Clearly something amazing had been going on.

Christine Keeler's 'confessions' started running in the *News of the World*. She described how she had met Profumo at Cliveden, the home of Lord Astor, and how she had had an affair with him and also with Ivanov, 'a wonderful huggy bear of a man'. She mentioned another guest at Cliveden, President Ayub Khan of Pakistan, and hinted at the involvement of more, as yet unnamed, celebrities.

This sparked off further rumours: an expensive call girl service had been providing young girls for men in high places; at least four Cabinet Ministers were involved; Christine Keeler had been passing Profumo's pillow secrets to Ivanov; she had also kept compromising letters from the other prominent men who had slept with her.

The rumours had it that an international blackmail ring was about to be uncovered; the FBI was conducting an investigation at President Kennedy's request; a special CIA team had moved into the American Embassy; a member of the Royal Family was involved with Christine Keeler; the national life was endangered; the Government was about to fall.

There were tales of organised orgies, including great whipping parties at a house in Mayfair where, it was said, one of the guests became over-excited and died of a heart attack. There were other sex parties in Pimlico where young girls, dressed only in little aprons, waited on MPs who had popped out of the House of Commons for a little diversion. Only some of this made the newspapers in Britain but it was widely and gleefully reported in full on the Continent and in the United States.

The *Washington Star* printed Mandy Rice-Davies's recollection of one sex party where the host who opened the door wore nothing but his socks. 'Then there was a dinner party where a naked man wearing a mask waited on table like a slave. He had to have the mask because he was so well-known.' The *News of the World* immediately identified the hostess at the dinner party as being Mariella Novotny, wife of a Chelsea antique dealer. She was interviewed by Peter Earle, the paper's crime reporter. Novotny, sitting up in bed wearing a lace dressing gown and dark sunglasses, said that the masked man was not a Cabinet Minister but a member of a titled family. She said that he had served the two stuffed peacocks which were the *pièce de résistance* of the dinner but that he had not done so naked — he had worn a pair of short striped pants.

The *Washington Post*'s gossip writer, Dorothy Kilgallen, under the headline, 'Profumo Case Rocking Palace Set', reported: 'The authorities searching the apartment of one of the principals in the case came upon a photograph showing a key figure disporting with a bevy of ladies. All were nude except for the gentleman in the picture who was wearing an apron. And this is a man who has been on extremely friendly terms with the very proper Queen and members of her immediate family!'

Addressing the Young Conservatives at Melton Mowbray, the Leader of the House of Lords, Lord Hailsham, announced, 'I am not the man without a head, the man in the iron mask, the man who goes about clad only in a Masonic apron, or a visitor to unnamed orgies. Nor have I indulged in any of the eccentric and disreputable activities contained in the rumours now circulating in the more credulous circles of the metropolis.' This light-hearted comment was taken by the Italian press as a clear indication of Lord Hailsham's guilt.

The *Daily Sketch* scored one back for Britain by printing on its front page a large photograph of the Russian, Ivanov, kissing an enthusiastic lady on the mouth. She turned out to be the wife of the assistant naval attaché at the United States Embassy, Captain Thomas Watson Murphy. The *Daily Mirror* roared, 'What the Hell is Going on in This Country?' The New York *Journal American* suggested that the scandal was not confined to Britain: 'One of the biggest names in American politics' – a man who held 'a very high elective office' – had been mentioned in Britain in connection with the investigation into the Profumo-Keeler affair. *Newsweek*, under the headline 'The New Pornocracy', said that Britain's sex and espionage scandal seemed to have assumed the proportions of 'a sort of World Parliament of prostitutes, whore-mongers, sex deviates, orgy-prone highbinders, and libidinous Soviet agents.'

French newspapers collected all the rumours and simply published them under the headline 'RUMOURS'. The more sensational ones said that Christine Keeler had been offered a bribe by members of the British Parliament to leave the country and that Ward had been promised an enormous sum of money, to be deposited in a Swiss or Mexican account, on condition that he pleaded guilty and gave no evidence.

Everyone appeared ready to cash in on the scandal. Christine Keeler incorporated herself as Christine Keeler Company Limited, the fastest rising fallen woman in Britain. Mandy Rice-Davies, interviewed at London Airport before leaving for a holiday in Majorca, announced: 'I will go down in history as another Lady Hamilton.' The ex-middleweight world champion boxer, Sugar Ray Robinson, said he planned to make a film about the scandal. Christine Keeler would play herself and he would play opposite her.

The calm that had followed Profumo's personal statement to the House of Commons in March had been quickly shattered. The scandal seemed to have a momentum of its own. Although the government had announced that Lord Denning, the Master of the Rolls, would conduct a judicial inquiry into the affair and would start work immediately, the Prime Minister, Harold Macmillan, still looked like being hurled from office with his reputation for political sagacity in tatters. The Conservative Party was in the greatest disarray since the Suez fiasco. Its Secretary of State for War, John Profumo, had ended his parliamentary career in a morass of lies and dishonour. Foreign relations with the United States had been strained because of the security implications of Ivanov's involvement. And the Royal Family had been dragged into the scandal, both by Profumo's acquaintance with members of the Royal household and by their relationship with Ward.

Public feeling was that London high society, apparently reeking of sexual decadence and debauchery, had been caught out. But only one person involved in this huge, sticky web had been brought to book. Clearly the Crown must believe that all the answers, all the responsibility, all the guilt must lie with the prisoner at the bar, Stephen Thomas Ward.

# 2 | The Crusading Osteopath

Stephen Thomas Ward, the second son of the Reverend Arthur Ward and his wife Eileen, was born at Lemsford, Hertfordshire, on 19 October 1912. The Reverend Ward was a quiet, scholarly man, who had been an Exhibitioner at Balliol College, Oxford, with a First Class degree in Modern History. Naturally shy, he was less attentive and more demanding of his children than his more extravert wife. He was handicapped by a spinal disorder which made him a virtual hunchback. Although his duties as local vicar required socialising, he was happiest when immersed in his library. Bridget Astor, a neighbour from his native Dorset recalls, 'I remember him like a mole creeping among his books. He hardly seemed to notice his children.'

Eileen Vigors, on the other hand, was a charming, lively woman from a sprawling Irish family from Burgage, County Carlow. She was scatty, colourful and extremely indulgent. She used to take her five children, John, Stephen, twins Patty and Bridget, and Raymond 'Peter' on camping holidays in Cornwall, where they would spend days pony-trekking. She loved horses and passed this interest on to her children.

It was evident that Stephen, from an early age, had a brilliant mind. His mother confided to a friend that she felt Stephen was destined for great things, and she spoilt and protected him.

In 1920 the family moved to Torquay when the Reverend Ward became Vicar of St Matthias, Ilsham. Stephen exasperated his father by his unwillingness to study and his inability to decide what career he wanted to follow. Despite his upbringing, Stephen had little regard for religion. He did, however, share one important belief with his father — that all people, whatever their background, race, colour or creed, were equal. This principle was not only to play an important part in shaping Ward's outlook but also to contribute, towards the end of it, to the way he was frequently misunderstood.

There occurred at this formative stage in Ward's life an incident at his school which must have greatly influenced his behaviour later, when he was caught up in the Profumo affair. He was a boarder at

Canford, a public school in Dorset. One night in the dormitory a fellow pupil crawled over Ward's bed to thump a boy who was snoring loudly. The next morning this boy would not wake up and the doctor found that he had a fractured skull. No one confessed. Ward said later that he knew who the culprit was, 'but one was not supposed to tell'. The upshot was that the masters decided that Ward was in the bed next to the injured boy, so Ward would be the one to be punished. 'I was thrashed with a cane in front of the whole school. Of course, all the boys thought I was a famous fellow. I knew who had done it but I hadn't split. Years later I went back to the school and asked one of the masters if they had all really believed I'd hit the boy. "No," he said, "but we thought that you must have known something about it, and in any case someone had to get whacked. It just happened to be you." No hard feelings, of course, but "*it just happened to be you.*"'

After Canford, Ward had to consider a career. At first he thought he would be a doctor. Ward had seen his father bravely tolerate acute back pain all his life and had watched his favourite younger sister, Bridget, suffer from permanent mental disorders since birth. This, plus his natural aptitude for Latin and Greek, inclined him towards medical school but, after being turned down by two colleges, he decided to live alone for a while in London.

At the age of 17, he took a job for 27s. a week in the Houndsditch Warehouse. His task was to take wholesale buyers to the various departments and turn over carpets for their inspection. It was a boring and exhausting job, so just before Christmas 1929 he resigned and went to Hamburg as a translator in the German branch of Shell. Although he loved the life there, playing tennis at the British Club and football for a Hamburg team, this job, too, did not last long. Ward played a practical joke on his boss and was asked to leave.

He moved on to Paris and enrolled in a 'Cours de Civilization' at the Sorbonne, living on an allowance sent to him by his mother behind the Reverend Ward's back. To supplement this small income he took casual jobs, at first working in the kitchen of a nightclub, Chez Florence, then teaching English privately to French children and working as a tour guide. He soon found out that tourists were more interested in the nightspots than in the Eiffel Tower and he extracted more lucrative tips by taking the male tourists around the seedier areas of Pigalle and the Bois de Boulogne, where prostitutes worked.

In 1932 Ward returned to Torquay but was thrown out by his father almost immediately when the Reverend Ward discovered that Stephen had hidden a French girl, who needed a place to stay, in the basement of the vicarage. The scandal threatened to cause the vicar deep embarrassment in the tight-knit Protestant community and Ward was told to find his own accommodation. According to Bridget Astor, Stephen's local friends, particularly the girls, missed him: 'Stephen was always considered a very glamorous figure around Torquay.' Ward again sought refuge in London, this time selling chests of Indian tea, and subscriptions to the *Spectator*.

Eileen Ward sought the advice of her brother, Edward Vigors, who worked in the House of Lords. His friend and colleague from Ireland, Jocelyn Proby, had just graduated from the Kirksville College of Osteopathy and Surgery, Missouri. The two men agreed to meet Stephen to sell him the idea of becoming an osteopath. Proby and Ward immediately liked one another. 'There is no doubt that Stephen had a very good brain but no direction,' recalls Proby. 'Edward Vigors and I really hijacked him and sent him off to Kirksville. But we were so confident that he would do well that we agreed to pay his fees.'

Ward often said that his five years in America had greatly influenced him, shaking his English middle-class values and broadening his horizons. He arrived in the USA in 1934 in the manner of millions of immigrants, third class on an ocean liner, and like those who had gone before him was deeply impressed by the sight of New York coming up over the horizon. From New York he took a Greyhound bus to St Louis, Missouri, and then a local bus for the final 200 miles to Kirksville. He arrived on a warm autumn evening, found rooms with no difficulty, and soon settled into the routine of medical studies at the University — anatomy, physiology, biology, pathology, with considerable emphasis on the educational value of dissection.

'There were rows and rows of tables on each of which lay a body in some state of dissection,' Ward recalled. 'These were mostly blacks, bought from local hospitals and poor homes for $50 each. Four students to a body which was luxury compared with sixteen or twenty in Britain. Two dissected the upper part and two the lower. The dissection took many months and students were often to be seen walking about with parcels which turned out to be homework in the shape of an arm or a head. The entire dissection part of the course lasted for over two years.'

Although the University was osteopathic in principle, it taught a full general medical course and provided medicine and surgery for a large surrounding area. As an assistant intern Ward helped deliver babies at remote farms, did surgery on kitchen tables, set bones broken during tornadoes and gave typhoid shots after floods devastated the area around the junction of the Ohio and Mississippi rivers. This experience confirmed his decision to be an osteopath. Other students opted for the glamour of surgery but Ward rejected this because of the distress failure caused. He was more in sympathy with a friend who chose dermatology, giving as his reason: 'The patients never die of the disease but on the other hand, they seldom recover.'

Ward worked to help pay his way, taking jobs as a clerk in a drugstore, a short order cook, a caretaker and furnace stoker, a lecturer in anatomy for junior students and an embalmer in funeral parlours. 'We used to pump the bodies full of formaldehyde with a pressure pump on the blood vessels of the thigh. I remember that once I left the pump on too long while I was reading a text book and out of the corner of my eye I saw a leg start to rise in the air.' His experiences in the funeral parlour shocked him. 'It was a disgraceful business. I remember with real horror the sort of half suits, complete with shirt and bow tie, that were placed like lids over the heavily made-up corpses. Bereaved families have been trained in America to pay enormous amounts for this sort of thing, a real racket.'

In the long summer vacations Ward devoted his time to travelling the United States, visiting every state in the Union, with occasional side trips to Mexico. There he twice ended up in jail. On the first occasion he and some of his Kirksville friends visited a local brothel after a bout of heavy drinking. One of the friends, William McClurg, remembers, 'Stephen created an uproar. I had seen him in the shower once at college and knew he was very well endowed but I didn't realise just how well until the girl Stephen chose in the brothel came running out of the bedroom banging on all the other doors and telling the girls to come to see Stephen's *pinga grande*.' This called for more drinks and on the way back to the hotel Ward was arrested for drunken and disorderly behaviour.

The second time was near the border in Baja California. Ward was travelling with his friend Burnham Brooke, a member of the well-known tea family, and Kalita Carney, a tiny attractive girl from Kirksville, and a direct descendant of Jesse James, the outlaw. There was an argument over whether they should turn back to collect Kalita's bathing costume which she had forgotten on a remote beach some hundreds of miles away. Ward refused and jokingly added, 'And if you don't like it, why don't you walk home.' To his dismay Kalita ran off into cactus scrub. He and Burnham Brooke ran after her, caught her, and were pulling her back to the roadway when they saw a car-load of Mexican police screech to a halt. Since they could not speak sufficient Spanish to explain why they were struggling with a girl in the middle of a desert, they were carted off to jail before being handed over to the San Diego police the next day.

Ward took his longest trip — three months — in a 1929 Chevrolet which he bought for $50. Again his companions were Burnham and Kalita. They drove first to Chicago, then across the Rockies to Arizona, stopping on the way to visit the National Parks. They stayed on an Indian reservation where Ward met an old Etonian who was compiling a dictionary of the Hopi and Navaho languages. On the West coast they went to Hollywood and paid the usual visit to a studio, arranged for them by Madeleine Carroll, a distant relative of Ward. From there they drove to Las Vegas and then to spend a week in Death Valley.

Then it was back to the sea at San Francisco, north to Canada, over the Rockies through Kicking Horse Pass, back into the USA at the Waterton and Glacier National Park and on to Butte, Montana to see the great refinery of the Anaconda Copper Company. In the Yellowstone National Park they usually hung their food from ropes strung between trees to keep it away from bears, but one night they were tired when they stopped so they put it on the roof of the car and went to sleep inside. In the middle of the night there was a tearing sound, then a crash and the car roof and the bear on it collapsed on top of them. 'You never saw three people scramble out from under that roof as fast as we did,' Ward said later.

They were nearly lost in a jewelled cave at Cody, Wyoming. They helped miners pan for gold in a stream in the Black Hills of Dakota. They hunted for fossils in the Dakota Badlands. They drove for hundreds of miles where no roads existed. They never slept under a roof or ate a meal indoors. They were nearly buried in a sandstorm, nearly drowned when a dry river bed they were driving along suddenly became a torrent after a thunderstorm in the hills.

In shorter breaks from his studies, Ward would hitchhike to Chicago, 'a much better city than New York; New York is international and lacks the true American flavours; Chicago is much more American.' He found endless pleasure there. He stayed at Winetka on the north shore, swam in Lake Michigan, went up all the skyscrapers, and spent hours at the stockyards, fascinated by the people who came to drink warm animal blood because they believed it cured anaemia.

When Ward went to Chicago alone, it was to explore a side of life that already fascinated him — brothels and prostitutes. Ward had already visited the famous Sphinx in Paris when he was a student. He wanted to compare it with the equally famous Eversleigh Club in

Chicago, run by two elderly ladies – the daughters of a parson. The Eversleigh Club was renowned for its gold spittoons and beautiful girls who, lavishly dressed, wandered through the club's bars and restaurants until they were chosen by a client.

Ward hitchhiked from Kirksville only to find that the club had recently closed. Undeterred, he visited another brothel. 'There was a line-up of about a hundred girls. They walked over a sort of bridge wearing very little. We sat in armchairs waiting for one we might like. The difficulty was always the knowledge that there were so many more to come that the one you fancied might be the last.'

By the time he had graduated, and then sat for the Missouri State Board examination which entitled him to practise as a doctor in the United States and hold a narcotics licence, Ward felt that he really knew the United States. Kalita agreed. 'She wrote to me years later to say that if it had not been for me she would never have seen her own country.' The effect on Ward himself was profound. 'I loved America and Americans, a warm-hearted, open and dynamic people. Their kindness and hospitality made me feel ashamed of the standoffish way the British treat people.' His American experience made Ward decide to cast off his English inhibitions, be more open in manner, and to give rein to his natural instincts.

The crowd outside the Mehta Clinic in Poona, India, was reluctant to make a path for a distinguished Indian and his companion, a rather casually dressed British army captain. It was a hot December day, 1944, and everyone was hoping to catch a glimpse of Mahatma Gandhi, one of the leaders of the Congress Party, recently released from jail where the British had confined him over his role in the Quit India movement. Eventually the distinguished Indian, who happened to be the son of the Maharaja of Baroda, located one of Gandhi's assistants and told him that the British officer sought an audience with the Mahatma. The Indian led the way into a courtyard garden where hundreds of spectators lined the surrounding roofs. Gandhi was walking slowly up and down, accompanied by Sardar Patel, another Congress leader. The Indian bent to kiss Gandhi's feet, but Gandhi pulled him upright. Then, as the Indian said, 'This is Captain Stephen Ward', Gandhi turned to the Englishman, greeted him Indian style with a *namaste* and, although it was his day of silence, broke it by saying, 'Well, it's a change to have a visit from an English officer who has not come to arrest me.' The two men then went indoors and Gandhi showed Ward his spartan room: a spinning wheel, a book rest, a bed, and in one corner a sunken bath.

When Gandhi said he suffered from headaches and a stiff neck, Ward revealed that he was an osteopath and offered to try and correct Gandhi's condition. He discovered a lesion in Gandhi's neck and manipulated it. Ward's treatment must have met with some success, because Gandhi agreed to several other meetings, the sum of which left Ward very impressed. 'Although much of his policy was opposed to that of my own country,' Ward said, 'I knew that when I was with him I was in the presence of greatness, and my encounter with him was certainly the most important meeting of my life.'

Ward was stationed in Poona at the time. He had ended up in India after a series of misadventures. On the outbreak of war, although he had just started a practice in his home town of Torquay, he had volunteered for the Royal Army Medical Corps, only to be rejected because it did not recognise his American qualifications. In 1941, called up for military service, he became a private in the Royal Armoured Corps, posted to the 58th Training Regiment at Bovington, Lawrence of Arabia's old camp.

There he had come into conflict with the military authorities. His skill in treating muscle injuries, back trouble and headaches attracted the attention of the commanding officer, who suffered from a bad knee. He relieved Ward of all his other duties and gave him a consulting room and surgery in a hut near the officers' mess. Soon Ward was treating men from other camps, including the Royal Air Force. For a pleasant two years Ward had private quarters, his own car, and was even allowed to keep a dog, a Gordon setter. Ward might well have seen out the war in these comfortable circumstances had there not been an incident with his rival, the camp doctor, who unfortunately was also called Ward. When a boxer was injured at a regimental boxing match, the Colonel shouted, 'Get Ward.' But when the medical officer came hurrying down the aisle, the Colonel said, 'Not you, you fool, the *other* Ward.' The medical officer complained and at the subsequent official inquiry Stephen Ward was reprimanded.

But the inquiry apparently recognised Ward's qualities and recommended that he should be commissioned in the RAMC in the newly-formed 'officer-stretcher-bearer section'. There had then arisen some misunderstanding. Ward thought that he would be free to practise osteopathy but soon discovered that the RAMC planned to use him entirely on non-medical work. Ward, who until then had been a reluctant osteopath, decided to become its crusader. He arranged for his MP to ask questions in the Commons about the army's attitude to osteopaths and he petitioned King George VI, and the Prime Minister, Winston Churchill. So the army court-martialled him, and again he was reprimanded. Whether the military authorities decided at this stage that the farther away from Britain it could send this dissident the better, or whether stretcher-bearers were in short supply in the East is not recorded, but in March 1944 Ward was posted to India.

The voyage out was a leisurely one, taking nearly three months. Ward did not mind. 'To my amazement I found that the ship was carrying three thousand women – entertainment groups and nurses for Egypt and India. Of course this is what we – about three hundred members of the Medical Corps – were waiting for. We zigzagged all over the Atlantic Ocean almost to New York and finally got to Gibraltar. The longer it took, the happier we were. We crossed the Mediterranean and lay up off Suez. It was getting hot in more ways than one and the noble three hundred were beginning to show some signs of strain.'

In India Ward and his companions began training for a landing in Malaya but this was abandoned when the Japanese surrender made the operation unnecessary. What Ward was doing in the last months of the war is unclear. He said later, 'We were put into a tented camp on the edge of the town, much to my horror, and from there [moved] to the hospital 3BMH where I remained until I left India at the end of the war.' But it appears as if the army had finally found a way of dealing with this trouble-maker. It officially admitted him to the hospital classified as 'emotionally maladjusted'. Dr Dorothy Ball, an army psychiatrist who served with Ward, explains, 'This was a term the army used for anyone who did not fit in and with whom they did not know what to do. It had absolutely nothing to do with Ward's state of mind.'

Ward was soon leading a busy professional and social life. The Maharajah of Baroda would send a car to fetch him from the hospital for bridge most evenings. He was a popular guest at dinner parties. But he despised what he called the 'true Poona sahibs' and spent most of his time with Indians. During the day he did anatomical drawings for surgical purposes and played chess with a fellow officer, Ellis Stungo, later to be a well-known Harley Street psychiatrist. 'We got on well together,' Stungo recalls. 'I liked him as a person and I admired his intellectual capacity. He was well-informed on many things. When the war ended we came home on the same ship and decided to keep in touch.'

Stungo went back to Harley Street, Ward to Torquay. But the war had unsettled him and the prospect of a lifetime in Torquay, no matter how successful, no longer appealed to him. He abandoned his practice and moved to the bright lights of London.

# 3 | *Ward Cracks the Social Scene*

At first Ward went to work at the Osteopathic Association Clinic in Dorset Square for £8 a week, sharing a room above the clinic with a Canadian osteopath, Dr Samuel Ball. The work, mostly with patients who could not afford to go to a private osteopath, was interesting and Ward might well have settled down to long-term employment had he not been asked to act as a locum for a Park Lane osteopath who had to go to the United States for a month. 'Suddenly I found myself in a world of smart men and women, with decisions to make that would have been dangerous if they had been wrong. It was then that I learnt to take responsibility . . . Confidence is what counts in dealing with patients and this was to be the keynote of my future relationship with them. I soon found that it worked wonders.'

The taste of high life in Park Lane and his newly-found professional confidence made Ward look around for an opportunity to start again on his own. It came almost immediately. Ward was near the Association's telephone in the clinic one afternoon when a call came through from the American Embassy. Could the clinic recommend a first class osteopath? 'Of course,' Ward said, thinking quickly. 'You should go to our best man. His name is Dr Stephen Ward and his rooms are at . . .' Ward hesitated and then gave the address of a friend. 'And', Ward concluded, 'if you give us a convenient time we'll be happy to make the appointment for you.' The time was arranged and, as Ward described it later, 'I put down the telephone and rushed around to my friend to ask if I could borrow his consulting room for an hour. He agreed and I sat there awaiting my first private patient in the West End. The bell rang and in walked the American ambassador, Averell Harriman!'

When Ward had overcome his surprise, he asked Harriman what his trouble was. Harriman said that he saw an osteopath twice a week, no matter where he was – 'It's the only thing that keeps me going.' Ward put everything he knew into the treatment and Harriman, pleased at the result, mentioned Ward's name to some of his friends. Ward began to get what he described as 'some big name patients'.

His real breakthrough probably came when Winston Churchill sought treatment. Ward had as patients Duncan Sandys and his wife, Diana, who was Churchill's daughter, and they recommended Ward when Churchill complained of back trouble. Ward was called to the Churchill house in Hyde Park Gate one morning, warned by Mrs Churchill not to let Churchill bully him, and was shown to the bedroom. Churchill was sitting up in bed smoking a large cigar. He opened the conversation by saying, 'I suppose you're another one who'll tell me to give up these?' And then, before Ward could answer, 'How old are you?' Ward told him and then set up a portable table he used for treating people at home. 'Mr Churchill, would you mind sitting on this?' Churchill, wearing only his pyjama top and still holding his cigar, sat on the table. 'Now I'd like to ask you a few questions,' Ward said. 'In that case,' said Churchill, 'you can ask me them in my bed,' and he hopped back again.

Ward felt he was losing the battle, so he said, 'As you wish, but I find it saves time to ask patients questions while I'm examining them.' Churchill grunted, got out of bed again and lay face downwards on the table, still smoking. Later Ward, trying to make small talk, mentioned that he had treated Mahatma Gandhi. 'Ah,' said Churchill, suddenly interested. 'And did you twist his neck, too?' Ward said he had. 'Evidently a case of too little too late,' Churchill said. He was then silent for a time. Finally he asked, 'When you twist my head like that what would you do if it came off in your hands?' Ward felt it was his turn to make a joke. 'Go and practise in Moscow,' he said. 'After such a thing I'd be very welcome.' Churchill was not amused. 'Don't you be too certain,' he growled. 'Mr Stalin was quite a friend of mine.'

Ward told his friends that each of the twelve treatments he gave Churchill was a battle of wills. Churchill wanted to know exactly what Ward was doing and the justification for doing it. If the answer was not convincing, Churchill went on the attack. Ward witnessed Churchill's browbeating of a distinguished dermatologist who was just leaving as Ward arrived. 'Do you know what I think of your advice?' Churchill was saying. 'First you tell me to put on this lotion, then that cream and then something else after my bath. What do you think I've got to do all day? I think your advice is a lot of balls.' The specialist was shocked. 'Well, Mr Churchill,' he said, 'if you find it too complicated I could make it a bit simpler.' Churchill pounced. 'There you are. I told you so,' he said. 'Not even certain of your own balls!'

Churchill and Ward got along very well. Churchill found out about Ward's portrait sketching and tried to persuade him to take up painting – 'It lasts forever.' Ward tried to persuade Churchill to go to the Tate Gallery with him to see an exhibition of romantic landscapes by Alexander Cozens but Churchill cried off, saying he was too busy. The two men often discussed international affairs and Churchill's views and plans. This insight into the way political decisions were made and what influenced them, Ward stored away for future use.

In osteopathy patients come almost entirely by recommendation. A word in Ward's favour from well-known people thus carried great weight. New patients liked the idea of being treated by Churchill's osteopath, and when they found that Ward's expertise matched his reputation, they spread the news. Ward had started with Harriman. Soon he was treating King Peter of Yugoslavia, six members of the Churchill family, Ava Gardner, Mary Martin, and Mel Ferrer. Within a year he decided he had sufficient private patients to set up his own clinic, so he took consulting rooms on the west side of Cavendish Square, on the fringe of Harley Street.

As well as his society practice, Ward enjoyed treating down-market show business people. His name went around the West End entertainment world as someone prepared to take a case at odd hours and help a strained back or a torn ligament. He was well known backstage at most London theatres and in hotels favoured by dancers, acrobats, jugglers, and in one instance, a team of midgets. On this case he was called out late one winter's night to go to Russell Square. As Ward told his friends, 'The door was opened by a man who could not have been more than thirty inches high. In the sitting room, perched on a chair knitting a brightly-coloured pair of socks, was another little man. They said that their sister had hurt her back and was in pain. They took me into the bedroom and there on the bed was the minutest women you have ever seen, but perfectly formed, only twenty-seven inches tall. The whole family was then appearing at the Palladium. The girl became quite attached to me and later I went to see her backstage. I made the mistake of popping into another dressing room to see a showgirl I knew. I had just opened the door when I got a crack on the head from behind. It was the lady midget. She'd taken off her shoe and hurled it at me.'

Ward's practice grew rapidly. People who came originally for treatment grew to like the quiet, competent osteopath with the deep resonant speaking voice, who was always smiling, and good-humoured, and who always seemed to have time to listen to their troubles as he eased away their aches and pains. Even when they were clinically cured, some continued to see Ward for a treatment when they wanted to relax and chat. Ward's professional life and private life began to overlap. His patients became his friends, and because of his healing skills and his charm London society, just getting into stride again after the war, opened its doors to him.

By the winter of 1946, 24 Wilton Row, Knightsbridge, the house of the Fleet Street artist and cartoonist Arthur Ferrier and his wife Freda, had already established itself as the venue for some of the best parties in London. One party, in particular, stood out from the rest, a fancy-dress ball held on New Year's Eve, *the* party that everybody in London hoped to attend, but to which only 300 people, a mixture of show business, artists and well known West End personalities, were invited.

The Ferriers always took a month to organise the party. The food was the best and most expensive, often arranged by such well known restaurateurs as John Mills of Les Ambassadeurs, Erwen Schleyen of the Mirabelle, and Siegi Sessler of Siegi's Club, all personal friends of the Ferriers. The bands were among the most popular of the day – Django Reinhardt and Humphrey Lyttelton. It was a celebration to remember, a way of getting through the drabness of those early post-war days.

The power workers were on strike, and the Prime Minister, Clement Attlee, had warned all electricity users to 'switch off or risk fines and imprisonment'. Unemployment threatened to reach three million for the first time and a disastrous harvest and a shortage of potatoes, flour, bread, milk, meat and fats, had forced the Government to announce that far from relaxing the strict food rationing, they were about to tighten it and extend it into the following summer.

Nevertheless, London was doing its best to enjoy life. The cinemas were packed. Danny Kaye was starring in *The Kid from Brooklyn*; Cary Grant and Ingrid Bergman were in *Notorious*; Margaret Lockwood in *Hungry Hill*. On the stage, Vivien Leigh had just finished a run of *The Skin of Our Teeth* at the Piccadilly; Coral Browne was 'Lady Frederick' at the Savoy, Constance Cummings was appearing in *Clutterbuck* at Wyndham's and the Drury Lane Theatre opened for the first time since the war with a dazzling musical by Noel Coward, called *Pacific 1860*, starring Mary Martin.

Everyone who was anyone wanted invitations to the Ferrier party. Canadian model Maxie Taylor, for instance, had been on the telephone to the Ferriers days before the party. 'Maxie was most anxious to bring an eligible young man,' Freda Ferrier recalls. 'Our instant reaction was to say no, but she was one of Arthur's favourite models and a good friend and she could be very persistent. She also intrigued us by saying that within a few weeks we would be able to

boast that this particular young man had been to one of our parties.'
So for once the Ferriers relented. Maxie Taylor's young man was in.

So was Stephen Ward. But this time the Ferriers refused to allow
him to bring two girls, as he often did. Faced with a choice, he opted
not for his current girlfriend, the actress Betta St John, but for Eunice
Bailey, an exotic redhead he had met a few weeks earlier.

Ward had barely arrived at the Ferriers' New Year's Eve party
when he had to cope with an attempt by Anthony Beauchamp, a
successful photographer, to lure her away. Ward told him that he was
too late: Eunice had promised to sit for his friend Baron Nahum, the
portrait photographer who had made Maxie Taylor so well known.

Someone standing nearby asked them to keep their voices down
because the actor/singer Theodore Bikel was doing an impromptu
act. Bikel wound up his act and went to join Peter Ustinov who was
sitting with Lauren Bacall and Burl Ives. But before he reached them
he was intercepted by a fresh-faced young man who was with the
actress Hermione Baddeley. The young man introduced himself as an
aspiring actor, Laurence Harvey, and asked if Bikel would introduce
him when he read something. Bikel agreed and later in the evening
everyone listened, entranced by the power and expression in
Harvey's voice. Zza Zza Gabor asked Hermione Baddeley who
Harvey was. 'None of your business,' Hermione said. 'Anyway,
tonight he's with me.'

Ward had left Eunice Bailey talking to the Labour peer Julian
Melchett and the American comedians Ben Lyons and Bebe Daniels
while he greeted Mary Martin and the young British actress Pat
Kirkwood. He invited them to sit with him to listen to Jon Pertwee's
act. The lights were lowered and Pertwee took his place on the
improvised stage. 'I see that we're honoured to have a naval officer
with us tonight,' gesturing towards Maxie Taylor's escort, 'so I'd
better keep my jokes dirty, otherwise the Navy will get a good name.'

At this the audience booed good-naturedly and the officer raised
his glass in salute. The pianist began the song, Jon Pertwee went
through the verse and, as he began the chorus, the naval officer joined
in so enthusiastically that he drowned out Pertwee altogether. The
musical comedy star Frances Day, sitting near Ward, leaned over and
asked him to do something. 'Jon hates being interrupted. Tell him to
shut up.' Ward said he could not do that. The officer was a friend of
his, Prince Philip of Greece, and would be a guest at his house-
warming party in Cavendish Square the following week.

Freda Ferrier acted. 'I'm terribly sorry dear. But will you be quiet.
Jon hates people joining in. He'll get dreadfully upset.' Prince Philip
ignored her. Freda was preparing a stronger reprimand when Ward,

Maxie Taylor and Frances Day surrounded her and whisked her towards the bar. 'That's blown it, Freda,' Frances said. 'Your head's for the chopping block.' Freda asked why. Maxie Taylor told her. 'Didn't you hear his name when I introduced you?' she said. 'That's Prince Philip of Greece. He's going to marry Princess Elizabeth. It isn't official yet but it soon will be.' Freda had no time to reply. Raised voices and some sort of a commotion in front of the stage sent them all hurrying to see what was happening.

Pertwee had come down from the stage and announced that he was going to kick Prince Philip's backside. 'I wouldn't do that if I were you,' Frances Day told him. 'You can't go around kicking royal arses. You'll be arrested for *lèse-majesté*.' And she told an astonished Pertwee who the naval officer was. Ward confirmed it. 'If you puncture the royal arse before the wedding day, then I'll be the one who will have to patch it up, so lay off!' Pertwee looked confused, mumbled an apology at Prince Philip, who was bemused by the whole affair, and hurried off towards the bar. Ward could not resist a last lance. 'That's it Jon,' he called to Pertwee's back. 'You can kiss your season at Buckingham Palace goodbye!'

# 4 | *A Magnet for Girls*

By the late 1940s Ward was leading the sort of life his spell in the United States, and later in India, had led him to choose as being ideal for his nature and personality. He enjoyed his work, but it was not the sole or even main reason for his existence. He got genuine satisfaction out of relieving a patient's pain, and made a comfortable living – he averaged about £5,000 a year (£50,000 by today's values) about the same as a Cabinet Minister. He could have earned more, but money meant little to him and he kept his professional hours down to provide time for his other lives. He saw his first patient at 9.30 a.m. and broke for lunch most days at 12.30. He went regularly to the Kenya Coffee House in Marylebone High Street, easy walking distance from his rooms in Cavendish Square. Most days he met his psychiatrist friend, Ellis Stungo, and they had a sandwich and a cup of coffee, each usually paying his own bill. But occasionally Ward would ask Stungo to pay.

'He was never hard up, he always wore nicely tailored clothes and his shirts were tailored with his monogram,' Stungo remembers. 'But he often did not seem to have ready cash. Money meant nothing to him. He'd just say, "I haven't any money with me. Do you mind Pop?" and leave the bill to me. I remember I'd arranged to meet him once at the RAC in Pall Mall. He turned up with two sisters, Joan and Jackie Collins. And Stephen simply said, "Are we going to have a meal Pop?" So we had a meal and I paid the bill even though he was the one with the girls. But he was like that. On the other hand, if anyone needed a place to stay they could always put up at Stephen's place. In his Cavendish Square flat there'd usually be five or six girls staying for a while.

'It was curious how they gravitated to Stephen. Some of them were country girls from Bristol or Yorkshire, or some place, and they were in London for some purpose, an interview for a job perhaps, and somehow Stephen got to know them and got them accommodation. You know, "If you're in London again, you can stay here if you want to." And a number of girls, very nice girls, would come to stay a while. You'd meet them at Stephen's, and he was very relaxed about it, and the girls seemed very secure there.'

Ward was so relaxed about who came to his flat that he never even bothered to lock the front door. Girls he had invited would arrive late at night, let themselves in, and either wake him in the morning with a cup of coffee or leave a note of thanks on the kitchen table. His osteopath friend, Jocelyn Proby, was staying in the flat once when Ward was away and, as Ward had requested, left the front door unlocked. 'I was woken in the middle of the night by voices in the sitting room,' he recalls. 'I got out of bed to investigate and found myself confronted by the whole chorus line from the Windmill Theatre. Before I could ask the girls what the hell they were doing there, one of them said, "Don't worry, love, Stephen said we can stay if we want to." And with that they all fell asleep on the floor. When I got up in the morning they had all disappeared.'

Ward was always having parties, small affairs compared with the others he went to, but his guests did not seem to mind. The food and drink might be scarce, but girls were plentiful. 'You had to bring a bottle,' Ellis Stungo says. 'The girls would produce sandwiches, and we would play music and dance. The girls would just be there, and not for any purpose. I emphasise that because I was there repeatedly and I never saw anything untoward. I never saw anyone disappear into bedrooms, or orgies, or anything of that kind at any time.

'I met some very interesting and attractive people at these parties. I met Miss Jamaica who was over here for a beauty competition. I met Eunice Bailey, who was then Ward's friend, and I met the girl he later married, Patricia Baines, a very nice person. And I met that associate of the Royal Family, Feliks Topolski.'

Some of these parties were very mixed. Michael Pertwee, the scriptwriter, remembers going to one and meeting in rapid succession Prince Philip, a junior typist, and a high-class prostitute. 'The typist and the prostitute were having a serious conversation that was very funny to listen to. The prostitute, who was apparently earning £200 a week, couldn't understand why the typist was slaving away five days a week for £5 when she could earn forty times that amount in a few hours. Unfortunately I was not around at the end of the evening to learn whether the typist had been convinced.'

The mix of people was deliberate. As Ward explained it, 'All my life I considered each person to be equally important as human beings. My father taught me this. All that was extraordinary about me was that I believed and practised this idea. I did keep *widely* different people apart. Each had prejudices of their own, their own snobberies, one might say. I could never understand these, but I was aware of their existence. Any evening at my flat would bring in as odd an assortment of visitors as it was possible to find — a barrister, a barrow-boy, a writer, a motor salesman, a peer, and always, for some reason, a steady stream of pretty girls of every type. This from early evening until two in the morning.

'What did we do? You'd be surprised. We sat and drank coffee and more coffee and we talked. I also ran a home for waifs and strays. Anyone who was homeless or unhappy was welcome. I don't say that I was not interested in female company. That would be humbug. But my attitude was always to make it quite clear that nothing was expected in return except good company and a steady stream of coffee. I don't think that the way I lived was sinful. It was unconventional, but as far as I was concerned, to hell with conventions that prevented kindness. To hell with barriers that prevented me from knowing people whose life and problems I found absorbing, far more absorbing than the little ingrown problems that beset the respectable. This was my life and I enjoyed it.'

Of course, Ward's relationship with women was much more complicated than this. Women fascinated him. He loved listening to their conversations, watching their movements, helping them solve their problems and sharing his life with them. But he seldom went to bed with them. There are several possible explanations. The obvious one is that Ward had homosexual tendencies. But his close male friends scoff at this suggestion and even his enemies never accused him of this.

Some say that he was ashamed of his hairless white body, others that he preferred group sex, or that he was a voyeur. There is evidence that he did not like undressing in front of others, but nothing to show that he preferred orgies. On the few occasions that we have been able to establish that he was present when group sex took place, everyone agrees that the only man in the room who never even removed his trousers was Stephen Ward. He did watch, but this took place so seldom he can hardly be called a voyeur.

In short, Ward's sexuality cannot easily be categorised. It can only be described. He liked women. He liked hearing all about their lives — including their sexual adventures. He liked having them around him. He enjoyed a bathroom full of underwear and stockings and closets full of shoes. He was fascinated by prostitutes and liked to listen to them talking about their lives and their clients' demands. If the circumstances were right, he occasionally went to bed with a prostitute himself. And sometimes he went to bed with a girl he had picked up in a coffee bar or a shop. His sex drive was not strong and it would seem that his main outlet came from discussing and watching other people's sexual activities — mainly from discussing them.

Then, in 1949, as Ward himself put it, he made the great mistake of getting married. At 36 he had been serious about only two women. The first had been Mary Glover, a local girl from Torquay, who had promised to wait for him while he studied in Missouri. Although they had kept up a correspondence of sorts during their four years apart, it was probably inevitable that by the time he had returned she had married someone else.

Then there was Eunice Bailey, the red-headed beauty whom Ward had helped launch on a highly-successful modelling career. (She was the top Dior model of the 1950s.) He considered marrying her and their friends say that she would have agreed, but Ward hesitated too long. She married Pitt Oakes, the son of Harry Oakes of the Bahamas, and when he died she married an American businessman, Robert L. Gardiner, of New York. Ward blamed himself for losing Eunice, and when he met society girl Patricia Baines, 21, in the spring of 1949, he plunged in.

Patricia's father was the director of a large textile company, and the family lived in the heart of Belgravia. She was a career model long before she met Ward. To a man just acquiring the skills of discovering girls from modest backgrounds and launching them into the world of fashion and high society, she offered him little challenge. Yet when they met at a bottle party given by the photographer Baron, they were instantly attracted to each other. Ward's friends suggested that the attraction for him was probably to do with the couple's striking physical resemblance to each other. On her side, Patricia was impressed by Ward's circle of friends and patients. There was no question in her mind but that Ward was professionally successful, earning a more than adequate salary and was socially very acceptable. She assumed, wrongly as it turned out, that Ward had the makings of an ideal husband.

They were married at Marylebone Register Office on 27 July 1949. The wedding photograph enhances their physical similarity. As they pose on the steps of the Register Office, a little east of the court where Ward was later to appear in the dock, Ward looks uncomfortably respectable and well-groomed in his navy linen suit and highly-polished shoes, with a crisp white pocket handkerchief, and a carnation in his buttonhole. Patricia, willowy, dark-haired, and confident in her maxi-length designer dress with its low neckline, a three-strand pearl choker and a cloche hat with chiffon flowers, looks relaxed and happy.

The first big fight came on their honeymoon. They had gone to the south of France and stopped off in Paris on the way back. Here Ward's financial irresponsibility surfaced. Patricia had been looking forward to a comfortable stay in an expensive hotel, a little shopping and good eating. Instead Ward announced that he had seriously miscalculated the cost of the honeymoon, had failed to bring enough money, and that they would have to stay in a cheap pension and eat frugally.

Patricia, perhaps thinking that Ward had arranged this deliberately to humble her, was upset. This was the first indication that Ward, with his fashionable address, his thriving practice, and his wealthy friends, was himself not as well off as Patricia had imagined. She was also beginning to wonder whether she and Ward had as much in common as she had at first thought. His modern views on sexual independence in marriage distressed her. His lack of interest in material things and his determination to experience life in all its variety clashed with her aims, revolving as they did almost exclusively around the home.

By the time the couple had arrived back in London the marriage was already virtually over. 'Stephen obviously still loved her,' one of his friends remembers. 'He strove hard to get her back. But apart from other problems they had, she was a normal healthy girl, obviously confused and demoralised by his inhibited sexuality, loving him in spite of it, but unable to face a future with him.'

Six weeks after Patricia Baines had moved into Ward's flat at Cavendish Square, she left. A story went around London that the final break had been over Ward's association with prostitutes in Hyde Park. Patricia had heard that Ward liked to chat with the girls, questioning them on how they had got into the business, whether they liked it, how much they earned. One afternoon, the story went, she hid herself in the boot of Stephen's car, and emerged in high anger when he was in the middle of talking to one of the prostitutes. The story sounds improbable and is more likely a joke put around by Ward himself, perhaps to disguise the genuine pain he felt over the failure of his marriage.

This expressed itself in several ways. He told everyone he was very happy to give Patricia grounds for divorce, including adultery. Yet it was two years before he finally agreed to allow the action to go ahead, undefended, and then the grounds were not adultery but mental cruelty. He refused to admit this, and ten years later was still giving his own version. 'In 1948 or 1949 I made the biggest mistake of my life. I got married,' he said. 'I don't know how she talked me into it. She was always wanting things and pretty soon I couldn't stand the sight of her. Two years later we both went along to a solicitor and soon she divorced me on the grounds of adultery, which wasn't difficult to prove.'

The marriage – or its failure – obviously influenced him more than he was prepared to admit. His friends say that he made a vow never to become emotionally attached to anyone again. It became a pattern in his subsequent relationships with women that, as soon as he realised that one was becoming too dependent on him, he would break the friendship and look around for someone else. He told Ellis Stungo, his psychiatrist friend, that this way he could be assured that he would never be hurt again.

So, in his fortieth year, Stephen Ward found himself once again a bachelor. He was determined to enjoy his status. In a London that was at last emerging from its post-war depression he had a circle of attractive and interesting friends and his profession was flourishing. Early in 1950 he added another famous name to his list of patients – Bill Astor, a member of the enormously wealthy Anglo-American family. Astor came to Ward complaining of a back injury after a fall from his horse while hunting. Ward had been recommended by Astor's half-brother, Bobbie Shaw, who swore by Ward's healing skills – he even went to Ward, rather than to a general practitioner, for treatment for an infected wound on his arm.

The relationship between Ward and Astor blossomed rapidly. It had a dual base. On the medical side, Ward proved a godsend to Astor. Always a hypochondriac, Astor had finally found someone who not only treated his aches and pains, but was prepared to listen patiently while he talked about them: his back always ached after riding; his new diet did not seem to suit him; his blood pressure was up again. As we shall see, there is evidence that Astor may have considered – in the manner of sovereigns – employing Ward as his full-time medical adviser. He certainly came to depend on Ward and to trust him as he had never done with any of his earlier doctors. 'If Bill wanted Stephen,' Astor's third wife, Bronwen, recalls, 'he'd send the chauffeur down with a note saying "could you come and do a massage?" Bill used to hunt practically every Saturday throughout the season, so it was great to have someone who would come and give you a massage after that.'

The second level of the relationship between the two men grew largely out of Astor's psychological problems. He was a complex, unhappy man. Those who knew him well – his few friends and his relatives – place the blame for Astor's difficulties squarely with his mother, the redoubtable Nancy, Lady Astor, a woman of powerful personality. Any relationship between such a remarkable woman and her sons was bound to be an awkward one, but Lady Astor exacerbated the inherent problems. Although she had many fine qualities – courage, generosity, a zest for living – she also had a streak of cruelty, and in favouring her son by her first marriage, Bobbie, over William, who was her eldest son by Waldorf Astor, she did so in a destructive and brutal manner.

Bill grew up a nervous, tense, insecure person who had great difficulty in forming relationships. His younger brother David says, 'The way I tried to describe him was being blasted by a lack of love.' He was clumsy, a fidget, and this nervousness turned people away, until he had few friends, only acquaintances.

Life became a constant disappointment for Bill. He went through Oxford with some credit, served in naval intelligence during the war, and won a safe Conservative seat in the Commons in 1955. There he could normally have expected to have fitted into some place in the lower echelons of the Government comfortably and usefully. But nothing was offered him, and when his father died he became a peer, and moved to the House of Lords.

He devoted himself to those pursuits where he felt secure. He was good at making money; he was an accomplished Orientalist, and he ran a successful horse-racing stable. In all these areas he felt in control. Business and horse-breeding did not require personal rapport and in the East his awkwardness, defensiveness and shyness did not provoke the same impatience as in Britain or the United States.

As can be imagined, Astor's relationships with women were rocky. His sensitivity and lack of aggression often brought forth a maternal instinct in women he met, but this was not always the relationship he was seeking. One of Ward's girl friends remembers finding herself alone with Astor, whom she considered shy and boring. Astor, knowing that Ward was away, came to visit her and asked her if she would like to 'slip into something more comfortable', hinting at 'baby doll' pyjamas, which were then the latest fashion. When she pretended not to understand what he meant, Astor's nerve deserted him and he left.

It would not have taken a man of Ward's perception very long to have realised that in Astor he had a patient who needed a lot more than adjustment to his back. Here was a man of some potential who had, for reasons not entirely his fault, failed to achieve anything of note. Ward saw a chance to remould him, to act as physician not only to his body but to the whole man.

What Ward had to offer must have seemed very attractive. He took Astor out of his stultifying existence, away from his board meetings, his charitable works and his formal dinner parties, into an exciting world of coffee bars, drinking clubs, bottle parties, stimulating conversations and pretty, available girls. Astor began to blossom.

Pictures of him at the time show a slightly balding, middle-aged man of medium height with rather large ears and a quizzical, uncertain smile, almost as if he was beginning to realise that life held more than he had previously imagined.

The traffic was not all one way. Ward gained from the relationship as well. His friendship with Astor confirmed his place in London society, won him acceptance to houses and clubs that might otherwise have remained closed to him, and extended his practice – Astor freely recommended Ward's skills to his acquaintances and business associates. And when Ward's trouble with the Inland Revenue threatened his practice, Astor came to the rescue. According to Philippa Astor, Bill's second wife, her husband bought the building at 38 Devonshire Street so that Ward could continue to use the consulting rooms and the flat above, rent free, thus easing his financial problems. He also made Ward a cash loan of £1,250.

The two men met frequently, dined together and shared their problems with each other. Some of Astor's friends say that Ward knew that Astor could be useful to him and exploited Astor's weaknesses to bind him more closely. But whatever Ward's initial motives, he grew to like Astor and to consider him his closest friend.

# A Rising Star
# in the Tory Party

5 |

St Columba's in Pont Street, Knightsbridge, is discreet yet fashionable, the sort of church chosen by couples who are aware of their place in society and who want a quiet wedding that nevertheless will not pass entirely unnoticed. It was here on 31 December 1954, a chill grey day, that John Profumo, 39, a rising star in the Conservative Party, married the actress Valerie Hobson, 37. As one gossip writer put it, 'The Profumos had an almost ostentatiously Quiet Wedding — no film stars, no producers, no directors, no political names.' But when the couple arrived at London Airport for the honeymoon flight to the south of France, their plane was parked on the VIP No. 1 bay and the authorities opened the royal lounge for a champagne toast.

Miss Hobson was a divorcee, her previous marriage to the film producer, Anthony Havelock-Allen, having been dissolved two years earlier. She was the daughter of a naval commander, born in County Antrim in Northern Ireland. Her upbringing was uncompromisingly conservative: Protestant, narrow, moral. Her acting career had been in the doldrums — she had not been on the West End stage for twenty years — until she won the star role in *The King and I*, then running at the Drury Lane Theatre. Now, back at the top again, she was throwing it all away for another try at marriage.

Profumo was a bachelor. A distinguished wartime career and his political activities had left him little time for romance. (He once complained that in the middle of the North African campaign, at a particularly sticky stage, he had received a letter that had made its way from the Conservative agent in Kettering, Northamptonshire, to the communications caravan in Tunisia where Profumo was doing his bit to win the war. The letter, he said, asked somewhat querulously why Profumo had not read the Beveridge Report and sent his comments on it.)

The marriage delighted the Conservative Party. It had been the one attribute lacking in a young MP who was clearly Prime Ministerial material. Everything else about Profumo was almost too perfect to be true. Descended from an aristocratic Italian family that had settled in

Britain in the 1880s, John Profumo had had a ruling-class upbringing. Educated at Harrow and Oxford, where he did better at sports than at his studies, he quickly found his real love, flying.

He was a member of the University Air Squadron and a frequent guest at the lavish weekend parties given in the 1930s by Sir Lindsay Everard, a Tory MP, at his estate, Ratcliff Hall in Leicestershire. The common interest was aviation and a weekend might begin with dinner for thirty at the Hall on Saturday night, then a flight to Deauville on Sunday for lunch, and end back at Everard's private aerodrome in time to motor to London on Sunday night or Monday morning.

All Everard's guests were influential people, or about to be (Hermann Göring, the Nazi Air Force chief, was a visitor) and Profumo made useful contacts there. Not that there was any doubt that if he chose politics as a career he would have any difficulty: the Profumo family was too firmly entrenched in the British establishment. His father was a barrister, a King's Counsel, with a lucrative practice in the Middle Temple. The family money was in insurance and in their social life the Profumos were very much a part of the English landed gentry.

They hunted with the Warwickshire, attended all the horse shows and the Conservative Party fêtes, played polo, gave dinner parties, and were active in charitable works. Young Profumo seems to have set his eye at an early age on the goal of Foreign Secretary. When he left Oxford he set off on a long overseas tour, visiting the United States, China, Japan and the Soviet Union. In 1938 he toured Germany, ostensibly to study economic conditions but also to assess for himself the strength of Hitler's regime. He took a keen interest in international and commonwealth organisations. He became chairman of the West Midlands Federation of the Junior Imperial League and he visited Geneva for the International Labour Conference and to watch the last gasps of the League of Nations.

But Foreign Secretaries have to start at the bottom, so Profumo's first political post was ward chairman of the East Fulham Conservative Association. He quickly became known to party headquarters as a young man who would never refuse a posting. By the time he was 21 he was chairman of the entire Association and a powerful supporter and friend of its MP, Bill Astor. At 24 he was the prospective Conservative Party candidate for the Kettering Division, the most memorable candidate the constituency had ever had.

A year later, in the lull of the 'phoney war' period, there was a by-election. Profumo won with a hefty majority of 11,000 votes over an 'anti-war' opponent. The youngest MP in Parliament, he soon showed his mettle. On 8 May 1940, he joined 29 other Conservative MPs in a revolt against their leader, Neville Chamberlain, and his appeasement policies. This vote had dual importance for Profumo: it showed his political courage, and it formed among the 30 rebels, men of the calibre of Harold Macmillan and Quintin Hogg (later Lord Hailsham), a lasting allegiance.

By the time he became an MP, Profumo was already in the army, a second lieutenant in the Yeomanry Armoured Detachment, in charge of a motor-cycle group whose job it would be to maintain communications if the Germans invaded. In 1941, promoted to captain, he became a liaison officer between the army and the Royal Air Force. His main task was to promote inter-services harmony and Profumo chose a striking way of going about it, one which showed his talent for organisation. He wrote and produced a musical, 'Night and Day', which was a sufficiently professional effort to star Frances Day in the lead, and which was seen by 2,500 servicemen and women.

In 1943 Profumo, now a major, was in the thick of the North African campaign, where he was mentioned in dispatches. By 1944 he was a lieutenant-colonel, the senior air-staff liaison officer with Field Marshall Alexander. He still made time for his parliamentary duties, and on one occasion he flew to London to make a speech raising questions about servicemen's welfare, including a headline-grabbing attack on the 'niggardly' clothing allowance paid to women members of the services.

When the Germans surrendered in Italy, Colonel Profumo, now the holder of the Order of the British Empire for his work in the campaign, won the coveted assignment of escorting the German generals to the surrender ceremonies at the headquarters of the American General Mark Clark. He wrote about it for his local newspaper: 'The meeting took place at night by the light of torches. It was very formal and quiet, save for the clicks of Nazi boots. There was no handshaking.'

The Labour landslide in 1945 swept Profumo out of Parliament, along with the Churchill Government. He remained in the army for another two years, now a brigadier, working in Japan with General Douglas MacArthur as chief of staff to the British Liaison Mission. In 1947 he returned to politics, joining the Central Conservative Office as the party's broadcasting adviser. A year later he was adopted as the Tory candidate for Stratford-upon-Avon and won the seat in 1950 with a majority of 9,000. Two years later he was in Government office, as Joint Parliamentary Secretary at the Ministry of Transport and Civil Aviation.

The dashing young aviator of pre-war days had matured. Thin, with a long handsome face, an easy charm, a quick sense of humour, and the assurance of his birth, Profumo was clearly a high-flyer. Politics had become an obsession. He narrowed his interests, dropping most of his sporting pursuits in favour of his career. (However, he could not resist a chance to fly in an air race to New Zealand, joining the race crew as steward and cook.)

Profumo's marriage enhanced his career prospects. He was honest – and amusing – enough to admit this. He said of his partnership: 'When I married my beautiful and talented wife I quickly found that I had become a most popular speaker. People used to invite me to open their bazaars, adding, "You'll of course bring along your charming wife". I tumbled to it all when a socialist asked me to open his bazaar. "You'll of course bring along your charming wife," he added. When I told him that that would be impossible, he replied, "Don't bother then. Come along yourself – next year!"'

In 1954, then, it appeared as if nothing could stand in the way of John Profumo's ambition to be Foreign Secretary. One day, in the not too distant future, he could very well be Prime Minister.

# 6 | *The Waif and the*
# *Crooked Businessman*

In the early 1950s, two people, a suburban waif and a crooked, cosmopolitan businessman, entered Ward's life. The waif was Valerie Mewes. When Ward transformed her into a star, she loved him for it. The businessman was John Lewis, one-time Labour MP. When Lewis thought that he had been betrayed by Ward, he developed an obsessive and dangerous hatred for him.

Valerie had left home in October 1949. She walked out of her grandmother's bungalow at 4 Chandos Road, Egham, carrying a brown fake-leather bag containing her collection of film fan magazines, her radio, and a change of clothing. She flagged down a green 701 bus, boarded it, and bought a 1s. 7d. ticket to carry her the 18 miles to London. At 17 years of age Valerie had embarked on the greatest adventure of her young life. Joyce Edmonds, who lived across the road at number 34, remembers Valerie's departure. 'She was one of our gang. We all used to talk about leaving home, living in London, becoming filmstars, meeting famous people, and marrying a prince. No one ever thought Valerie would actually do it.'

The 701 bus arrived at Park Lane at 8.35 p.m. and Valerie immediately had her first glimpse of Mayfair's varied night life. Prostitutes loitered, singly and in groups, under the street lamps. Kerb crawlers drove slowly past them, holding up the traffic in the late evening rush hour. There was a procession of chauffeur-driven limousines arriving at the Dorchester and the Grosvenor House hotels. Valerie wandered slowly to Hyde Park Corner, turned, headed for the bright lights of Piccadilly, and was swallowed up by the London crowd.

She resurfaced a year later. A heavy April cloudburst found her sheltering in the doorway of a shop in Oxford Street. She had obviously been walking for a long time. The rain had pasted the hair to her head and her damp clothing clung limply to her body. As Valerie, shivering with the cold, waited for the shower to pass, Stephen Ward joined her in the doorway. They smiled at each other.

As Ward told his friends, 'It was a smile you could never forget, spontaneous, uninhibited and genuine.'

Journalist Freddy Mullally wrote later, 'One can only guess what a mess she looked. But what Stephen saw at once with his artist-osteopath eye, were the cheekbones, the clear, opaque skin, the superbly-turned legs inside the laddered hose. And he must have seen something else, something most of us would have missed. Valerie was about 18, of poor parents, uneducated, out of work. Her accent was plain working class, but she was an original.'

Ward offered her a cup of coffee and on the way to Cavendish Square Valerie chattered incessantly − her year in London had not dulled her dreams. In Ward's flat she dried her hair, and at Ward's invitation changed into some clothes that Ward's wife, Patricia, had left behind when she moved out. When Valerie had curled up in front of the fire, her hair piled on top of her head, Ward sketched her. She should be a model, he said, and offered to introduce her to people who could help her.

Valerie slept on the sofa but in the early hours crept into bed alongside Ward saying that she felt lonely. Ward kissed her chastely on the forehead, and said that he knew how she felt. They spent the rest of the night talking. Valerie told him how she had quarrelled with her boyfriend and was about to lose her accommodation. She had been sharing a room with Ruth Ellis (later to become notorious as the last woman in Britain to be hanged for murder after shooting her lover). Ellis had just found a job as the manageress of the Little Club in Knightsbridge. When she moved from the room Valerie would no longer be able to afford the rent.

Ward listened intrigued. As he later confided to a friend, 'Valerie was a born optimist. She never showed her unhappiness although it was evident she had no one to turn to. And her talk was constantly punctuated by her smile. I used to try to keep her laughing just for the joy of seeing her face light up. I never got tired of her laughter. She bubbled over with the sheer love of life.'

During the next few weeks Ward transformed Valerie from a delightful teenager into a sophisticated, socially-acceptable young woman who nevertheless lost none of her originality. The exercise cost him time and money but he took a delight in every minute of it. They began with a new name, something simple, catchy, and easy to remember − Vickie Martin.

Next, Ward spent patient hours ironing out the harsh parts of Vickie's cockney accent. Some lessons on how to walk like a model, a regular reading of the newspapers to give her a reasonable grasp of current affairs and Vickie was about ready. There was one last thing.

Realising that behind Vickie's confident air there lurked a deep homesickness, he insisted that she re-establish contact with her grandmother, Mrs Alice Reynolds, and he drove her to Egham himself, a gesture that made Mrs Reynolds a firm friend for the rest of her life.

Ward chose the bar of Siegi Sessler's new club, the Fine Arts, in Charles Street, to introduce Vickie to Mayfair society. Mullally was there. 'The euphoria hadn't quite mounted to its heady pre-dinner peak when Stephen and Vickie made their entrance. There were girls in the room far lovelier than Vickie, and all of them were more expensively and elaborately dressed. It just didn't matter. They all lost their escorts, for as long as they stayed in the bar, to a girl-of-the-people with short-cropped hair the texture of hemp, a laughing, unguardedly-avid face, and a body you would commit crimes for.'

Vickie Martin was launched. She became a model for photographers Baron Nahum and Anthony Beauchamp. The society artist Vasco Lazzolo did her portrait in oils. She was taken to the best London nightspots and to the Royal Meetings at Ascot by princes and earls. Her escorts showered her with jewels and flowers. She became the darling of the gossip columnists: 'the Golden Girl', 'the Girl from Nowhere', 'the Girl with No Past'. She got a part in a film. And she became the toast of London.

She was seen at expensive restaurants, film premières, first nights at the theatre, and at a seemingly endless round of cocktail parties. The smart young men of London liked her because she was different. She had picked up Ward's views on the British class system and took a delight in crossing social barriers. After a night out in Mayfair, she would order her titled escort to Covent Garden where she would spend the early hours talking to market workers. Or, instead of a lavish dinner in the West End, she would take her escort to a pub in Whitechapel where she would stand on the table and lead the community singing.

Her money — she was earning well by then — meant nothing to her. She gave most of it away to friends, hangers-on, and street buskers. Some sensed in her a certain desperation. Film producer Kenneth Harper, who gave Vickie a major role in the only film she made, *It Started in Paradise*, said of her, 'Vickie always lived too close to the wind. One had the feeling that something had to happen to her.' But in four short years, Vickie Martin achieved almost all her dreams. She even found her prince.

He was there that first night at Siegi Sessler's club. The Maharaja of Cooch Behar — of Harrow and Cambridge, palaces in India, two flats in London and a £20,000 a year tax-free princely purse (£200,000 by today's values) – was a well-known international playboy, a friend of Aly Khan, Clark Gable, Errol Flynn, and the Marquess of Milford Haven (Prince Philip's cousin). At the age of 34, still a bachelor, he could have had virtually any girl in London. He chose Vickie Martin.

Cooch Behar knew Ward from Ward's time in India, so he asked for an introduction to Vickie. Ward obliged and after a brief conversation Cooch Behar invited Ward and Vickie to dine with him the following night at Les Ambassadeurs. In the meantime, to show Vickie what an impression she had made on him, he walked into the Dorchester Hotel, bought the entire contents of its flower shop and ordered it all to be sent to her at Ward's flat.

Vickie had a dangerous love of speed. In three years she was involved in eleven car crashes. Newspapers began to refer to her as 'the unluckiest girl who ever rode in a car'. This did not deter her. She took long, fast drives with Cooch Behar in his midnight blue Bentley, urging him to see how fast the car could go. Cooch Behar and Vickie in another of his cars were speeding along the highway near Baldock, Hertfordshire, when they hit the kerb. The car flipped over and landed on its roof.

Cooch Behar broke his collar bone and five ribs. Vickie had concussion, minor leg injuries and a black eye. In Ward 11 at the Lister hospital, Hitchin, Vickie held court for the Press. Journalists could hardly get in, most spare space being occupied with hundreds of vases of flowers which Cooch Behar had ordered from his sick bed across the corridor. Fleet Street scented a romance. 'London Model to Wed Prince' and 'Vickie's Romance with the Maharajah', said the headlines.

But there were problems which the newspapers did not know. Cooch Behar was worried that if he wed a foreigner the Indian Government would stop his princely purse. When he went off to stay with his cousin, the Maharaja of Jaipur, in East Grinstead, Vickie, consoled by his parting gift of a gold Cartier brooch of a leaping Indian tiger, decided to consult Ward. Cooch Behar was prepared, she said, to sacrifice the princely purse and go ahead and marry her. But he would be unable to keep up his London life. They would have to live in India. She was agreeable, she told Ward, but would it work?

Ward said he did not think it would. He pointed out that Cooch Behar had become used to his ostentatious lifestyle and that, if he gave it up and was unhappy he might well come to blame her for it. Ward also warned Vickie of the limitations of a sedate palace life in India. After the initial thrill, he said, a girl like her – headstrong, capricious and fun-loving – would soon become bored. She would miss the freedom and independence she enjoyed in London.

Vickie listened. When Cooch Behar returned from his convalescence, Vickie explained why she felt she could not marry him. He told her that if there was ever a way he could marry her without losing his princely purse he would do so.

For the next four months they went everywhere together. They shared a passion for horses and they often drove to Newmarket for the thoroughbred sales, or to Windsor to see the polo, or they would fly to Paris for the racing at Longchamps. Sometimes, on the way to Windsor, they would visit Vickie's grandmother at Egham. Once Joyce Edmonds, Vickie's old friend, was outside when the couple arrived in the blue Bentley. 'A beautiful blonde waved at me and shouted "Hello Joyce". But I thought she'd made a mistake and I turned away. It was only later that I realised that the Vickie Martin I kept reading about in the newspapers was my old friend Valerie Mewes.'

They had one more summer together. When Cooch Behar left for India he promised Vickie that next time she would accompany him as his wife. And for Christmas he commissioned Vasco Lazzolo to paint her portrait. Although the painting did not have to be ready until the summer of 1955, when Cooch Behar would arrive for his annual visit, Vickie, perhaps from a premonition, began sitting for it immediately, begging Lazzolo to finish it by the New Year.

'The last time we all saw Vickie,' recalls Freda Ferrier, 'was when she came walking down the staircase at our New Year's Eve party. She was dressed in a top hat, white tie and tails. She had these wonderful long legs in black tights. She looked absolutely stunning. As she swept down the stairs everyone held their breath for a moment and just stared.'

Nine days later Vickie Martin was in her 13th car crash. At 3.30 a.m., just outside Maidenhead, her car, which was being driven by journalist Terence Robertson, was in collision with another. Robertson suffered leg injuries and amnesia. The driver of the other car was killed instantly. Vickie Martin died shortly afterwards from massive and horrific injuries. She was 23.

There was a public funeral for Vickie Martin in the small chapel at Golders Green crematorium. The titled and the rich from Mayfair wept openly. Cooch Behar sent a huge wreath of red roses with a card that read 'Goodbye to Méchante. My love always Tigre.' (A year later he married Vickie's best friend, Gina Egan − without losing his princely purse.)

Afterwards there was a short burial service in the little village cemetery at Englefield Green for Valerie Mewes. Only a handful of people attended: bandleader Paul Adams, club-owner Ruby Lloyd, producer Kenneth Harper and his wife, and Stephen Ward. Harper said later, 'Stephen Ward was magnificent. The moment he heard the news he went down to stay with Vickie's grandmother to console her. Vickie and Stephen were always very close. Her death was a great blow to him.'

Ward's part in transforming Valerie Mewes into Vickie Martin had given him a lot of satisfaction. This was the first time he had played Professor Higgins and he had enjoyed transforming a girl from a humble background into the toast of London. But, as became apparent with others who succeeded Vickie, in order to be a success the girl had to have her own originality. Ward's search for someone as unusual and as enchanting as Vickie Martin, his first 'Fair Lady', was to contribute to his downfall.


John Lewis was to bring nothing but trouble to Ward. Outwardly he was a charming, upwardly mobile and ambitious Labour MP, successful in business and devoted to his wife. But there was another side to him. He was unscrupulous, falling foul of Harold Wilson, who was President of the Board of Trade at the time, by trying to influence Board officials. Wilson banned Lewis from the Board's offices.

In 1955 his company won a very lucrative contract from the National Coal Board to supply conveyor belting to bring coal from mines. Once Lewis was certain from his negotiations with the Coal Board that the deal would eventually come off, he told all his friends to buy shares at the depressed price. When the contract, the biggest the Coal Board had ever awarded, was announced, the price of shares in his company, Rubber Improvements, soared fifteenfold. Friends who had bought them made a lot of money from this inside information. One who did not was the actor, Jon Pertwee. He recalls, 'Lewis told me to buy all the stock I could. I had nothing to do with the stock market so I didn't bother. Next time Lewis saw me he said, "Well, where's the Roller?" When I looked blank he said, "You must have got a Rolls-Royce out of it at least." When I said I hadn't bought any shares in his company, he said, "You're a bloody fool."'

Lewis's social life was not the success he wished. Many of the people who accepted his hospitality made fun of him behind his back for his desperate desire to be accepted in the London scene, his vulgarity over money, his heavy drinking, his woman-chasing activities, and his vanity. He was half aware of this and blamed his wife. He told the divorce court that he had hoped for a bride who would 'grace the life of a public man'. Instead, he said, when he had chided his wife for not shaking hands with a receiving ambassador at a reception, his wife had replied, 'Let the bloody ambassador come to me.'

His wife confided to women friends that Lewis's sex education seemed to have come from prostitutes and that he expected her to perform services like washing his genitals after intercourse. Their sexual relationship declined to the point where Joy Lewis had consulted the family doctor, David Minton, about her repugnance for her husband and Minton, she said, had advised her, 'Find yourself a lover.'

Lewis, dissatisfied, convinced that there was more to the social scene than he had experienced, at this stage met Ward and was immediately entranced. Ward appeared to be leading exactly the life that Lewis had imagined for himself – friends with famous names from all levels of London life who genuinely seemed to like him; plenty of pretty young girls and opportunities for sexual gratification with few inhibitions. Ward, in turn, introduced Lewis to Freddy Mullally, former *Sunday Mirror* journalist and *Tribune* editor who had started a Mayfair public relations company, Mullally and Warner, with his wife, Suzanne Warner, an American who was Howard Hughes's publicity officer in Britain. Lewis began to meet film starlets and models, and to attend parties where girls were to be had for the taking. 'I've screwed every pretty girl in London' became his oft-repeated boast.

But Lewis's sexual morals were essentially provincial and sexist as Mullally soon discovered. 'He called me one morning, said he was in bed with a cold or something, and demanded that I come to Abbey Lodge immediately. It was absolutely vital.' Mullally was busy and tried to get out of it, but Lewis was insistent and eventually Mullally went. 'He was sitting up in bed and he launched straight into it. "Joy's left me," he said. "I know she's been unfaithful. I want you to help me. Freddy you're my friend, I want you and Suzanne to find out the names of the men Joy's been involved with."' Mullally said that he did not intend to spy on Joy Lewis and he was certain that his wife, who was very friendly with Joy, would not do so either. Lewis's mood changed and he said, 'All right, then. But remember, those who aren't with me are against me. You'd better watch out.'

The same day Lewis summoned a journalist friend, Warwick Charlton. 'He was in bed looking desperately worried and he said, "Warwick, I'm going to kill myself." And, knowing he was being melodramatic, I said, "Do you mind not doing it while I'm here, John." He said, "Do you know Stephen Ward?" and when I said yes, he said, "He's a bastard. Not only did he introduce Joy to Freddy

Mullally but to some Swedish beauty queen as well. I'm going to cite seven men and one woman in my divorce case." He was livid with anger, appalled that Joy had done anything at all. He blamed Stephen entirely and swore that one day he would pay him back.'

Mullally discussed Lewis with Ward. 'What had happened was that Joy Lewis had had a terrible fight with John and had walked out into the night with nowhere to go. Knowing Stephen and knowing how hospitable he was to people in trouble she went to Stephen's flat and, in great distress, asked him to put her up for the night. I'm positive nothing happened between them – Stephen was too conscious of his image as a gentleman to have tried to take advantage of her predicament – and the next day Joy went back to Lewis. Lewis was a tremendous bully with women and he put her down in a chair and third-degreed her. She told him she had stayed at Stephen's and from that moment on Lewis developed an obsession about Stephen and decided to get him any way he could.'

Mullally was part of Lewis's obsession too, perhaps with some justification – the divorce court judge found that he had had an affair with Joy Lewis – and Lewis moved quickly to avenge himself. Lewis could be ruthless – he once ordered a racehorse he owned to be put down after it finished last in an important race – and his tactics to punish Ward and Mullally barred no holds. He began to gather evidence for his divorce case and let it be known that he planned to name both Ward and Mullally as co-respondents in the action.

As a warm-up to the main bout, Lewis brought libel and slander actions against Mullally, claiming that Mullally had accused him in public of having paid £200 to a one-time employee of Mullally's to give false information in the divorce action. Lewis won. The court awarded him £700 damages and ordered Mullally to pay the costs, estimated at £1,000. Lewis won again in the divorce action, despite some curious sidelights to the case. (In one of these, another former employee of Mullally's gave a statement against him, then later retracted this evidence under oath and flew off to Canada. Lewis followed him there and persuaded him to revert to his original evidence. In another, a witness who gave evidence for Lewis had cosmetic surgery on her nose after the trial, the surgeon's bill being paid by Lewis.) Lewis was given custody of his daughter and Mullally was ordered to pay his own costs and one third of those of both John Lewis and his wife. These were estimated at £7,000 (£70,000 at today's values) and the total payout crushed Mullally financially.

But Lewis was having less success in his efforts to ruin Ward. Ward had been dropped from Lewis's divorce action in a legal *quid pro quo* deal. Ward had issued slander writs against Lewis because Lewis had been telling anyone who would listen that Ward had procured Joy for Freddy Mullally. Solicitors for both parties reached a compromise – Lewis would not name Ward in his divorce action if Ward would drop his slander action against Lewis.

So Lewis turned to other methods to avenge himself on Ward. He wrote to the taxman. The Inland Revenue suddenly swooped on Ward and began a long and detailed investigation into his financial and business affairs. The investigators told Ward that they were acting on 'information received'. The investigation showed that Ward's bookkeeping was chaotic and he received such a large bill for back taxes that it was to take him several years to pay it off. But the incident which was to have the most serious repercussions on Ward's life – and one that can positively be traced to Lewis – concerned sex.

Mullally was in his office at Hay Hill one summer afternoon in 1951 when he received an agitated telephone call from Ward. As Mullally recalls, 'He sounded very angry indeed. He said he had just kicked out a reporter from the *Daily Express* who had called on him "to discuss a tip-off that you [Ward] and Frederic Mullally had been operating a call girl service in Mayfair." Stephen said the reporter was on his way to see me and wanted my okay to ring the *Daily Express* and create hell. I told him to leave it to me.'

The reporter duly arrived and Mullally told him to get out before he was thrown out. Then Mullally made an appointment to see Arthur Christiansen, the editor of the *Daily Express* and a friend. 'I told him what had happened and he sent for the News Editor, Morley Richards, and in my presence demanded to know the source of the allegation. Morley, clearly embarrassed, hemmed and hawed, turned red, pretended to be ignorant of the source and said he would have to look into it. Lewis's name was mentioned and Morley's reaction left me in no doubt that he was the source. Christiansen said he would see that we would not be bothered again and asked me to forget about the incident. I told Stephen what I'd done and he reluctantly accepted my advice that an action against Lewis for slander would be a waste of time and money.'

When Lewis realised his plan to get Ward in this manner had failed, he began to telephone the Marylebone Police Station anonymously, saying that Dr Ward was procuring girls for his wealthy patients. The police treated the calls as coming from a crank, and ignored them – for the moment.

# 7 | *Delightful Days at Cliveden*

In the days when Bill Astor entertained at Cliveden guests could wander at will, or go boating, play tennis, bowls or croquet; visit the stud or go riding. An invitation to spend a summer weekend at Cliveden in the 1950s was to step from the competitive hurly-burly of London into a pre-war haven of luxury and privilege that had, somehow, managed to survive.

Ward was a frequent guest at Cliveden. Bill Astor had invited him most weekends during the hunting season to treat his back after a vigorous ride and, as the two men had grown closer, took to asking him throughout the summer months to enjoy his company. One Saturday afternoon in July 1956, Philippa Astor suggested a ride in Cliveden's motor launch. From the boat Ward noticed for the first time a rather impressive, though dilapidated, cottage in a secluded corner of Cliveden's grounds. It was a large, double-fronted place built in an almost Tyrolean style with twin, deeply-pitched roofs, stucco walls, and leaded-light windows, and a very distinct gabled balcony around the first floor. It was a mile from the main house down a winding drive through beech woods to the river and then along the bank, past the boathouse.

Ward tentatively suggested that he might be interested in doing the cottage up and using it at weekends instead of staying in the main house. Philippa Astor, who looked on Ward as a good friend, supported him. She had considered living in the cottage herself – her marriage to Bill Astor was breaking down and she left Cliveden four months later – but had decided too much was wrong with it. 'It's a lovely cottage to look at but it's incredibly damp. I decided it was a rather unhealthy place, so sodden you felt like living death after being in it for more than ten minutes.'

Bill Astor was won over. Ward was to pay him a 'peppercorn rent' of £1 a year. In return, there was an understanding that when Ward was in residence at the weekends or on holidays, he would be available to give treatment if Astor or any of his guests needed it.

Ward was delighted. 'I cannot express how much I grew to love that cottage,' he said. 'It represented a haven from the turmoil of London. The garden was a wilderness. The stream was choked with huge weeds and nettles with roots like hoop-iron. Gradually I overcame them.' Ward was helped in his work by the new love in his life, Margaret Brown, a tall, striking redhead.

They had met at a New Year's Eve party on the Embankment. She was already a successful model, very independent and earning a good income. Ward was instantly attracted to her. 'She was probably the most beautiful girl in London. She was very hard-working, very professional. She never went to bed late when she had a modelling assignment the next day. She knew that a modelling career did not last long and that therefore she had to be serious about it until she was no longer on the top.' They met a couple of times at parties given by mutual friends. Soon afterwards Margaret moved into Ward's flat and they shared expenses. Their friends considered them a 'couple'. Ward went further, saying that they had become engaged.

The cottage was theirs, rather than his. They would drive down there on Friday evening or as early as possible on Saturday morning, just the two of them. Unless guests were prepared to help, they were discouraged on Saturday because it was a work day. Margaret tackled the painting indoors while Ward wrestled with the garden. As he said: 'With infinite effort and backache I carried tons of rocks to surround the little waterfall that ran down to the river from alongside the cottage. I planted it with every kind of alpine plant and in the spring and for most of the summer it was a glorious sight. Down by the water's edge I planted irises, marigolds and primulas. Campanulas trailed into the water and in the summer I fitted the huge ornamental tubs with hanging plants.'

Gradually the cottage became a home, although it never had facilities for luxury living. The electricity supply cable was able to cope with lighting but nothing else, so heating was from oil fires, cooking by bottled gas, and the outside spring substituted for a refrigerator. Not that Ward or Margaret Brown wanted to entertain. Instead they invited friends to 'muck in'. Anyone could stop by on Sundays without notice — there was no telephone — as long as they were prepared to eat whatever was on the stove, sleep wherever there was space, and contribute to conversation or entertainment in the evenings.

Ward kept some old clothes at the cottage for girls who used to come from London expecting something grander. He provided no alcohol, not even wine. Guests who wanted a drink were expected to bring their own. No one can remember Ward himself drinking anything at his cottage other than coffee, his favourite beverage. During the day, the guests would sit around and watch the pleasure craft going to Cookham Lock, or the fishermen who lined the opposite bank. If they were lucky, they might catch sight of a fox, a hedgehog, a badger, or even an otter which would sometimes sit at the waterfall watching the people watching him.

Sometimes there would be a picnic. The other two cottages on the estate were rented by Alan Brien, the writer, and Philip de Zulueta, secretary to the Prime Minister, Harold Macmillan. According to Brien, Macmillan would sometimes visit de Zulueta and on these occasions Ward and Brien would be invited over for tea on the lawn of de Zulueta's cottage. This means that when the scandal developed, Macmillan knew only too well who Ward was.

Lunch and dinner at Ward's cottage were usually the same – a big pot of stew or curry, enlivened by gifts from guests. Then everyone would sit around a fire – it could be chilly in the cottage even in the summer – and Ward would conduct the conversation in much the same way as a conductor directs an orchestra. He would open a topic – sex, religion, black magic, science, art, politics – and provoke his guests' opinions by making some outrageous statement. 'He was a philosophical spectator,' Margaret Brown said later. 'He liked to make a shocking remark and then sit back and see what effect it had on people. He was well-informed, highly intelligent and able to bring both political and historical subjects alive in a manner no one else could. And he was often right. I can remember that very early on he said that the United States would one day get around to recognising and accepting Red China.' As a break if the talk became too dull or heavy, Ward would lead his guests in a game of 'ghosts' in the misty woods. The aim was to disperse, hide and then see who could give whom the most nerve-shattering fright. 'It all sounds very childish,' Ward said later. 'But we all loved every moment of it.'

Ward did not demand conversation from his guests. They were allowed to contribute in other ways if they wished. The conductor, Sir Malcolm Sargent, dropped by Ward's cottage with Bill Astor one Sunday evening to find three judo experts giving a demonstration of their skills on the lawn. Sargent insisted on joining them and nearly got tipped into the river. On another occasion Tommy Steele had been invited for Sunday afternoon. He lost his way, so he stopped his car before some impressive gateway and said to a man standing inside, 'Excuse me, but do you know how to get to Cliveden?' 'Yes,' the man said. 'Straight in here and follow the signs. But you've got to pay an entrance fee of 2s.' Steele paid, found Ward's cottage, and that evening Bill Astor came over from the main house. Ward introduced

Steele to him. 'Ah,' Steele said. 'You're the man who took my two bob. Do you mind if I have it back.'

Astor was fascinated by Ward's friends and spent a lot of time at the cottage. He looked to Ward and his crowd to entertain him and his guests. 'Astor was always over at Stephen's place,' one of Ward's friends remembers. 'And on the rare occasions when he didn't turn up then sure enough the chauffeur or someone would arrive with a message, "Come on Stephen. Bring some amusing people up and we'll meet by the pool." Astor was a lonely old man who had nothing in his life and Stephen had exciting friends. There was always someone of interest every Sunday, and they enjoyed it as much as the rest of us because Stephen entertained them too. He was a great conversationalist, one of the best I've ever met. He loved conversation and he loved people. Those weekends at his cottage were really something.'

The hospitality was not all one-way. Astor would invite Ward and Margaret Brown to some of the big parties at the main house. Ward often sat near Nancy Astor, then in her mid-seventies but still a major presence at Cliveden, because they got on well together, Ward reacting to her thrusts in kind, until she acknowledged defeat. 'I've seen her reduce people to tears with her jibes,' he said later. 'She pulled legs unmercifully.' It was a different Ward at these formal gatherings. He wore his dinner jacket. He was not too outrageous. He played the role expected of him — an amazing bohemian, an unconventional novelty, a fascinating Londoner, a 'visiting' member of the establishment. He enjoyed it.

'I sat next to Lord Hailsham and discussed the future of commercial television. I played bridge after dinner with Lord and Lady Dartmouth. Duncan Sandys was a frequent visitor with his red dispatch boxes from his Ministry. Frank Pakenham, later Lord Longford, was another peer who visited frequently. I also remember Lord Shackleton, Lord Derby, the Duchess of Roxburgh, the Duchess of Rutland, the Duchess of Westminster and Lord Gladwyn. Ayub Khan would come with several shy Eastern women. The visitors' book at Cliveden read like a private edition of *Who's Who*.'

Sometimes Astor would allow a friend to use Cliveden for a private party and on these grand occasions Ward and Margaret would be invited. Probably the most spectacular of these parties during Ward's time was given by Douglas Fairbanks Jnr for the coming out of his daughter Daphne on 18 June 1957. There were 450 guests, of some 12 nationalities, drawn from a cross-section of the international set. The Queen and Prince Philip, Princess Margaret, the Duchess of Kent and Princess Alexandra all attended. From the United States a contingent of prominent families made the Atlantic crossing to attend the party:

'Jock' Whitney and his wife Betsy, his stepdaughter Kate Roosevelt; 'Doc' Holden; the James Fosburghs; the Winthrop Aldrichs; Michael Canfield and his wife, Lee, who is John F. Kennedy's sister-in-law; Johnny Schiff's son David, and three friends from Yale; Peggy Bancroft and the Gilbert Millers.

From India came the young Maharaja of Cooch Behar, his cousin the Maharaja of Jaipur and his wife; from France the Marquise de Bousset-Roquefort and the Rothschilds; from Greece the Stavros Niarchos family; from Germany, Prince Frederick of Prussia. Professional friends of Fairbanks included Ben Lyons and Bebe Daniels, Oliver Messel the international interior designer, and the Richard Todds.

The guests drank champagne at four long bars, dined on cold Scotch salmon, turkey, ham, Scotch beef, hot dogs, hamburgers, sausages, kedgeree and bacon, strawberries, raspberries and chocolate éclairs, and danced to the music of two live bands, Paul Adams and Bobby Harvey. The house and grounds were floodlit, there were thousands of floral decorations. Tony Armstrong-Jones, a young photographer just beginning to make a name for himself, took the official portraits. Dancing did not begin until 10.30 p.m. because many of the guests attended dinners in London first – Sir Henry ('Chips') Channon, the Spanish and Swedish ambassadors, the Whitney Straights, the families of John Mills and Henry Tiarks, were among those who entertained Fairbanks's guests and then drove them to Cliveden.

They approached the house, which had lights in every window, along the wide driveway lined at every yard's distance with 3-feet-high flaming torches. All these lights were extinguished at midnight for the fireworks display. This ended with a set-piece, which spelt out Daphne's name in letters 6 feet high. For the display Astor had invited the patients and nurses from nearby hospitals, all the farmers, workers and staff on the Cliveden estate, and the chauffeurs and special police. They had been shepherded through a side gate to the grounds and given a party of their own with beer and sandwiches.

There were elaborate precautions to keep out the Press and gatecrashers. Two secretaries and a plain-clothes detective checked invitations and uniformed police patrolled the grounds. Two reporters managed to get past the first security check but were uncovered by Fairbanks's private secretary and were escorted from the grounds by a policeman.

Ward's comments on the party reveal his ignorance of, and lack of interest in, financial matters. 'While I was in my cottage there were two great parties at Cliveden. Both were coming-out parties for debutantes. All the trees lit by coloured lights, barbecues, two orchestras, river steamers alongside. All that sort of thing. Both parties were great successes and must have cost the hosts an enormous sum of money. At least £2,000 each. However, these parties were nothing to do with me. The house was just lent for the occasion and I was invited like the other guests.'

Ward, then, led a double life at Cliveden. We can picture him on a typical Saturday at his cottage, deeply engrossed in his gardening, happy at the progress he and Margaret are making in transforming their cottage, suddenly realising the time, and making a desperate dash to clean up and change into his dinner jacket in time to go to a formal dinner with the Astors. We can see him the following day, again in his old clothes, greeting the wide assortment of guests arriving from London, this one bringing a few bottles of wine, that one a leg of lamb, another a pound of cheese, or some fruit, chocolates, or tins of soup. And then Sunday lunch, outdoors if it was fine, with everyone sitting around with plates on their laps, talk flowing freely, tempers rising to one of Ward's outrageous remarks and then fading as newcomers realised what Ward was doing. Then the washing-up with everyone helping, the walks in the woods or along the river banks, friendships flowering, liaisons beginning and, more often than not, the arrival about teatime of the shy, awkward Astor, an outsider, but anxious to be part of Ward's glamorous gallery. Later, perhaps, a change of venue, as Ward and some of his guests made their way to the main house for a brief encounter with Astor on his home ground. The whole weekend gathered over the years a ritual quality that both Ward and Astor found extremely comfortable.

Ward's break with Margaret Brown was sudden, amiable and painful. She said later that she had genuinely wanted to marry Ward but he wanted to carry on the way they were. She came to realise that not only did he want to avoid the emotional responsibility of marriage but that the thought of any major change in the established pattern of his life disturbed him.

Ward had often talked about his ambition to open a holistic health centre, a clinic in the heart of London which would offer patients an alternative to conventional medicine. Margaret encouraged him and when an ideal location came on the market – a house at 46 Chelsea Square owned by Lord Parker, a judge later to play an important role in Ward's life – she persuaded her bank manager to loan her some of the £18,000 purchase price. They paid £1,800 deposit and then lost it because Ward dithered about raising the balance.

'Stephen had absolutely no material ambition whatsoever,' Margaret said later. 'When I realised this I was deeply disappointed in him.' She now knew that she could not rely on Ward to provide her with financial security when her modelling days were over, and when she was offered a film contract in Hollywood she accepted.

When she had gone Ward realised, too late, what he had lost and made frantic but unsuccessful attempts to persuade her to return and marry him. There is little doubt that she was the love of his life; as he confided to a friend, 'I know that she will always have a large part of my heart.'

# 8 | *The Promiscuous Showgirl*

On 22 March 1958, *Tit-Bits*, a popular but light-weight magazine, carried a pin-up picture of a long-legged girl in a bikini. There was nothing sensational about the girl's figure — in fact she appeared rather flat-chested. But what was striking was the contrast between the innocence of the pose and the maturity of the girl's face: the body might be that of a 15-year-old, but the expression suggested that here was a girl who knew a lot more about the world than the caption suggested.

'Though she is only fifteen,' it began, 'Christine Keeler is pretty enough to be a professional model. But the idea doesn't appeal to her because, quite frankly, she rather prefers animals to people and her hobby is dog-, cat-, or even bird-sitting.' The caption ended, 'It's not surprising that pretty Christine's ambition is to have a large house full of animals. Like any other young girl, or older girl for that matter, she loves dancing, the theatre and gay parties.'

This was Christine Keeler's first essay into modelling, part of her plan to break out of the restrictions of her upbringing in the Thames-side village of Wraysbury, and make a name for herself like Vickie Martin. Christine had been at school with Vickie's sister and had read in the newspapers about Vickie's exploits. She had even remembered Vickie coming home in Cooch Behar's Rolls-Royce to visit Vickie's parents, she told Ward later, just like a glamorous film star. The opportunities of London in the 1950s had attracted many girls like Christine, and Vickie Martin's story was taken as proof that their dreams were not unrealistic.

Wraysbury contained a strange mixture of old villagers, London middle-class on weekend retreats, and the improvised homes of the underprivileged, driven from London by the shortage of decent housing. Keeler's mother, who had re-married and who was now called Huish, lived in two converted railway carriages a few yards from the river, the carriage wheels half sunk into the damp ground. The carriages had no bathroom, no running hot water, and, until Christine was twelve, lighting came from oil lamps.

Christine did not get on well with her stepfather and for long periods did not exchange a word with him. At the age of 15 she told a psychiatrist that she hated her stepfather because he tried to make her come home in the evening by 10 o'clock. He locked her out once when she was late and let her in only when her mother interceded for her. He said she was going to end up in trouble.

At school, Christine was at first a tomboy – good at sports (discus and javelin), physically daring and competitive. But she matured early and quickly realised the power that her sexual attractiveness gave her. There were many secluded, abandoned gravel pits in the area which the local youth used for swimming parties in the hot summer months. The queen of these gatherings was Christine Keeler in her home-made, brief bikini and word of this nymphette spread widely.

By the age of 16 Christine had been thrown out of several local pubs for being hopelessly drunk. She had been banned from baby-sitting by many local women because she had flaunted her sexuality in front of their husbands. She had dated workers at the local tyre factory and, later, American servicemen at the Laleham Air Force base near Staines. We know this because on 17 April 1959, when she was barely 16, Christine gave birth to a baby boy in the King Edward VII Hospital in Old Windsor. The father was an American, serving at the base. She had tried all the usual methods a desperate girl used to employ to cause a miscarriage, and had not told her parents. The child was premature and lived only six days. When she came out of hospital she left home.

But did stories about the fascinating Christine also reach the nearby Thames-side cottage of Dr Edward ('Teddy') Sugden, the well-known gynaecologist, who had a lucrative practice in Half Moon Street, Mayfair? Sugden was an amazing man, especially for his time. He believed – when such beliefs were not only unfashionable but illegal – that women had the right of easy access to contraception and abortion. So he provided contraception to those society girls who wanted it – he was known around Mayfair, Knightsbridge and Belgravia as 'The Debs' Delight' – and abortion for those who could afford it. (If he liked the girl he would sometimes do it at cost – which, even so, was not cheap, because to stay within the law he had to have the opinion of two psychiatrists that the girl's mental health was at risk if Sugden did not perform the operation.)

Sugden was an eccentric. The walls of his waiting room were lined with glass cases filled with an assortment of live snakes, lizards, iguanas and exotic reptiles. In his cottage were hundreds more. And in this cottage at Wraysbury, not far from the gravel pits where Christine held court, Sugden indulged his other pleasure – group sex.

For Sugden had a problem. He was a gregarious, fun-loving man and a great womaniser, but outside surgery hours women steered clear of him. Michael Pertwee remembers meeting Sugden in a Chelsea club one evening. 'He was alone at the bar and looking very miserable. I asked him why and he said, "Well, I know every girl in this room and I also know that not one of them dare say hello to me." ' So Sugden created a 'scene' at Wraysbury and the word quickly spread. An assortment of Londoners who moved in a fringe world of property dealing, antiques, show business and import-export, and whose other similarity with Sugden was an ability to remain just on the right side of the law, would turn up at Sugden's open-house parties. After fine food and wines, inhibitions vanished. 'It was a case of grab whoever you fancied,' one guest recalls. 'Most of us knew each other anyway, but Teddy always managed to invite a local girl or two.'

The modelling job for *Tit-Bits* was only part of Christine's plan to change her life. The other was to cut her ties with Wraysbury, her family, and her boring job in nearby Slough. She moved to London, took a room in St John's Wood and found a job as a salesgirl/model in a Soho gown shop. No one spotted her; no prince came to spirit her away to the bright lights of show business. Instead she became the mistress of the black man who worked as a sweeper in the gown shop. He told her that he was a student and asked her to his room to help him with his studies. They ended up in bed.

The affair with the black sweeper did not last. Christine changed jobs and became a waitress in a small Greek nightclub in Baker Street. There she met a girl called Maureen O'Connor who worked for Murray's Cabaret Club in Beak Street, Soho. Maureen offered to introduce Christine to the owner, Percival Murray. Murray ran an unusual club. It was open only to members and their guests. Membership cost a guinea (£1.05 today) and the entrance fee was a guinea a time. Members could eat, drink, and watch the cabaret which consisted of a series of not very original dance routines performed by not very talented dancers. But they danced to a backdrop provided by showgirls, girls chosen for their beauty, who appeared bare-breasted, but who stood – as required by the law at the time – motionless. By later standards, the floor show at Murray's was very tame, and Murray himself, fat, balding and bespectacled, would boast that his was a most respectable club 'catering for the upper crust, the crowned and uncrowned heads of Europe'.

Certainly the dancers and the showgirls were obliged to follow strict rules. Unpunctuality, ungroomed hair or chipped nail polish were punished by a fine, deducted from the wages. Parents who wanted to check on where a daughter was working were invited to the club for dinner and assured by Murray that he would watch the girl like her father. If a customer liked a particular girl he could ask the head waiter to invite her to his table during the two hour break between shows. The girl then earned a commission on the drinks that the customer consumed, and he was expected to add a tip for the girl when he came to pay his bill.

Of course there was nothing to stop a customer from arranging to meet a girl — for whatever reason — after the club closed. There are two views on Murray's attitude to this. One is that he frowned on it. As one girl said, 'He had a knack of being able to sniff out any hint of a blossoming liaison and he would then stamp it out fast. A lover's tiff could lose the club a good client. By forbidding romance Perce was protecting his investment.' The other view is that the first is an example of typical British hypocrisy; that Murray's was a high-class pick-up place and that Murray not only knew that many of his girls met customers outside the club for sex and sometimes were paid for it, but that this — and discretion — was an inferred condition of employment. (Former showgirls have said that Murray not only knew that some of the girls sold sex for money, but how much they charged because he did business himself with those he fancied, Christine included.)

Murray is dead and the club has closed; its girls are naturally reluctant to talk about those days, and its customers, mostly middle-aged then, are old men now with old men's memories, so the truth about Murray's remains ambiguous. But certainly the club had the *appearance* of respectability, and although Murray's boast about the 'crowned and uncrowned heads of Europe' being members was exaggerated, the club did attract more than its share of titled Englishmen and foreigners, Members of Parliament, businessmen, and wealthy playboys from Europe, the Americas and the Middle East. In some circles in the 1950s to have been one of Percy Murray's girls said something about your beauty, your personality, and your attitude to life.

The club employed 45 girls. Hundreds were always waiting to fill any vacancy. Most were turned away. Christine Keeler was one of the lucky ones. She went to the club with her introduction, was interviewed by Murray, and was told that she could start immediately. Murray saw in Christine a quality which has instant appeal for a certain type of man — she was a child-woman. Her photographs do not capture this quality. Keeler was very small but perfectly proportioned. Her dark, oval eyes set wide apart and her high cheek bones were, she said, part of her Red Indian ancestry. She had little skill in applying make-up or wearing clothes and always managed to look slightly scruffy. She spoke quietly and with effort, as if always trying to remember lessons. She moved very sensuously and let men know that she was fully aware of the effect that this had on them. Overall – and this is the previously-unrevealed secret of her attraction – she appeared like a sexually-aware 12-year-old girl who has dressed up in her mother's clothes, put on her mother's make-up and is prepared to play at being a woman, no matter what that involves.

She was a nymphomaniac in the true sense of the term, in that she felt emotionally secure only when she was giving her body to someone. There is evidence that she did not really enjoy sex but tolerated it for company or reward. She was prepared for anything except to be kissed. She once admitted that she would allow a man to use her in any way that pleased him as long as he did not want to kiss her on the lips.

This desire to please extended to her social relationships. She had no views of her own and tended to agree with everything people told her. She had great difficulty in distinguishing between fact and fantasy and was a persistent liar, largely to cover up for her wild behaviour and to explain the trail of devastation she constantly left in her wake.

But as far as Murray was concerned, as long as she followed the club's rules while at work, she could get up to whatever she liked in her own time. On 26 August 1959, Christine Keeler became a Murray's showgirl, wages £8 10s. a week. Wraysbury was behind her; there would be no more jobs as a shopgirl or waitress. Standing semi-naked on stage twice a night might not be everyone's choice but Christine believed that it would open the path to a glamorous future.

Christine was in her dressing room at the club one evening in 1959 when Murray came backstage to say that one of Christine's boyfriends, a rich Arab called Ahmed Kanu was out front with a couple and wanted Christine to join them. Ahmed made the introductions. The girl's name was Claire Gordon. The man's was Dr Stephen Ward. He asked her to dance. He asked if he could take her home. He asked for her telephone number. Christine fobbed him off.

As she recalled in her Confessions: 'I remember it so well. There was something about Stephen which fascinated me from the start. Perhaps it was his eyes . . . or his soothing voice, or his broad athletic shoulders . . . that wonderful grace he has whenever he moves . . . or his brown, muscular hands, or the astonishing flash of his teeth as he half-smiled and half-laughed. I don't know. I only know he had me enthralled. I forgot all about the Arab, who was paying the bills.'

Ward persisted. He was clearly not going to leave without Christine's telephone number so she finally relented and gave it to him. Ward had succeeded in charming her and, without her realising it, had set the pattern of their future relationship.

Ward telephoned three times the next day. He took to telephoning every day, ignoring Christine's feeble excuses explaining why she could not meet him for a cup of coffee. Then, after she had told him that she was going home to see her mother at the weekend, he turned up at Wraysbury on the Saturday morning on his way to Cliveden. Ward quickly charmed Christine's mother and received her permission to take Christine to his cottage. Once there, Christine was impressed. Ward sketched her, kept up a running conversation, largely about his life and friends, and at the end of the afternoon drove her home. He felt he had made a good start.

The following week Ward invited Christine for coffee at his regular coffee bar in Marylebone High Street. She went. Two days later he invited her again, and out of the blue suggested that she should come and live with him. Christine protested. She did not know him very well. She told him she'd need time to think about it, that she wasn't very sexy. Ward explained that sex wasn't everything in a relationship. He told her he did not expect her to go to bed with him. He made it clear he only wanted her around for the company. 'I've had relationships with beautiful women,' he explained, 'and never had sex at all.' Christine thought about it for a day. The more she considered Ward's suggestion, the more she liked it. Stephen treated her differently from other men she had known. He discussed politics with her. He amused her with anecdotes about well-known celebrities. He reeled off jokes and kept her laughing. If she felt lost for words he would rescue her. His carefree attitude to life succeeded in charming her again.

Two days later Christine packed her bags, left her boarding house and moved in with Ward. It was not a sexual relationship and they never had intercourse throughout the time they knew each other. Their friends found it difficult to understand the attraction. Ward probably thought he had found another Vickie Martin. Christine may have looked on Ward as a father figure.


When Christine decided to move in with Ward, he was living in a studio apartment in Orme Square. It proved too small, and in November 1959, Ward began to look around for something larger. He went to a West End estate agent who offered him a double-fronted first floor flat in Bryanston Mews West, between Baker Street and Edgware Road. He arranged for Ward to meet the owner at the flat. His name was Peter Rachman, later to be known as the notorious slum landlord.

Ward took Christine with him. It turned out that the flat was already occupied. A friend of Rachman, Peter Nash, kept his mistress 'Chérie' there, but Rachman promised to see what else he had that might be suitable. He then invited Ward and Christine to dinner, during which Chérie suggested that Christine call on her the next day. Rachman was there, and with his suave charm and obvious sexuality he quickly persuaded Christine to leave Ward and move into Bryanston Mews with Chérie. Christine packed her things when Ward was out and left.

She was soon under few illusions as to what the arrangement would be. 'Rachman's love-making was clinical and joyless. After lunch every day, he would push her straight into the bedroom and, dispensing with any romantic preliminaries, make her sit astride him with her back towards him. "I never even saw his face."' In return Rachman gave Christine all the expensive clothes she had ever wanted. He paid for her hairdresser, bought her expensive gifts, handed over ten or twenty pounds any time he felt like it, and when the hours that Rachman was not around began to bore Christine he gave her a white sports car so that she could drive around London visiting her friends.

One of those she visited was Ward. He had not forgiven her for leaving him. He told her she would ruin her reputation being seen around with Rachman and his friends. He warned her about Rachman's disreputable business dealings and told her she would regret moving in with him. When Christine mentioned this to Rachman he brushed it aside. He could not imagine a man and woman having a friendly relationship and thought that Ward's outburst was purely one of sexual jealousy.

The end came quickly. Barely six months after she had met Rachman, Christine, who had been driving to Wraysbury regularly to see her mother, resumed an affair with a childhood boyfriend. 'Rachman must have sensed it because one weekend he and a companion, driving his Rolls-Royce, followed Christine down to Slough. Rachman waited until she had picked up her boyfriend and had driven him to a nearby pub for lunch before revealing himself and demanding the keys of the car. As he left Rachman, who was, by this time, trembling with rage, shouted, "And if you come back, this time see you behave yourself!" (Rachman later said that Christine was the only person he was afraid of, because he believed if she wanted revenge on someone she would be quite capable of shooting him dead in front of a roomful of people.)'

As she was to do so often, Christine went straight to Ward. He was delighted to have her back. He had found a little house in Wimpole Mews just around the corner from his consulting rooms, and had prepared a spare bedroom for Christine. Rachman, furious at first, calmed down and allowed her to collect her clothes and gifts from the Bryanston Mews flat. She persuaded Murray to let her return to her job and she soon slipped back into the easy routine of life with Ward: people dropping by for a cup of coffee, the occasional mid-week party, and long pleasant weekends at Cliveden.

# The Artist and the Royals

10 |

One of London's more popular coffee bars in the late 1950s was the Brush and Palette in Queensway. For the price of a meal, a cup of coffee, or a glass of wine, customers were allowed to sketch or simply look at whichever pretty girl was posing nude among the tables. The owner never made a fortune because he enjoyed the company of his customers, never pressed anyone to leave, and stayed open until the last one had finished his sketch or his conversation.

In January 1960 one of the wine waiters at the Brush and Palette was a young man called Noel Howard-Jones who was working at night to help pay for his law studies. When business was slack, Howard-Jones would sit and chat with the customers. One evening he noticed a new arrival, a tall, slim man, casually but neatly-dressed, wearing dark sunglasses, his thick, light-brown hair swept from his forehead. The man took out his sketch book and pencils, drank endless cups of black coffee, and chain-smoked Senior Service cigarettes. When he had a chance, Howard-Jones sneaked a look over the man's shoulder and was surprised to see that he had sketched only the girl's face.

Later he spoke to the artist who introduced himself as Dr Stephen Ward. They had a brief conversation and had barely resumed it the following evening when they were interrupted by the arrival of a fellow student from Howard-Jones's boarding house. 'You'd better come back,' he said. 'The landlady's putting your stuff out into the street.' An embarrassed Howard-Jones explained to Ward that he was two weeks behind with his rent and had no money until pay day. Years later he recalled, 'Without a second's hesitation Ward pulled out £5 and told me to go and pay the landlady quickly so that I'd be able to stay. He hardly knew me. And I saw him three or four times in the next week and I just didn't have the money to pay him back. He never mentioned it. When I did pay him back about a month later he went through a whole rigmarole of saying, "Look, you paid me back the other day. I remember it distinctly." He gave me every opportunity to let myself off the hook gracefully and I really had to insist before he would accept the money.'

Howard-Jones was deeply impressed by Ward. 'He was well-informed, articulate and amusing. He was enthusiastic about everything, a wonderful listener, and full of good advice. He had open house at his flat in London. You could pop in at any time and be certain that you'd find an interesting crowd of people there, with Stephen at the centre of things, steering the conversation, enjoying everyone's company.

'On one visit I met Christine Keeler. I was a randy 20-year-old and here was this pretty girl who seemed available. I asked her out and we started a half-hearted affair that lasted a couple of months. I couldn't take her to my room, so we'd go to bed in Stephen's flat when he was at his consulting rooms. Sometimes I'd pick her up on a Saturday and we'd buy a couple of bottles of wine and some food and I'd take her down to Stephen's cottage on the back of my motor scooter.

'But it fizzled out after a while. I didn't drop her. She didn't drop me. We just dropped each other. She was disappointingly dull in bed and after a while it was a struggle to make conversation with her. Once you got beyond clothes and gossip there was nothing left. I mention this because of the way things later got twisted.'

Ward's practice was still expanding. Every week saw a new patient who had usually been recommended by someone Ward had cured. Most were bad backs and painful joints. But he still found time to take on cases that really interested him. One of these was a young girl, Alexandra Wilson, who had been knocked down by a car and had lost the power of hearing and speech. Alexandra had had several operations before her parents, in desperation, turned to Ward.

With great patience Ward acted as physiotherapist, speech therapist, counsellor and doctor, spending nearly 17 years treating the girl. Eventually she made a complete recovery. Her parents had told Ward at the beginning that they could not afford his fees and although they later offered him money he refused to accept a penny. When Alexandra invited him to her 21st birthday party and told him that if she ever had a son she would call it after him, Ward was deeply moved. He later said to a friend, 'It was sufficient payment for me to see that girl alive, happy, and leading a normal life. If she ever names a son after me that'll be more than I could ever have hoped for.' (This remark made the friend wonder if perhaps Ward was sterile. 'I know he would have loved a child of his own. But he never spoke about children, or having made any girl pregnant. I believe that he couldn't have kids.')

Another of Ward's patients was able to further his art career. This was Hugh Leggatt, a well-known West End dealer and gallery owner. 'I had a frightful backache and Ward took one look at it and said, "Just a touch of lumbago. We'll soon cure that." And he did. Three treatments later it was gone.' During the last treatment Ward rather diffidently told Leggatt that he was an amateur artist and that he would be happy to show him some of his work if Leggatt had time.

Leggatt recalls: 'He wasn't pushing himself and I was so pleased that he was curing me so quickly that I agreed to have a look. They turned out to be very good, extremely lifelike. So I said to him, "Well, I've never held an exhibition of work for any one artist. Would you like to have one? But it'll be on a strictly amateur basis. I don't deal in modern works of art because I don't want to make money out of living artists. So I won't take a commission or anything like that. What you get from your sitters is your business. I'll just give the exhibition as thanks for what you've done for my back." I did it for him partly out of friendship, because I liked him as a person; partly because he was hopeless over money and always forgot to charge you; and partly because he was good — there are very few artists capable of catching a living likeness.'

Ward and Leggatt agreed that the exhibition would work only if there was a variety of portraits. Ward had sketched most of his friends and could persuade them to lend the portraits for the exhibition, but more sketches, especially of well-known people, were needed.

Ward set out to get them. He gave himself six weeks. He wrote to everyone he could think of, going through his professional lists and appointments book, calling in favours and dropping names shamelessly. Most of those he contacted were flattered to be asked and agreed, especially as Ward said he needed only one half-hour sitting to complete the portrait. He began with Paul Getty, then reputedly the richest man in the world, doing three chalk studies at the Ritz Hotel on the very afternoon he had reached agreement with Leggatt for the exhibition. He went to the House of Commons and sketched the Prime Minister, Harold Macmillan, and then, the same day, across the road to the Home Office to draw the Home Secretary, Rab Butler. He sketched the Foreign Secretary, Selwyn Lloyd, in his vast room sitting behind a huge desk.

Nubar Gulbenkian's portrait took only 20 minutes. 'His face is a wonderful rococo creation,' Ward said. 'Black eyebrows that curl up in spirals, a white beard and hair, and a monocle. It's hard to go wrong on a face like that.' He drew the Labour leader, Hugh Gaitskell, early one morning, going straight from a party at the Getty house to Gaitskell's, stopping off at his flat only to change. He did a portrait of Sophia Loren at Elstree Studios where she was making *The Millionairess*, staying to lunch with her in her dressing room.

Some of his sitters were patients and he drew them either before or after their treatment. Douglas Fairbanks Jnr was one of them – 'difficult to draw; his face is all movement' – and A. P. Herbert was another: 'He sat in one of my armchairs and had a gin.' Stanley Spencer sat for Ward in Spencer's own studio at Cookham. 'This took two hours which is a long time for me,' Ward said. 'But it was the only exciting portrait of Spencer in his later years and it ended up hanging at Cliveden.' Ward did Sir John Rothenstein at the Tate Gallery, Mylène Dymengeot at the 'Compleat Angler' at Marlow, and Lord Shawcross in his chambers.

The exhibition, on 12 July 1960, went very well and the *Illustrated London News* published a page of the drawings. Leggatt remembers: 'I thought his most successful portrait was of Lord Shawcross, but a number of the others were extremely good too. Ward was, at that time, the toast of what I call artistic society, in the sense that he was creating something of which there was a serious vacuum in the London art scene. Everybody who was anybody approached me to arrange for them to have their portrait sketched by Ward.' The exhibition marked Ward's transition from amateur artist to professional. The day after it opened he had a call from Sir Bruce Ingram, editor of the *Illustrated London News*, who offered Ward a contract to do a series of portraits of famous people for the magazine.

Ward accepted and began to travel all over Britain on these assignments. He went to Jodrell Bank to draw Professor Lovell and to Oxford and Cambridge Universities for the portraits of the masters of several colleges. He drew John Diefenbaker of Canada, and Archbishop Makarios of Cyprus when he was staying at the Carlton Towers. Cardinal Godfrey sat for Ward in the palace attached to the Cathedral at Westminster. 'You found me without any trouble?' he asked Ward. 'There's a pub next door called The Cardinal and sometimes when people ask for me they get sent to the pub.'

The climax of the *Illustrated London News*'s assignments was to be a series of portraits of royalty. Ward went to a lot of trouble to get these exactly right. He began with Prince Philip.

I took up a suggestion that I should go the day before and look at the lighting and so on. I sat an equerry in various positions until I thought it was about right. Next morning Prince Philip arrived on time. I sat him down and we were off. There is on these occasions a horrible presentiment of failure when you know that this is likely to be your only chance to do the job. But, as it happened, the Prince had been to a party of mine at Cavendish Square before his marriage and he remembered me. 'By Jove,' he said. 'You're the osteopath. I never connected you with this appointment.' We discussed the old days, polo, and the fact that he had a rare condition called 'rider's bone' in the thigh. He was a wonderful sitter, still as a rack and yet relaxed. I usually do what I call a safe drawing first and then, if there's time, a more informal or bolder effort. There was time, and I did an informal one, but it has never been published yet.

The Duchess of Kent sat for Ward in a well-lit room in Kensington Palace. He had arranged for an hour to do both the Duke and the Duchess but took longer with the Duchess than he had planned and had only 20 minutes left for the Duke. 'He had a strange and difficult face. I never thought I'd make it, with the sun throwing a pattern from the window across him, but in the end it came out, in my opinion, the best drawing of the series.' Ward sketched the Duke's mother, Princess Marina, in a great drawing room at Kensington Palace. He found her the most difficult to capture. 'The mouth is ever so slightly askew, the sort of thing in a drawing that is extremely hard not to overdo. The result didn't please me and I don't think it pleased her.'

This was not his only disappointment. He found Princess Margaret's the most difficult face he had ever tried. 'I was conscious of failure when Mr Armstrong-Jones, who was to be my next sitter, came into the room, looked at what I had done and pointed out that I had got the nose too long. I thought so too, so I shortened it a bit. But then it didn't look like Princess Margaret any more. I started on Armstrong-Jones, but once things go wrong it is difficult to get them on the rails again. I was feeling quite despondent when I left.'

The Duke and Duchess of Gloucester were more successful. 'The Duke has an interesting Hanoverian face. This assignment had made me realise the strong family likeness I had encountered in things like the shape of the skull. Here it was again with the Duke. I got engrossed and spent too long, neglecting the Duchess's portrait as a result. I gave the Duke's portrait to the British Red Cross Association and it later presented it to the Duchess. On my way out, the guard at York House, mistaking my exit for that of the Duke, came smartly to attention.'

Ward not only enjoyed doing people's portraits for artistic reasons, but because his chats with his sitters gave him a fund of anecdotes. Ward, who loved gossip, was notoriously indiscreet, and would never keep a good story to himself. He polished them, rehearsed them and then dined out on them: 'A. P. Herbert wrote this poem, never published, which starts, "The portion of anatomy which appeals to man's depravity". When he was in the Navy as a petty officer, even after his remarkable work as an author, a playwright, and a very active MP, it was often the case that some distinguished officer, an admiral or someone of high rank, would come upon him and say, "You're that chap Herbert, aren't you, the one that wrote that poem." And they'd quote the first line and ask him to sign a copy.'

And another: 'Stanley Spencer had some odd eccentricities. He came down to the cottage one weekend and it was a bit quiet so we decided to go for a row on the river. I was at the oars and Spencer sat next to Tommy Steele's agent, John Kennedy, in the stern. Kennedy kept looking at Spencer's ankles and finally Kennedy said, "Haven't you forgotten to take your pyjamas off?" And Spencer said, "I never do, old boy. When I go out I just put my trousers over my pyjamas. Saves a hell of a lot of time."'

# 11 | *Enter Ivanov, Soviet Spy*

On 27 March 1960, the 63-strong Soviet Embassy in London welcomed a new member. He was Captain (second rank) Yevgeny M. Ivanov, 37, who was taking up the post of assistant naval attaché. Ivanov's welcome was particularly warm – not only his boss, Captain (first rank) Zucherushkin, turning out to meet him, but also the ambassador himself, Alexander Soldatov.

There were two reasons for this. One was that everyone in the Embassy knew Ivanov's background. The son of a Russian army officer, he had joined the navy in 1944 and had served in the Far East, the Black Sea and the Arctic as a gunnery officer with the Red Fleet. An intelligent man, he had been marked early as leader material and had been given special intelligence training by the GRU, the Soviet military intelligence service, before his posting to Britain. He had enhanced his career prospects by marrying well. His wife Maya, a pretty and amusing girl, was the daughter of Alexander Gorkin, chairman of the Soviet Supreme Court. Ivanov's brother-in-law was Colonel Konstantinov, head of the GRU *residentura* at the London Embassy.

The second reason for Ivanov's warm welcome was that he had gathered a reputation as a jolly fellow, someone to liven the restricted social life that Soviet diplomats serving abroad usually lead. He was a keen sportsman, excelling at volleyball, and soon dominated the regular games held on the Embassy court behind 10 Kensington Palace Gardens. He was a keen party-goer, a vigorous singer, ready to perform after a vodka or two. He and Maya were good hosts and good guests, affable, friendly, and both capable of sustained, intelligent conversation. The Embassy staff looked forward to their influence on diplomatic receptions and cocktail parties and to staff weekends at the Embassy's retreat, a large and elegant house in the village of Hawkhurst, Kent.

The British security services also noted Ivanov's arrival with interest. He had not come to the MI5's notice before, but no one in its D-Branch (counter-espionage) or in the London Station of

MI6, whose combined job it was to keep an eye on Soviet bloc diplomats, was under any illusion about Ivanov's assignment in Britain. By tacit diplomatic agreement the senior naval attaché, be he British in Moscow or Russian in Britain, is a strictly naval man who confines himself to open naval business. His two assistants are a different matter. Both countries accept that the assistant naval attachés are collectors of intelligence, by both open and covert means. This intelligence is principally to do with naval matters, but since no GRU intelligence officer would reject choice items of information if they came his way, it is also accepted that GRU officers may have a political intelligence role. They are expected to keep within generally understood limits. They must not be too ambitious, too active, and, above all, too obvious. If they are, then the security services are forced to take notice of them, there is a diplomatic flurry, a burst of expulsions and counter-expulsions, and Anglo-Russian relations cool for a while until the status quo can be restored.

It is a diplomatic/intelligence game that suits everyone while the rules are observed. It provides a two-way flow of intelligence that has a calming effect and avoids dangerous guess-work. It opens a channel of communication between Moscow and the West on a 'deniable' level. It would be impossible for the Kremlin ever to claim that a Soviet ambassador had spoken without the authority of his Government. But exploratory balloons can be floated by military or naval attachés and, if they explode, then the Government can say that the lowly attaché had acted on his own initiative and send him back to sea to punish him.

Ivanov knew the rules. But he was playing for high stakes. Within days of his arrival in London he began to put himself about. His office at 16 Kensington Palace Gardens seldom saw him. Ivanov was out and making contact with the British. He wanted an entrée to London society, to the world of the decision-makers. MI5's D-Branch watched and took note.


One of Ward's patients who had become a friend was Sir Colin Coote, editor of the *Daily Telegraph*. Coote had suffered from lumbago for years and had gone to see Ward on the recommendation of Sir Godfrey Nicholson, MP. 'To my complete astonishment . . . the pain was tamed and then expelled,' Coote said later.

Coote and Ward had started to play bridge together, attending the Connaught Bridge Club in Edgeware Road. Occasionally Coote had asked Ward to his house to make up a four. Then, after the success of Ward's series of portraits for the *Illustrated London News*, Coote decided to implement a scheme he had been considering for some time. 'I had long been pondering whether black and white drawings might not be an interesting substitute for photographs [in the *Daily Telegraph*]. The trial of Eichmann in Israel was about to begin and I thought I would try the experiment of employing Stephen Ward to do sketches of the personalities in court.'

Ward duly went to Israel and a series of his drawings appeared in the newspaper. Coote got many complimentary letters about the drawings and decided that when there was another opportunity to use Ward he would do so. Ward, too, was thinking about an encore. He knew that the impact made by his exhibition, his *Illustrated London News* series, and his Eichmann trial sketches would not last for ever and that his art career needed another imaginative boost. He had an idea: he would go to the Soviet Union and sketch the Soviet leaders, the whole Politburo if he could get them. He raised the idea with Coote who encouraged him, promising to commission him if the Russians agreed.

Ward realised that trying to negotiate permission to sketch Soviet leaders through the Soviet Embassy in London could take ages. He decided that his best chance would be to go to Moscow with his portfolio of British leaders, somehow show it to Khrushchev and ask permission to draw him. If Khrushchev agreed, Ward reasoned, then other Soviet leaders would prove easy. The only problem was that the Soviet Embassy apparently would not give him a visa, even for a tourist trip to Moscow. The Embassy never actually refused him a visa, but weeks went by and nothing happened.

One afternoon when Coote's lumbago was playing up again, he went to Ward for treatment. Ward took the opportunity to complain about his visa problems and Coote promised to do what he could to help. Two days later an opportunity occurred. The doyen of the naval attachés of the London diplomatic corps, Vice-Admiral Victor Marchal, had earlier asked Coote's permission to bring some of his colleagues on a tour of the *Daily Telegraph*.

After the attachés had seen over the building and watched the presses begin their nightly run, Coote, as was his custom, invited them to his office for a drink. One of the attachés turned out to be Captain Yevgeny Ivanov, representing the Soviet Embassy. 'He seemed to be an agreeable person and spoke excellent English,' Coote recalled. 'I remembered Stephen Ward's difficulty about a visa and thought that this link might be useful.' Coote decided that the way to go about it was to have Ward and Ivanov to lunch and there introduce them.

The luncheon took place at the Garrick Club. The other guest was the *Daily Telegraph*'s correspondent on Soviet affairs, David Floyd. Ivanov and Ward got on very well. Ward was impressed at the way Ivanov held his own in debate with Coote and Floyd: 'I listened with fascination as they argued backward and forward on issues which I had never heard discussed before in an intelligent and informal manner.' Ivanov liked Ward's enthusiasm and informality and when Ward suggested that they take a walk together after lunch, Ivanov readily agreed. They called on Jack Hylton, the television mogul, at his office in Savile Row, chatted a while and listened to Hylton play a waltz on the piano. Before Ivanov left Ward at his consulting rooms the two men had arranged to meet again. Ward suggested that Ivanov should drive down to the cottage at Cliveden and Ivanov readily accepted the invitation.

As Ward's friendship with Yevgeny Ivanov blossomed, the original purpose for meeting him – to get a visa to go and sketch Soviet leaders – appears to have been forgotten. The two men met often and went everywhere together. Ivanov would call at Ward's flat unannounced and the two of them would go out – either to visit a club, to play bridge, or to dine with one of Ward's friends. Not all of these approved of Ward becoming so close to a Russian and some of them would provoke Ivanov into a political argument. He usually held his own. Helen Cordet, who ran the Saddle Room Club, recalls, 'Ivanov often came into the bar with friends, Ward among them. There would be terrific political arguments. We thought it was amusing to argue politics with a Russian diplomat. But he really shut us up, because his answers were quite accurate. When he thought he was losing ground, he recovered by laughing or turning the whole thing into a joke.'

But if the discussion became too heated or Ivanov considered he or his country had been maligned he could be very tough. Ward took him on one occasion, along with Christine, to the house of John Kennedy, the theatrical agent. Another guest was the actor Paul Carpenter. On this occasion Carpenter was drunk and baited Ivanov about Gagarin, the Soviet astronaut, who had recently made the first space flight. 'He's the first one you've got back,' Carpenter said. 'How many others have you got up there that you can't bring down? How many thousands are floating around up there?' Ivanov tried to shrug off the question but Carpenter suddenly thumped his fist on the mantelpiece and shouted: 'All Russians are full of fucking shit.' Kennedy recalls: 'Ivanov got really angry. He went bananas and took a swipe at Paul, but Paul moved and Ivanov hit the fireplace instead. Stephen, Sid James and I grabbed Ivanov and we could hardly hold him. This guy was really strong. We'd just got him under control when Paul shouts, "I still think you're full of shit" and that started Ivanov off again. So we said to Paul, "Get out", and we finally succeeded in getting him out of the place. I mean we had to. Ivanov was going to kill him.'

But this was an exception. Other encounters ended in agreement, agreement to disagree, or jokes. Tom Corbally, an American businessman and friend of Ward, who described Ivanov as 'a man who looked like a capitalist serving as a communist', remembers arguing with Ivanov over the Russian's description of the West as decadent. Corbally asked for evidence. Ivanov replied, 'You see Piccadilly and you see girls and you see dirty magazines.' Corbally challenged him: 'You mean you don't have that in Russia?' Ivanov said, 'No. No. We have nothing like that.' Corbally persisted: 'No faggots in Russia. No lesbians?' 'No. No,' Ivanov said. 'We don't permit them.'

Ivanov had an earthy sense of humour. Ward described the time Ivanov came to visit him and met a friend of Ward in his flat. Ivanov and the girl finished a bottle of vodka between them, and then Ivanov began to tease her. Pointing at her red hair he said, 'In Russia women do not dye their hair in false colours.' The girl, who was proud of her genuinely red hair, became very angry and proceeded to show him that her hair was the same colour all over her. Ivanov roared with laughter and shouted, 'Ah, a true Red.'

He was always prepared to help any of Ward's friends who were having difficulty with the Soviet bureaucracy. Howard-Jones, by now working in an advertising agency, wanted some recordings of Russian music for a client. Ivanov brought them back from Moscow where he had been on leave. But Howard-Jones found the quality of the recording to be very poor, so he suggested that the Soviet Union should do a deal with EMI by which EMI would send technicians and modern equipment to Moscow in return for the right to market the recordings in the West on a royalties basis. 'Ivanov got very excited about this and it went ahead very fast,' Howard-Jones said. 'Someone came over from Moscow and there was a meeting at the Soviet Embassy – me, Ivanov, the man from Moscow, and Sir Joseph Lockwood, then the head man at EMI. It all fell through in the end, but it would never have gone as far as it did if it had not been for Ivanov taking the initiative in a matter that obviously did not fall within his official sphere.'

Under Ward's tutelage Ivanov's bridge improved, his English improved, and their friendship deepened. Ward took Ivanov into English homes he could never have hoped to enter as a Soviet diplomat. He spent Christmas with Lord Ednam and his wife Maureen, formerly the actress Maureen Swanson. He stayed at an Ascot house party with Lord Harrington, visited Cliveden often, drank and argued with MPs in Ward's flat, had dinner at the House of Commons, and played bridge with businessmen, journalists and publishers.

The hospitality was not all one way. Ivanov invited Ward to most of the Soviet embassy parties. He had obviously told his colleagues of his friendship with Ward because at all these functions Ward was treated as a VIP. At the huge reception to meet Yuri Gagarin, Ward was one of 5,000 guests and it took nearly an hour to reach the top of the reception line. After Ward had patiently queued and finally shook Gagarin's hand, he passed into the main hall where he met a friend, Harry Myers, who was taking photographs. Myers said that it was a pity that he had not seen Ward being presented to Gagarin: he could have taken a photograph for Ward to keep as an historic souvenir. 'Easily remedied,' Ward said. 'I'll go out and come in again.' An hour later Ward reached the head of the reception line. But when he shook hands with Gagarin the Russian turned to his interpreter and said something which made them both laugh. Ward looked inquiringly at the interpreter who explained, 'Major Gagarin says "a second time in orbit."'

On another occasion Ward was invited to meet Madame Furstova, the Soviet Minister of Culture. Ward was impressed by her face and told Ivanov he would like to draw her. Ivanov pushed his way through the crowd, spoke to Madame Furstova and then told Ward, 'She will talk to you here tomorrow morning.' Ward spent an hour with her and drew her portrait. While he worked they talked on a wide variety of subjects including the Hungarian uprising, Pasternak, and the problems and hopes of Russian émigrés. Ward wrote an account of the conversation, hoping to sell it as a package to his friend, the editor of the *Daily Telegraph*, Sir Colin Coote. He checked with Ivanov whether this would be all right, only to discover that Ivanov was horrified that Madame Furstova had spoken so openly. Ivanov begged Ward not to publish the article. Ward agreed and only the portrait appeared in the newspaper. 'Probably more than anything else this cemented the confidence which grew up between us,' Ward said.

Sometimes they got into trouble like two unruly schoolboys. Ivanov's vodka-induced sense of fun would be matched by Ward's pleasure in creating mischief. One Saturday afternoon they drove from Ward's cottage to Paul Getty's house, Sutton Place, in Guildford. Getty was not there, but his guests included Madame

Tessiers whose cousin would have been the Czar of Russia but for the Bolshevik Revolution. 'When two Russians get together,' said Ward later, 'it's vodka and more vodka; toasts to this and toasts to that, and then songs and more toasts.'

Ivanov and Ward persuaded five or six of Getty's guests to pile into two cars and drive to a nearby pub where there was more drinking. Ivanov and Ward were expected for dinner at the house of Lord Harrington at Ascot so eventually they loaded Getty's guests into one of the cars and sent them back to Sutton Place. Ivanov and Ward set off for Harrington's dinner party, with Ivanov driving – 'I am a captain in the Russian Navy,' he said, 'and I can navigate anywhere.' Two hours later they found themselves hopelessly lost in the middle of some rifle range. At this point, one of the Getty guests emerged from under a blanket on the rear floor of the car where she had been asleep. They decided to take her to Harrington's with them, but when they finally got there, she mutinied, refused to go inside and insulted Harrington when he tried to persuade her.

Ward took over. He put the girl into a taxi and told the driver to take her to Getty's house 30 miles away where Getty would take care of the fare. 'From then on we had a series of horrifying telephone bulletins of the girl's progress across the country. As the butler came in with each bulletin we laughed louder and louder. The last one was to say that the girl had finally arrived at the Getty house but that Getty had refused to pay the taxi fare and was blaming the whole thing on some Russian naval captain who had been at Sutton Place earlier in the day.'

Ivanov met Christine and Mandy at Ward's flat. Both girls found him warm, humorous and charming. They were impressed by the money he had to spend, the gifts of vodka and caviare he brought – usually accompanied by a joking, 'I know you capitalists appreciate a few little luxuries.' But Ivanov showed no physical interest in either of them. Mandy became sufficiently curious about Ivanov to ask Ward – and then Ivanov himself – what his real job was. Was he a spy? Ivanov dodged the question. He said that of course he was not, but that all diplomats picked up information and that when this was all put together back at intelligence headquarters it might make a clear picture. Significantly – in the light of accusations that Ward was naïve in his relationship with Ivanov – Ward replied to Mandy's question by saying, 'Everybody at the Russian Embassy is a spy.'

Ivanov did not know it, but there were others in London at that time interested in his true role as a Soviet diplomat. Ever since his arrival the London Station would have kept a wary eye on him and would have passed information to MI5's D-Branch. He was in MI5's files as an unconfirmed GRU or KGB officer. He was watched automatically but nothing he did served to harden suspicion into fact. Then early in May 1961 that all changed. A game the Secret Intelligence Service (SIS) had been playing with a potential Soviet defector began to pay off.

The potential defector was Colonel Oleg Vladimirovich Penkovsky, formerly assistant military attaché at the Soviet embassy in Ankara, now a low-level protocol officer in the foreign department of the Soviet State Committee for Science and Technology. (This was the body which arranged visits to the USSR by foreign scientists and technologists and which controlled visits overseas by their Soviet counterparts.) Penkovsky's post concealed his real status. He was a GRU officer and as such had access to secret material of some importance. Penkovsky had been 'courting' SIS through several Embassies abroad, when he had wanted to pass information to the West. He had provided a package containing an account of his GRU career and sufficient secret material to convince SIS that he was genuine.

Two weeks later Penkovsky had arrived in London as part of a Soviet trade delegation. SIS were immediately in contact with him and each night after his official duties were over, Penkovsky met SIS and MI5 officers in the hotel where he was staying. They questioned him into the early hours of the morning. One of the early demands made upon a defector is for him to name fellow Soviet intelligence officers. There are two reasons for this: one is to enable Western officers to cross-check that the defector is who he says he is and not a hoaxer; the other is to try to establish that he is not a KGB plant. For if a defector is prepared to betray Soviet fellow officers then the likelihood is that he is genuine. This is not an infallible test – the KGB might be prepared to sacrifice a low-level spy to help establish a plant's 'bona fides' – but it is a quick and easily executed step towards checking out a defector.

Penkovsky passed it. He quickly named the KGB and GRU officers in the Soviet Embassy in London, providing their ranks, their real names, their cover names and their cover postings. One of those he named was his colleague from their student days at Moscow Military Diplomatic Academy, Yevgeny Ivanov, GRU intelligence officer, under cover as an assistant naval attaché; actual mission unknown, although taking into account Ivanov's career prospects and his connections in Moscow's ruling élite, it must be an important one.

Of all the Soviet intelligence officers Penkovsky named in the

London Embassy, no one interested MI5 more in its overall surveillance role than Ivanov. The 'watchers' on assignment for 'D-Branch' had not failed to notice Ivanov's life-style, his heavy drinking, his socialising with Westerners, his party-going, his night-clubbing and his obvious enjoyment of London. If Ivanov was as important an officer in the GRU as Penkovsky made out, then he would be a major catch if he could be persuaded – or blackmailed – into defecting. New information makes it clear that there was a meeting of senior MI5 and SIS officers on 6 or 7 June and the decision was taken to target Ivanov for a 'honey-trap'. He would be subtly 'encouraged' to continue his high life. At the right moment he would be forcibly reminded what he would be giving up if he returned to the Soviet Union. If this failed to persuade him to stay, then by this time MI5 might have sufficient material on Ivanov to blackmail him into defecting anyway. What was needed as a first step was a trustworthy person close to Ivanov who could help MI5's scheme. There was one obvious choice: Stephen Ward.

MI5 already knew quite a lot about Ward, having checked him out when their surveillance of Ivanov revealed Ward as one of his frequent contacts. It is inconceivable that MI5 did not also take the opportunity to carry out two specific checks on Ward. MI5 officers knew that one of Ward's friends was Bill Astor. Astor, as we have seen, had worked in naval intelligence during the war and still kept in close touch with his wartime colleagues – some of whom were now serving in MI5. As well, Sir Colin Coote, the editor of the *Daily Telegraph* who had introduced Ward to Ivanov, had served as an agent controller for SIS in Italy in the 1920s and it is possible that Coote himself may have early on drawn MI5's attention to the opportunities the Ward-Ivanov friendship presented. Either way, with two 'friends' of MI5 and SIS well placed to advise on Ward's suitability for recruitment for the Ivanov mission it would have been highly remiss of MI5 not to have consulted them. Subsequent events suggest that it did.

A D-Branch officer got in touch with Ward and proposed lunch. Ward recalled the first contact as being by letter from Room 393 at the War Office, but a telephone call would have been more likely – a letter would give Ward evidence that he had been approached and MI5 might later want to deny this. The officer used a cover name – 'Woods' – and said, rather vaguely, that he was attached to the War Office. The two men lunched on 8 June 1961 and later went back to Ward's place for tea.

What was agreed at this extended meeting is crucial to what followed and, as is frequently the case in the murky world of

espionage, all the accounts conflict. Ward said in his tape recording
that Woods revealed that he was an MI5 officer, that the service
had noticed Ward's association with Ivanov and thought that they
should have a chat about it. Ward asked Woods whether the service
had any objection and Woods replied, 'No. On the contrary. I think
that it might be a good thing. But if anything happens that you feel
we should know about, I want you to contact me immediately.'

Woods's version as given in Lord Denning's report to the Prime
Minister was:

> Ward asked me if it was all right for him to continue to see Ivanov.
> I replied that there was no reason why he should not. He then said
> that if there was any way in which he could help he would be very
> ready to do so. I thanked him for his offer and asked him to get in
> touch with me should Ivanov at any time in the future make any
> propositions to him ... Ward ... was completely open about his
> association with Ivanov ... I do not think that he [Ward] is of
> security interest but he is obviously not a person we can make any
> use of.

The difference is striking. Ward's version gives the impression that
MI5 wanted him to continue the relationship with Ivanov and
encouraged him to report on it. Woods's version was that Ward was
putting himself forward to help MI5 in any way he could and that
Woods considered him unsuitable. But, it should be remembered,
both Ward and Woods had reason at the time to conceal the truth.
Ward, when he told his version while awaiting trial, still imagined he
had an arrangement with MI5 that he did not want to damage by
revealing too much about it. Woods would have been under orders
from the Director-General of MI5, Roger Hollis, not to reveal all the
details of the operation to entrap Ivanov – even to Denning – so he
'doctored' his report accordingly.

There is a third version which we have established is true. Nigel
West in a semi-official book about MI5, *A Matter of Trust*, published
in 1982, says that at the lunch 'Ward agreed to co-operate' and that
although Woods had some reservations about Ward himself, he
became Ward's case officer for the entrapment operation. Journalists
who followed up West's revelations spoke to Woods and other MI5
officers (all by then retired) who had been involved in the Ivanov
operation. They confirmed that Ward would have deliberately been
given the impression that he was being recruited for MI5 and that he
would have been encouraged to see himself as a patriot working for
his country. West explained the haste with which the matter was
pushed: 'Penkovsky had gone back to Moscow promising to

Early days: 1, *above, left,* Stephen Ward in Kirksville, Missouri, 1937; 2, *above, right,* at his wedding to Patricia Baines, 1949; and 3, *below,* his close friend, Eunice Bailey

4, *above*, Stephen Ward with Kim and Kay Kendall and Freda Fairchild Ferrier
5, *below*, Stephen Ward with actress Maureen Swanson and the artist Arthur Ferrier

Principals in the Lewis
divorce case: 6, *above, left,*
John Lewis; 7, *above,*
*right,* Frederic Mullally, the
co-respondent
8, *below,* the two wives,
(left) Joy Lewis and (right)
Suzanne Mullally

9, *above*, Cliveden, the home of the Astors; 10, *below*, *left*, Nancy, Lady Astor, her son
Bill (Lord Astor), and grandson William, 1959; 11, *below*, *right*, Douglas Fairbanks, Jnr
and his wife, with their daughter Daphne at her coming-out party, 1957

12, *above,* Ward's cottage on the Thames at Cliveden; 13, *below, left,* Vickie Martin, Ward's waif, 1954; 14, *below, right,* Margaret Brown, Ward's great love, 1958

John Profumo: 15, *above, left,* as a Second Lieutenant, 1939; 16, *above, right,* as an MP, with his wife, Valerie Hobson, 1955, and 17, *below,* an engagement portrait by Vivienne, 1954

18, *right,* Christine Keeler,
Murray's Club showgirl,
1959
19, *below,* her family home
at Wraysbury

20, Mandy Rice-Davies, model

21, *above,* Mandy's lover, Peter Rachman, and his wife Audrey

22, *below,* one of Rachman's properties in Paddington

23, *above*, *left*, Yevgeny
Ivanov, Russian assistant
naval attaché, with his wife,
Maya; 24, *above*, *right*,
Ivanov as sketched by his
friend, Stephen Ward
25, *below*, Sir Colin Coote,
editor of the *Daily
Telegraph*

26, *top*, *left*, Sir Roger Hollis, Director-General of MI5, 1956-65; 27, *top*, *right*, Oleg
Penkovsky; 28, *above*, President Kennedy and the Soviet leader, Nikita Khrushchev, meet
in Vienna, 1961

29, *above left*, Bronwen Pugh, model, 1959; 30, *above, right*, Lord Astor receives the Grand Cross of Merit of the Knights of Malta, 1957; 31, *below*, the swimming pool at Cliveden

32, *left*, Hod Dibben
marries Mariella Novotny,
1960
33, *below, left*, Mariella and
a detective arrive at the
New York court where she
faces prostitution charges,
1961
34, *top, right*, Harry Alan
Towers; 35, *above*, Dr
Teddy Sugden, abortionist

Christine's lovers: 36, *left,* John Profumo, Privy Councillor; and 37, *right,* Lucky
Gordon, jazz singer; 38, *opposite,*Christine Keeler

Some notable patients of Stephen Ward:
39, *above, left,* Nubar Gulbenkian, his wife, with John Profumo
40, *above, right,* Paul Getty, with Madame Mary Tessiers
41, *below,* Ward's consulting rooms at 38 Devonshire Street

continue to report to the British Secret Intelligence Service. If he were to be caught by the KGB he might admit that he had named Ivanov as a candidate for entrapment. Then Ivanov would quickly be recalled and MI5 would have missed its chance to suborn him. An operation that is usually conducted with slow, painstaking care had to be speeded up if it was to work.'

One other matter was discussed at that crucial first meeting. Woods asked Ward what political subjects seemed of interest to Ivanov. Ward thought for a moment and said that one of Ivanov's interests had been 'the time of delivery to Germany of nuclear warheads'. In view of the importance this topic was later to assume, it is essential to note that it originated with Ward himself.

But why did Ward, who said at the time that he had loved Ivanov like a brother, agree so readily to betray him? There is evidence, both from Ward's behaviour and from letters he wrote later, that he did not see what he was doing as a betrayal because he was playing a deeper game. Shortly after the two men had met, Ward had asked Ivanov, 'What would happen in Russia if a British diplomat became very friendly with a Russian?' According to Ward, Ivanov replied, 'The Russian would receive a visit from our Security Police.' Ward said he had protested that Britain was different: 'We've nothing like that over here.' At this Ivanov had just smiled.

When Woods approached Ward and revealed that he was an MI5 officer Ward realised that Ivanov had been right. Ward would have considered telling Ivanov about the meeting with Woods and then would have rejected the idea, not necessarily because he owed any loyalty to MI5 but because he would quickly have realised that it was unnecessary — *Ivanov would automatically have assumed that Ward had been approached and therefore anything he told Ward would be passed on to MI5.*

Once Ward had worked this out his subsequent behaviour is at once understood. Ward was criticised as behaving like a man living a fantasy, the fantasy being that he was acting as a messenger between British and Soviet intelligence. Yet we have established that this is exactly what Ward was doing. Since Ivanov knew that anything important he told Ward, Ward would pass on to MI5, he told him only that information which his Soviet masters wanted MI5 to have, either to mislead it, or, more likely, as a deniable, unofficial way of talking about mutual problems.

Such an arrangement is not unusual in the intelligence world and this one might have run its course until Ivanov either defected or went back to Moscow. But political events abroad and human frailties at home upgraded Ward's minor role to centre stage.

# 12 | *Mandy and Christine Run Riot*

A year had passed since Christine Keeler had started work at Murray's Club. She was Murray's most troublesome girl. When she had money she vanished, off with a new boyfriend or enjoying a few days doing nothing. When she was 'skitters', as she described it, she would come back to work. The other girls could not understand why Murray put up with her. Perhaps one of them got it right when she said, 'Everybody puts up with Christine.'

The year had not worked out quite as Christine had hoped. She was still a showgirl. Fame and fortune had not come her way. She had met many men but most of her affairs had been unsatisfactory. She seemed to be attracted mainly to men who treated her badly. The one who did not, Michael Lambton, a rich young publisher and the nearest she ever had to a regular boyfriend, was a heavy drinker. (He used to keep a baby's chamber pot in the back seat of his Bentley in case he found himself too far from a toilet. Then he would steer with one hand, reach with the other into the back of the car, and say to his passenger, 'Pass the potty, dear.')

No matter how much Christine earned, it was never enough. The money seemed to disappear. Rent days arrived and went and irate landladies lectured her, but she seemed incapable of managing her finances. This failed to worry her: periods of being 'skitters' were, she believed, a normal part of life. Something would turn up. She would meet someone who would change her life, organise her, make things happen. Strangely, when she did, it was not as she believed it would be, a man. It was Marilyn Rice-Davies.

Mandy, as she preferred to be called, was the daughter of a failed actress from Wales and a Welsh-born Birmingham policeman. She was a rebel at school, but enjoyed games and art, and sang in the choir in the local Anglican church. Her main interest was horses and she managed to buy and keep a pony of her own by doing a paper delivery round, helping in a racing stable and, later, working on Saturday mornings in a Birmingham dress shop.

She left school at 15, found a job in a department store, and bullied her way into helping organise the store's fashion show, which was arranged to coincide with the local preview of a British film *Make Mine Mink*. Her hair backcombed and lacquered into a towering bouffant extravaganza, Mandy posed with the stars of the film, Terry-Thomas and Hattie Jacques, for the *Birmingham Post* photographer. Then the company limousine drove her home. This was heady stuff for a Birmingham teenager and soon afterwards when a man stopped her in the street and offered her a job modelling at the Earls Court motor show, she accepted with alacrity.

The Mini was the most photographed car that year and many of the photographs show a cheeky, open-faced young girl with bobbed hair, thick black eyebrows, a turned-up nose and an appealing smile. Mandy was also photographed at receptions, cocktail parties, dinners, and on the way to lunch with the Mini's brilliant designer, Alex Issigonis. She returned to Birmingham with £80 in her purse and her mind made up: she was going to live in London. When her parents objected, she packed her luggage in secret, waited until they were out, and left for the station.

Two hours later Mandy opened the pages of the London *Evening Standard* and ran her finger down the 'situations vacant' column. One advertisement seemed to stand out: 'Murray's Club requires dancers.' She auditioned that same afternoon, forged a letter of consent from her parents, and started work the next night.

Mandy was at Murray's for several weeks before she met Christine. The dancers were considered a professional cut above the showgirls and had separate dressing rooms so it was possible for two girls to work at Murray's and seldom meet. In the end another girl formally introduced them. It was not a happy meeting. Christine made a few uncomplimentary remarks about Mandy's excessive use of green eye shadow. Then she hid the top half of Mandy's Red Indian squaw costume just as she was about to go on stage to sing her fans' favourite number, 'Redskin Girl with Fire in Her Eyes, Bang! Bang! Bang!' Mandy retaliated by flinging a handful of talcum on to the ceiling fan over Christine's dressing table, coating her newly-applied makeup with white powder. Christine laughed, called a truce, and the next night fixed Mandy with a blind date.

The two girls quickly became firm friends. Christine often stayed the night at Mandy's flat. She enjoyed cooking late breakfasts and amusing Mandy with stories about her love affairs. Mandy, for her part, made fruitless efforts to sort out Christine's finances. It is difficult at this distance to decide who was the leading character. Mandy implies that Christine's life was chaotic and she needed Mandy to organise it. Christine says that Mandy was an over-confident 16-year-old and that she took her in hand and was always the boss. The truth is probably that the girls complemented each other, each providing something the other lacked, and in their friendship at that time they found emotional comfort and security.

Christine Keeler was soon restless again. Living with Stephen Ward might be comfortable but was not exciting enough. One morning after a night out with Mandy, the two of them decided that they were fed up with their Arab boyfriends, tired of Murray's Club, and bored with their lives. Christine suggested they leave the club and get a flat together. She convinced Mandy that if they worked as models they could earn as much in one day as they did in one week at the Club. They'd also be free in the evenings to go out or to entertain at home. Mandy agreed, and after some searching found a small flat in Comeragh Road, Fulham, at £12 a week.

Christine's faithful publisher friend, Michael Lambton, was persuaded to bring his Bentley to carry the girls' luggage. Mandy tried to skip without paying her landlady but was caught and Lambton had to pay £40 to settle her bill. Christine could not face Ward so she left him a note saying that she was going to share with a girlfriend. The night after moving in, they threw a house-warming party. Christine invited Ward and Rachman, and Mandy met them both for the first time. Rachman impressed her; Ward did not.

'I was attracted by Peter's manner and by the fact that I knew he was attracted to me. We all drove off to dinner in Peter's car, a navy blue Rolls-Royce convertible with a white hood. When the bill came, it was Peter, peeling off the notes from a thick roll, who paid. Wealth impresses ... Ward was a good conversationalist, quite charming. But I didn't like him. I suspected that the charm was superficial, that beneath it he was cold. There existed a sort of unspoken truce between Rachman and Ward, who had no liking for each other but maintained a polite relationship.'

Yet it was first with Ward that Mandy went to bed. He invited her to spend a weekend at his cottage. He cooked dinner and they sat for a while in front of the fire. Then Ward played one of his practical jokes. He said he was going to the pub to buy more wine and would be away about half an hour. Soon after he had left, Mandy heard a tapping sound at the window. It was a huge, grotesquely-deformed hand. Ward had driven away, parked the car, and crept back to the window with a trick, rubber hand.

'It had unnerved me so much,' Mandy said later, 'that when we went upstairs to bed I knew there was no way I was going to stay alone that night, so instead of sleeping in the guest room where he had put my suitcase, I crossed the tiny passage and climbed into bed with Stephen. He was a good lover, but he was not my trip and I was not his. It warmed our friendship but neither of us had any desire to repeat the performance.'

The next day Bill Astor called at the cottage and Ward introduced him to Mandy. Astor invited her to tea that afternoon and the two became friends. Mandy often went to Ward's cottage after that, sometimes alone with Ward and sometimes with other friends. 'Later I read in the newspapers that the parties at Cliveden during this period had assumed the proportions of a long-running orgy. How laughable. Nothing could have been further from the truth. Nancy Astor was there, and her sharp eyes missed nothing.'

Most weekends there would be at least one visit to the main house and sometimes Bill Astor would call at the girls' flat in Fulham. So when money became desperately short Mandy turned to him for help. Three months' rent was due in advance and neither Christine nor Mandy had the money. Mandy asked Astor for a loan of £200. Astor wrote out a cheque. 'Poor, good-hearted Bill,' Mandy recalled. 'That small act (to him) of kindness cost him plenty when it came out at the trial.'

Why the girls should have been short of money is a mystery. They later gave conflicting accounts of where their money came from and where it went. For a short period both of them worked at the 21 Club in Mayfair. There, Christine met Major Jim Eylan, who could always be relied on for money. She slept with him regularly at her flat and, later, at Ward's flat. She had other 'clients' too and she later confessed that she and Mandy competed to see who would be the most daring. Sometimes they indulged in group sex.

According to Mandy, when the girls decided to go off together to France for a break, they later disagreed again on where they got the money. She recounted a long story about winning considerable sums in the casino at Cannes and about a friend from Murray's Club, Robert Sherwood, the Canadian steel millionaire, who slipped her 1,000 francs under the table at lunch one day.

Christine told a very different story. They had tried to get into the casino but the casino officials barred them after checking their age from their passports. Instead, said Christine, they had met a wealthy film producer who knew Mandy from the 21 Club and Mandy had explained to him that they were available for money. According to Christine they returned home richer than when they had left. They were able to fly back and Christine still had enough money left over to buy her mother a new bicycle.

Both girls were looking for something more secure. Mandy quickly found it with Peter Rachman. 'I felt safe with Peter from the first time he took me out to dinner . . . Sexually he was not aggressive. I knew he was attracted to me but there was no pressure.' Eventually they became lovers and on Rachman's suggestion Mandy left the Fulham flat. 'I don't want you living with Christine,' he said. 'Will you move into my flat in Bryanston Mews?'

Mandy agreed. Rachman proved a generous man. For Mandy's seventeenth birthday he gave her a white 3.2 litre Jaguar, complete with forged driving licence. He gave her £80 cash as spending money each week, and paid all the bills at Bryanston Mews. 'It was the perfect bachelor girl apartment,' Mandy wrote later. 'Comfortably furnished with the best that money could buy, the sitting room boasted an antique Welsh harp and an ornate drinks trolley in glass and gilt filigree. There was a huge mirror in the sitting room which gave a view of the bedroom next door. It was a two-way mirror installed by a former tenant, Denis Hamilton, just like the one he and his ex-wife Diana Dors had had at their home in Maidenhead. This was slightly shocking in his [Rachman's] puritanical view. He did not have long to worry about it. A few months after I moved in we had a fight and I threw my wooden hairbrush at him. He ducked and it hit the mirror, shattering it completely. We hung a painting over it to disguise the mess until it could be repaired, and it never was.'

Christine took Mandy's departure philosophically because she was deep into an affair with Manu, a rich Iranian student, and was spending a lot of time in his rooms in Victoria. She told friends she was madly in love but Manu treated her badly. She used to follow him around the clubs in the West End looking for him and, when she found him, implored him to come home. He paid little or no attention to her. He would sit talking and drinking with his friends ignoring her while she created a scene. He was strict and demanding and used to thrash her if she misbehaved. It was the first time Christine had been treated this way and this reversal of roles appeared to have left a deep impression.

Inevitably, Manu threw Christine out. Once again she went back to the only man she could live with for any length of time, the only man she knew well but with whom she never had sex: Stephen Ward.

The life Christine, Mandy and the Ward crowd were leading during this period reflected in extreme terms the general change in social and sexual attitudes occurring in the rest of the country. Some sections of society welcomed the changes, but others were alarmed by it. The reformers, anxious to end persecution of homosexuals and liberalise the draconian laws on obscenity in literature and the arts, were opposed by a vociferous group who believed that Britain was being destroyed by a collapse of family life encouraged by sexual licence.

The struggle had its lighter moments. In May 1959 when the House of Lords debated the Street Offences Bill, aimed at making soliciting for prostitution in the streets an offence, Lord Massereene and Ferrard said he had been frequently accosted by prostitutes and it had never annoyed *him*. Baroness Ravensdale (63), well ahead of her time, said that if the streets were to be cleared of women then they should also be cleared of men. This brought the Earl of Arran to his feet for his first speech in the Lords, one which created uproar when he stated that one in every 540 women in London was a harlot.

It seemed that for every advance there was a step backwards. The Wolfenden Report recommended wide-ranging reforms that would decriminalise much homosexual activity, but a motion in Parliament calling for its early implementation was heavily defeated. Penguin Books, prosecuted as a test case over its publication of *Lady Chatterley's Lover*, was found not guilty. (It immediately printed 300,000 copies and sold a total of two million in the next eight months.)

But Paul Raymond, owner of the Revuebar, a drinking club that included striptease acts and sex tableaux in its floorshow, was fined £5,000 in April 1961 for running a disorderly house. When Raymond's defence counsel said membership of the club included almost every well-known name in London, the judge said, 'Your establishment and others have been vying with each other to see what degree of disgustingness they can introduce to attract members from all classes who are only too ready, out of lust or curiosity, to see the filth portrayed in this establishment. This, I think, is the fourth or fifth case I have had, and this is by far and away the worst.'

The 'moral majority' clearly felt threatened. A parliamentary association was formed in February 1961 by Sir Charles Taylor, Robert Mellish and Leslie Lever, with the aim of 'defending moral principles in public life'. A week later the novelist Barbara Cartland showed a 'girlie' magazine to a startled Conservative Party audience at Lemsford, Hertfordshire, and then set light to it, declaring to loud applause, 'I hope our small fire at Lemsford will start a big fire all over the country.'

# Astor's Summer Swimming Party

Saturday, 8 July 1961 saw the start of the hottest weekend of the year. Bill Astor had planned a large house party and early on the Saturday morning, as the temperature climbed steadily into the seventies, the guests began to arrive, grateful for a chance to get out of London's oppressive humidity. Later reports about this party, destined to become notorious, spoke of it as glittering with the stars of London society. They included Lord Mountbatten, President Ayub Khan of Pakistan, Sir Isaac and Lady Wolfson, Mr and Mrs Nubar Gulbenkian, Sir Gilbert Laithwaite, former High Commissioner to Pakistan, and John and Valerie Profumo.

Profumo's career had continued its steeply upward curve. After a spell as Parliamentary Under-Secretary at the Foreign Office he had been made Minister of State for Foreign Affairs in 1959. He had performed creditably in both jobs. In July 1960, Macmillan thought Profumo was ready for high office and appointed him Secretary of State for War. Profumo had had a tough week in the House and was looking forward to a chance to unwind.

Like Astor, Ward too was planning a weekend party. He expected two sets of guests, one on Saturday, another on Sunday. The Saturday crowd was small: Christine, and Noel Howard-Jones. For Sunday Ward had invited Ivanov and, if the weather remained fine, other guests were expected to drop by, unannounced. Christine could not get away on Saturday morning, so persuaded a friend of Ward's, Gerry Weedman, to drive her to Cliveden late in the afternoon. On the way they stopped to pick up a girl hitchhiker and she accepted an invitation to come to the party as well.

When they arrived Ward was still working in the garden and Howard-Jones had not yet arrived. It was too hot to do much, so they all lounged around until Ward prepared some food. They cleaned up after the meal and then all drove up to the main house to go swimming, which they were entitled to do because Astor had told Ward he was free to use the pool at any time.

There is some slight difference in what the participants say happened next, but the broad outline is the same. Christine discarded her swimsuit — either because it was too big and kept slipping down (Ward's version) or because Ward dared her to (her version) and swam naked. It was getting dark when Bill Astor and Jack Profumo, both in dinner jackets, walked out of the house and approached the pool. Ward, seeing them coming, snatched Christine's swimsuit from the pool's edge and threw it behind a shrub. Christine spotted a towel at the deep end, swam to it before Ward could get there, and wrapped it around herself in the water.

She climbed out and tried to recover her costume but Astor and Profumo, who had come straight from the party, decided to intercept her. There were a couple of minutes of chase, with Keeler, a nimble 19-year-old, finding no difficulty in avoiding two out-of-condition, middle-aged men. Then, just as the other guests arrived from dinner, Ward switched on the floodlights.

It is a pity no one photographed the moment: Christine, her hair streaming water, trying to cover herself with a towel that was obviously too small; two out-of-breath husbands looking slightly guilty; a party of men in dinner jackets and women in long gowns standing slightly on one side, spectators at an event the import of which has escaped them; all frozen for a moment in the sudden glare of white light. Then the scene comes alive as Astor, ever the perfect host, breaks the silence in the best British manner, 'Let me introduce . . .' Soon Christine is shaking hands with Profumo, then with Valerie Hobson and the other guests. The party proceeds.

But Profumo was obviously enchanted with Christine. When Astor invited Ward and his guests to come back to the main house for drinks, Profumo volunteered to show Christine round the house. According to Christine, the tour began very sedately but deteriorated. 'It was in one of the rooms which Jack was showing me over that he grabbed me. It was just a bit of fun I thought.' And Christine, amused by the idea that Profumo's wife was a famous film star, did nothing to discourage his advances, 'I liked it,' she said later, 'I don't mind admitting.'

Everyone seemed to have had a good time. Christine struggled into an old suit of armour, and with Profumo's help, clanked into the room where the guests were having drinks. She was greeted with a burst of laughter. Then she announced that she would have to leave because she was driving back to London that night so as to show some friends of Ward's the way to the cottage in the morning. Astor invited them all to a poolside picnic lunch. Ward accepted on behalf of his guests and the party broke up.

Sunday was even hotter and as soon as Ivanov and Christine

arrived they all went to the pool where they found the picnic in full swing, with nearly everyone in swimsuits. Ward introduced Ivanov and encouraged him to join in the swimming events which Astor was organising. The first was a race the length of the pool. Swimmers could use any armstroke they preferred but were not allowed to move their legs. Ayub Khan and Ivanov, both with powerful armstrokes, were nevertheless quickly passed by Profumo, who put his feet on the bottom at the shallow end of the pool. When there were shouts for him to be disqualified he turned to the other contestants and said, 'That'll teach you to trust a Minister of the Crown!'

Then there was a double wrestling match. Each man took a girl on his shoulders and tried to tip opposing couples into the water. The winner was the girl who was not unseated. Needless to say, Christine and Profumo were a team. This time there *were* photographs. Some show Profumo, Christine, Ward and other guests. Some were captioned by Profumo himself: 'The new Cliveden set' but they were later stolen from Ward's flat. One of the surviving pictures shows Ward, slim and smiling, handsome behind his sun-glasses, with Christine in a one-piece black swimsuit leaning on his shoulder. Resting her head on his thigh is a brunette, Sally Norie, and sitting by his feet is a blonde, both women later to figure in Ward's trial as prosecution witnesses.

Late in the afternoon Ward took Ivanov aside and asked him to drive Christine back to London. He said he had an hour or so's work to do on Bill Astor's back but he encouraged Ivanov to wait for him at Ward's flat so that later that evening they could play bridge. Ivanov agreed, but Ward never kept the appointment. What happened at the flat is unclear. Christine said later that Ivanov took a bottle of vodka from the boot of his car; they drank it and when it became obvious that Ward was not coming to play bridge, they went to bed together. But, as we will see, Christine was encouraged by newspapers to say that she had slept with Ivanov whether she had or not. Ivanov's version was that he got very drunk on vodka while waiting for Ward and when it became late he decided to leave. He said he was so drunk he could hardly find his way home.

Christine's story must be treated with great scepticism. As the barrister John Zieger points out, Christine was quite frank about her sex life and if she had slept with Ivanov she would have said so *at the time*. On the contrary, at the time she actually said she had *not* slept with him. 'Two or three weekends later she was gossiping about it,' Zieger remembers. 'She said Ivanov had been drunk and she was amused by his wavering along the line of being a Russian married man and amorous at the same time. And she said he went off. It was only 18 months later when people were pursuing her and she had a story to sell, and it was only a good story if Ivanov and Profumo were sharing a mistress, that Christine decided she had slept with Ivanov. I don't believe she ever did.'

What is more important was Ward's motive in deliberately throwing Christine and Ivanov together. If he really had to treat Astor, what was to prevent Ivanov and Keeler from waiting for him at the cottage? Then they could all have driven back to London together. If he was baiting the 'honey-trap' for Ivanov then it was a strange way of going about it, since Ivanov was smart enough to see what was happening, having been trained to recognise such risky situations and having learnt to avoid being compromised. (Would a Soviet GRU officer really have intercourse with a girl steered his way in the flat of a man he knows is in contact with the British security services? Any intelligence officer, Soviet or Western, would automatically assume in such circumstances that he would be photographed and blackmailed.)

What is not speculation is that first thing on Monday morning Ward telephoned his case officer, Woods, and went to see him. He gave him several significant pieces of information: that he had pushed Keeler in Ivanov's direction; that Ivanov and Profumo had met at Cliveden; that Profumo had shown interest in Christine (Profumo had asked Ward for her telephone number); and that Ivanov had asked him when the United States was going to arm Germany with atomic weapons. This flood of information was almost too much for Woods to handle. The routine entrapment operation was becoming complicated.

Woods was not concerned about Ivanov's interest in Germany and atomic weapons – that was to be expected of a serving GRU officer. But Profumo's interest in Keeler could interfere with the honey-trap. The aim was to catch a Russian in an indiscretion, not a British Cabinet Minister. Woods decided he was out of his depth. This was a matter for his Director-General, Sir Roger Hollis.


On Tuesday Profumo telephoned Christine and asked her if she would come for a drive with him. The chauffeur-driven ministerial car took them around London for an hour or so, Profumo keeping Christine amused with light conversation. When he dropped her back at Ward's place, he asked to see her again. The second time, later that week, Profumo came in a Mini. He took Christine to his house in Regent's Park and there, according to Christine, they made love for the first time.

We have discovered that this was the beginning of a longer and

more serious affair than has hitherto been realised. Profumo
showered Christine with presents, gave her money, and proposed
setting her up in a flat of her own – mainly because he felt that their
relationship could not long remain a secret while Christine continued
to live with Ward. Most of their meetings took place in Ward's flat
when Ward was out. Christine later vigorously and convincingly
denied that their relationship was ever any threat to national security.
'Christine told us at the time,' Noel Howard-Jones recalls, 'that
Profumo was only interested in her sexually.' They hardly ever spoke
and, if they did, the conversation 'would have dwelt mainly on her
since that was about the only thing she could talk about with any
authority. The idea she could ever have discussed anything serious in
bed is quite preposterous! You only have to know Christine to know
that's true!'

Early in August MI5 tried to recruit Profumo for their operation
against Ivanov. After reading Woods's report Hollis decided that one
way of ensuring that Profumo was not compromised by the
operation would be to make him aware of it. Rather than approach
Profumo directly, Hollis asked the Cabinet Secretary, Sir Norman
Brook, to act for him. On 9 August Brook saw Profumo and put
MI5's request: would Profumo be prepared to help MI5? Profumo
said no. Brook did not press the matter, but said that the operation
would continue and it might be advisable for Profumo to keep away
from Ivanov during this time. Profumo agreed and said that since
Ivanov spent so much time in Ward's company it might be a good
idea if MI5 were to warn those members of the Cabinet who were
acquainted with Ward about the Ivanov operation.

The same day Profumo wrote a letter to Christine.

Some accounts say that this was to break off the relationship
because Profumo had mistakenly assumed from his conversation with
Brook that MI5 knew of his affair with Keeler and had told the Prime
Minister. But there is no evidence for this conclusion. Firstly,
although MI5 probably did know of Profumo's affair with Keeler, its
Director-General, Hollis, would certainly not have considered that
this was any concern of the service. It is not part of MI5's charter to
monitor the sex lives of Cabinet Ministers and Hollis would have
been particularly wary of this issue because he himself was having an
affair at this time with an MI5 secretary.

Next, Profumo might have wanted to break off his relationship
with Christine because of his own assessment of the risk to his career
of sharing her with Ivanov. But there is no testimony that Christine

slept with Ivanov other than on the Sunday when he drove her home
from Cliveden — and, as we have seen, there is only Christine's word
for this.

Finally there is the letter itself:

Darling,

In great haste and because I can get no reply from your phone —
Alas something's blown up tomorrow night and I can't therefore
make it. I'm terribly sorry especially as I leave the next day for
various trips and then a holiday so won't be able to see you again
until some time in September. Blast it. Please take great care of
yourself and don't run away.

Love J.

P.S. I'm writing this 'cos I know you're off for the day tomorrow
and I want you to know before you go if I still can't reach you by
phone.

This letter is no more than what it appears to be — a note breaking
an appointment — and Christine accepted it as such. She hid it away
and forgot about it for the time being. Christine herself is vague about
when the affair ended but she is precise about the underlying cause —
her refusal to stop living with Ward and move into a flat provided by
Profumo. The most likely date for the break is not therefore just a
month after the affair started, but towards the end of the year — three
or four months later.

But why was Profumo so concerned about the fact that Christine
lived in Ward's flat? It is unlikely to have been jealousy — Profumo
was not *that* deeply involved with Keeler — or Profumo's scarcely
concealed dislike for Ward. There are two feasible reasons. Profumo
was aware of MI5's interest in Ivanov. Ivanov was a frequent visitor
to Ward's flat. As long as Profumo had to use the flat for his meetings
with Christine there would be a danger that Ivanov might turn the
tables: it might be the British Secretary of State for War who found
himself being blackmailed by the Russian. The other risk was Stephen
Ward's big mouth. Ward already knew too much about Profumo's
affair with Christine, and Profumo knew Ward could not be trusted
to keep quiet about it.

Ward was enjoying his role in the shadowy world of espionage and diplomacy. Christine said he was an avid reader of spy novels and now he was a leading figure in a real-life spy drama. The entrapment operation had turned into something far more important for him: he and Ivanov would play a major part in negotiations between Britain and the Soviet Union on a wide range of issues. Ivanov had Moscow's ear: 'Anything important you tell me can be on Khrushchev's desk in 20 minutes,' he once said. And Ward, he believed, had quick access to Britain's power élite and MI5. When open diplomacy broke down, the Ward-Ivanov duo took over.

At first glance this all reads like a Ward fantasy, a dramatised story invented to entertain guests after dinner, or to provoke a discussion on ethics one Sunday at his cottage. Yet at least some of the fantasy came true.

On Monday, 7 August 1961 Khrushchev appeared on Soviet television to make a speech about what came to be called 'the Berlin crisis'. The West had declared that it would not accept that East Germany could control Western access to Berlin. Khrushchev hinted at a Soviet arms build-up on her Western frontiers. In this tense atmosphere, probably at Ivanov's instigation, Ward took steps to bypass normal diplomatic channels and intervene in Soviet-British relationships. He first went to Bill Astor and persuaded him to write a letter to the Foreign Office. Astor had too much experience in the workings of British government to word it as bluntly as Ward wanted, but even so it was a fairly remarkable letter.

Astor said that he had a friend called Stephen Ward who was close to a Russian diplomat, Captain Ivanov. If the Foreign Office wished to ensure at any particular moment that the Soviet Embassy was absolutely correctly informed about Western intentions, then Stephen Ward could be useful. He could pass on information himself or he could very easily arrange for Ivanov to meet anyone. The Foreign Office must have been amazed at this approach. For one thing, it carried the implication that the Foreign Office officials could not be doing their job properly in communicating with the Soviet Union through normal diplomatic channels. But it was sufficiently intrigued by Astor's description of Ward to arrange an interview with him. There he told officials that he was anxious to turn his friendship with Ivanov to some use and that the Berlin crisis seemed a good opportunity to do so. He was turned down.

Undeterred, Ward next arranged for Ivanov to have dinner at the House of Commons with a long-serving Conservative MP, Sir Godfrey Nicholson. Ward had known Nicholson, one of his patients, for several years, and thought that he would have an open mind on anything Ivanov might suggest to ease East-West tension. This was more successful. Nicholson was impressed by Ivanov and agreed to make enquiries at the Foreign Office about the British attitude on disarmament and the Berlin crisis.

Nicholson duly did so and wrote Ivanov three letters on these matters. The fact that there were three letters suggests that Ivanov must have asked for clarification on some point or another. All these letters were approved by the Foreign Office, so although they were not on Foreign Office letterhead, they represented official British policy. All these were passed by Nicholson to Ward who then delivered them personally, the first two direct to Ivanov, the last to the ambassador because Ivanov was in Moscow on leave.

The Foreign Office had done an about-face. An unofficial line of communication with the Soviet Union *had* been opened – the Foreign Office to Nicholson, Nicholson to Ward, Ward to Ivanov, Ivanov to Khrushchev. And Ward had been accepted as a part of it: otherwise why did Nicholson not simply post the letters to Ivanov?

There was more to come. Nicholson had been in touch not only with Foreign Office mandarins but with the Foreign Secretary, Lord Home himself. Home had warned Nicholson against seeing Ivanov, but Nicholson said that as an MP he felt it to be his duty to be free to talk to Ivanov if he wished. Encouraged by Nicholson's independent attitude, Ward suggested that Nicholson should arrange for him to meet some high-ranking Foreign Office people. His ideas might not have got through the lower-level red tape, he said. Why not go direct to the Permanent Under-Secretary of State, Sir Harold Caccia? Nicholson obliged. On 5 April 1962 he arranged a luncheon where Ward met Caccia. Ward was frank. He was worried about the state of Anglo-Soviet relations. So were his Russian friends. He could put Caccia in direct touch with Ivanov. Caccia politely declined the offer.

Later, when Ward was in the dock at the Old Bailey, the prosecution painted him as something of a fantasist, an incorrigible name-dropper who lived on the fringes of London society and who had deluded himself into believing that he was playing some role in international affairs. Yet the truth is that in the autumn of 1961 Ward did play such a role. This becomes incontrovertible if we simply list what Ward was doing, what meetings he had, and the matters he discussed.

Ward was discussing international political issues with an important Soviet GRU officer, Ivanov. Since Ivanov automatically assumed that everything he told Ward made its way to MI5, anything he said would have to have had official Soviet approval. But Ivanov wanted something in return. At his request, Ward was openly seeking official information about British intentions. He was consulting a leading Conservative MP on the issues; he was passing Foreign Office-approved letters on to Ivanov and the Soviet ambassador; he was meeting with Foreign Office mandarins to put forward ideas and plans.

All this was no fantasy, and the British authorities now admit that it all took place. Ward was acting as an unofficial pipeline to convey information between the Russians and the British. The fact that he was unable to persuade the Foreign Office to make greater use of the channels he had opened did not discourage him. There would be other, more important opportunities.

# 15

*Wigg Seeks Revenge*

George Wigg was one of the most colourful Members of Parliament this century. When he first entered the House of Commons he was appalled at what he found. 'Perhaps my greatest shock in politics was to find how corrosive of human decency the search for place and power can be,' he said later. 'Never in my life before had I found men hating other men to the point where they hoped the wounds would fester.'

Wigg, who had spent eighteen years in the army, gradually established a reputation as an MP who had the interests of the ordinary man, especially the ordinary soldier, close to his heart. Not for him the detached rhetoric of politics. His speeches conveyed passion and sincerity, a tremendous sense of personal involvement in whatever cause he was championing. He failed to understand those of his Labour colleagues who would bitterly tackle the Conservatives on points of political principle in the Commons and then join them for friendly drinks later at the bar. The Conservatives were the class enemies, Wigg believed, and he would, if pressed, say so. 'I hate their guts,' he said once in Parliament. 'I always have, and I always will.'

One reason for this was the sly jibes some Conservatives would make about Wigg's background – snide class prejudice based on the Establishment dictum that it is all right for a self-made man to rise to the top provided he never forgets that he does not really belong there. 'Has not the time now come', said Sir David Renton on one occasion, pointing a finger at Wigg, 'for the hon. Member to be sent back to his regiment?' This raised an easy laugh because, as every MP knew – since Wigg made no secret of it – Wigg never *had* a regiment; his years in the Regular Army were served in the ranks; and he never saw action in the war.

Wigg made exceptions for certain Conservatives. If they were ex-army men then he felt they shared a common background which transcended party political lines: 'I'm an old soldier; he's an old soldier; we can trust each other.' In the early 1960s one such Conservative was the Secretary of State for War, John Profumo. Since

Wigg was always raising questions about the army — the quality of recruits, educational and recreational facilities, medical matters — he and Profumo got to know each other, establishing a formal friendship based on mutual respect and the conviction that they both had the interests of the British Forces at heart. In 1962 this relationship ended abruptly.

The breach centred on British troop landings in Kuwait in July the previous year. The operation, launched on the plea of the ruler of Kuwait to repel an alleged threat of invasion by Iraq, had been hailed as a 'model', putting to rest at last the ghost of the Suez débâcle. Wigg was immediately sceptical. Knowing the area and its politics as he did, he doubted both the need for the operation and the efficiency with which it was said to have been carried out. He began to ask embarrassing questions in the Commons and soon had the Minister of Defence, Harold Watkinson, in an awkward position.

As reports of Wigg's stand reached the troops in Kuwait, many began to write to him. Most confined themselves to the logistics of the operation and said that there had been insufficient drinking water, unpalatable food, and inadequate medical advice. All this was something Wigg really understood. Even generals acknowledged that when it came to running an army few men knew as much about pay, rations, leave, hospitalisation, transport and equipment as Wigg. When he had digested the soldiers' letters, and reports from those journalists he trusted, Wigg decided that the Government had not told the whole truth about the operation. This opinion was reinforced in July 1962 when an official report on the medical aspects of the Kuwait expedition was published. Its conclusion was damning: if there had been any fighting there would have been heavy British casualties from heat exhaustion. As many as 10 per cent of the troops were out of action from heat-related illnesses in the first five days.

Wigg decided to build up a case against the handling of the operation by the War Office, to challenge the accuracy of some of the Defence Minister's answers in July, and to press for a Parliamentary Select Committee of Inquiry on Kuwait.

The opportunity to do this did not arise until the following November. Wigg spent a lot of time preparing his case. He visited the War Office frequently to gather information for his speech and since he regarded the issue as one of national importance and therefore above politics, he discussed it with his friend, the Secretary of State for War, John Profumo, and they agreed to work together on how best to air the issues. They discussed the form the debate would take, the principles that would be raised, and what they hoped would be achieved. On the eve of Wigg's speech Profumo telephoned Wigg at his home to double check the arrangements.

Wigg's speech was one of his best. He used the Kuwait operation as a launching pad to criticise the state of the British Army. It was under strength, badly trained, without an effective anti-aircraft weapon or medium artillery, and without mobility. Reporting the speech the next day the *Daily Telegraph* said:

The matter is vivid, personal and picturesque: the thirsty troops reduced to drinking water from truck radiators; HMS *Devonshire*, which should be called HMS *White Elephant*; the piles of rusting jerricans at Chilwell, Didcot and Bicester.

The Heads of the Services being banged together; the soldier who died through drinking beer in Kuwait (not so, said Mr Profumo, Secretary of State for War; the soldier had indeed drunk some beer, but he had become ill through exhaustion and had now recovered).

Mr Wigg's gestures are as ample as his material. With his right hand he picks up a division or two here and drops it there. At the sweep of his arm great forces march, squadrons fly, Lord Mountbatten rules the waves.

'I've looked it up!' he cries, suggesting with pointed finger great piles of tomes outside, ransacked by armies of orderly room clerks and research assistants.

When, instead of Profumo, the Air Minister, Hugh Fraser, rose to reply, Wigg had his first suspicion that he had been set up. Fraser answered the main thrust of Wigg's allegations by saying simply that the faults in the operation had been grossly exaggerated and that where there had been errors they had been corrected. Then Profumo rose. He repeated Fraser's assurances and then produced two letters from two commanding officers saying, in effect, that Kuwait had been a rather good show.

When Profumo sat down Wigg realised how he had been slyly outmanoeuvred. Parliamentary procedure gave him no right of reply, so he could not produce other letters to balance those from the commanding officers. The debate fizzled out. Wigg said later that Profumo had failed to keep their agreement on the way the debate was to be conducted, had not told him in their pre-debate discussions about the letters and had used them to dodge the real issues. 'I felt he was playing politics with a matter of gravest national importance.'

Wigg told his friends that he felt betrayed. Even an ex-soldier, if he were a suave Tory like Profumo, could not be trusted, he said. Wigg smarted over the way Profumo had treated him, and pondered the chances of revenge. He had been wondering what to do about an anonymous telephone call he had received some ten days earlier. It is not unusual for Members of Parliament to be telephoned by people who do not wish to identify themselves, but this call had two strange aspects. The first was that it did not come to Wigg's own home but to the house of a friend whom Wigg was visiting — and no one, or so Wigg thought, knew he was there.

Next there was the nature of the call. Wigg had been in the forefront of those MPs who had pressed the Government over the issues involved in the case of William Vassall, the homosexual Admiralty clerk who had been convicted on 22 October of spying for the Russians. The caller's message had been brief and to the point: 'Forget about Vassall,' the man had said. 'You want to look at Profumo.' The most likely person to have made the call was John Lewis, who was later to become a regular informant of Wigg's. But at this stage Wigg did not know him well, did not recognise the voice, and had been half-convinced that, whoever the man was, he was probably a crank. Now he began to have second thoughts.

# 16

# The FBI and the London Call Girl

Mariella Capes was a London nightclub dancer who also used the names Henrietta Chapman and Maria Novotny. She had different stories of her life to go with each name: Mariella Capes was born in London and became a striptease dancer to support her old mother; Henrietta Chapman was a budding author waiting for a publisher to discover her talent; and Maria Novotny was a refugee, the niece of the former President of Czechoslovakia, and worked part-time for the British secret service.

The truth is that Mariella was a fantasist who told so many lies in her brief but tempestuous life that it is now extremely difficult to unravel the truth from her fairy tales. The only certainty is that she was a prostitute and a police informer, whose real name was Stella Capes. At least that is the name she used when, on 29 January 1960, she was married at Caxton Hall to Horace ('Hod') Dibben, a wealthy antique dealer and nightclub owner, 36 years her senior. Mariella (the name she used most frequently) denied that she was marrying Hod for his money. 'I've met a lot of rich men in my time as a dancer,' she said. 'But none has shown me the care, love and attention that Hod has.'

As one hundred guests drank champagne at Dibben's West End club, The Black Sheep, and cut slices from an 18-tiered wedding cake, Dibben announced that he had given Mariella a 20-room, sixteenth-century mansion in Sussex and a luxury flat in Eaton Place for a wedding present. Her engagement ring was a 200-year-old diamond and sapphire antique. Dibben said, 'You may think I'm showering her with gifts but nothing is too good for this wonderful girl.'

Less than a year after they were married, Mariella went off to the United States. Dibben told the newspapers that their married life had been hectic. 'She used to tie me to a chair in my leather suit, whip me and then make me watch while she screwed someone in front of me.' According to Dibben, Mariella performed similar acts for some prominent men and women in London and was well paid for it. 'I liked her to earn a few bob on the side,' Dibben said. 'It made her feel independent.'

But a few bob was not enough, and when a friend of Mariella's, a television producer called Harry Alan Towers, invited Mariella to join him in New York where, he said, he would introduce her to his American colleagues, she snapped up the offer. 'I wanted to be famous and show my mother that I could make a go of life myself,' she said.

Mariella arrived in New York in December 1960 and immediately set herself up in a call girl service. She used four numbers in New York to arrange meetings with clients. One was Towers's apartment at 4A, 140 West 55th Street, another was registered in her name at 18D, 300 East 46th Street, another one at the same address registered in Hod Dibben's name, and one at 54 East 83rd Street in the name of E.M. Adams. In addition she employed an answering service.

It was a call to the answering service which put the New York police on her trail. Someone tipped off the District Attorney, William F. Reilly, who passed on the information to the FBI. The FBI passed it to the police who intercepted a client's call to the answering service. Then, posing as a potential client, a detective from the 54th Street police station arranged to use Mariella's services for $30.

She told the detective to go to 140 West 55th Street, Towers's address, between 11.30 a.m. and noon on 3 March 1961. When he arrived Mariella was waiting for him. But as she undressed two other detectives crashed into the apartment and arrested her. They also arrested Towers who, according to FBI files, was concealed in a clothes' closet at the time. Towers was charged with maintaining a disorderly house. Mariella was charged with soliciting.

Towers was held in the Manhattan House of Detention on $10,000 bail until his hearing, set down for 7 March. Mariella was released on $500 cash bail put up by Dibben. The bail was low because Mariella had told the Attorney General that she would be willing to be a prosecution witness in a more serious case. This was filed in the Southern District of New York on 6 March and charged Towers with violation of the White Slave Traffic Act (WSTA), title 18, section 2421, alleging that he had transported Mariella Capes Novotny from England to New York for the purpose of prostitution.

On 15 March Towers's bail was reduced to $5,000 and he was released. He appeared before a grand jury on 12 April on five counts of violating the WSTA. On 25 April he came up before Judge Charles M. Metzner and pleaded not guilty to all five charges. The District Attorney asked that bail be increased to $25,000 because 'a large number of influential and wealthy persons involved in this case would like to see the defendant out of the country.' The judge refused the request and set Towers's trial for 16 May. In the intervening period Towers jumped bail — to avoid being framed, as he says — and Mariella absconded.

On 31 May she boarded the Cunard liner, *Queen Mary*, in New York using a ship's visitor's pass. Few noticed an attractive blonde woman, dressed all in black, who made her way to a first class cabin, number B-63, for which she held a ticket in the name of Mrs R. Tyson. During the five-day voyage to Britain, Mrs Tyson had all her meals in her cabin and took no part in the ship's social events.

By the time the *Queen Mary* docked in Southampton, the British immigration authorities had received word from the FBI that Mrs Tyson, *alias* Mariella Novotny, Marie Capes, Stella Marie Dibben née Capes, Maria Novotny, Henrietta Chapman, Mrs Harry Alan Towers, and Mrs Horace Ronald Dibben, was wanted in the United States in a 'sex-for-sale' case which, the FBI said, involved men in 'high elective office in the United States government'.

The FBI requested British immigration to hold Novotny until such time as they could arrange for her extradition. However, since Mariella was a British subject, the immigration authorities had no choice but to allow her to land, and then leave for London with her husband and her mother, who had come to meet her.

Mariella was quick to recognise the value of what had happened to her. She put the word around Fleet Street and then sold to the highest bidder, Peter Earle, the crime reporter of the *News of the World*. In her story, ghosted for her by Earle, she blamed Towers for setting her up in the call girl business. (Towers, whose case was eventually dropped, later blamed her and Dibben, and said he knew nothing of what was going on in his flat while he was at work.)

But because of Britain's strict libel laws, Mariella was unable to publish the names of her 'wealthy and highly-placed clients' in New York — if they ever existed other than in her imagination. The whole sordid story would not be worth recounting, except that it had two significant repercussions. The first was that the Mariella-Earle combination – whore and writer about whores – was a potent one and they would have other chances to exploit their respective skills.

The second was that the case came to the attention of the head of the FBI, J. Edgar Hoover. Hoover was obsessed by the idea that the United Nations was a risk to the security of the United States. He was convinced that many of the UN diplomats were easy prey for Soviet intelligence which had set up vice rings to trap and blackmail them. Hoover's other obsession was the sex lives of the Kennedy family. Mariella Novotny, with her references to her important clients one of whom held 'high elective office', now made Hoover begin to wonder whether his two obsessions might be linked.

Christine Keeler met Lucky Gordon in October 1961 when she visited the Rio Café in Notting Hill with Ward and some friends. (Ward had taken to visiting West Indian haunts, both as an outing to excite his friends and to sketch faces.) Lucky had come to Britain from Jamaica in 1948 in one of the early waves of West Indian immigration. A small but well-built man, his real name was Aloysius, but his parents called him Lucky because they won £4,000 in a lottery on the day he was born.

He had joined the army in 1954 but lasted only two years because he assaulted an NCO. Then spells in and out of prisons, usually for assault, made him decide to try another country and he went to Sweden to work as a nightclub singer. He returned to Britain in 1959 and made a subsistence living singing around the West Indian clubs in Notting Hill and Soho.

Christine's version of how she met Gordon is that Ward encouraged her to buy some marijuana, that Gordon sold it to her, and that remembering Ward's wish to try a West Indian girl, she had asked Gordon to find a sister for her brother to make a foursome. She says that she gave Gordon her number to call when he had found a girl and that she and Ward had then tried the marijuana for the first time.

Gordon's version is that Christine was already a user of the drug, that Ward was not, and that Ward did not like Christine smoking it. Christine's version continues with Gordon later luring her to his room and raping her at knife-point. Gordon says that she willingly became his lover. What is not in dispute is that Gordon was jealous and possessive of Christine, that he telephoned her frequently, often in the middle of the night, called at Ward's flat and tried to seize her, and lay in wait for her in the street. Yet on one of the few occasions that he managed to persuade Christine to spend some time with him, she confessed she enjoyed herself.

'She told me at the time that she was very happy with me,' Gordon told us later, 'because I treated her like a queen. She told me she'd never experienced love or been looked after that way before.' For a man with a history of violence, Gordon attended to Christine's every need with a tenderness that she must have found surprising. Gordon had transformed himself from the axe-wielding maniac she described to the police to a gentle, considerate and unselfish lover. The room they shared in his brother's house was small, dark and sparsely furnished, a sharp contrast to the more affluent homes of her wealthier boyfriends. 'There was very little privacy there,' Gordon recalls, 'but my family were good to her. They liked Christine.'

Ward had begun behaving like an over-protective father so Christine started to spend longer periods away from him. In November 1961, she took a flat in Dolphin Square, a large modern block on Chelsea Embankment overlooking the river. And there she entertained a succession of men. Some were friends or casual lovers, others were clients. Gordon recalls, 'One time Chris let me stay and watch her with one of them. She told me he was a barrister. I looked through the keyhole while she was whipping some guy with a broomstick while he was on his hands and knees on the floor.' According to Gordon, Christine had messed up the flat before the client arrived so that she could make him clean it up. She kept shouting orders at him, beating him and telling him he was a lousy maid. She threatened to fire him and then left. When she returned the flat was spotless. No sex was involved. The man paid her and left.

This period of Christine's life was one of the few times when she seemed to have enough money to enjoy herself. Life was a continuous party, either at her flat, or in the pubs and clubs of the West End. The agent John Kennedy, who had met Christine at one of Sugden's parties, remembers bumping into her one day outside her Dolphin Square flat.

'She asked me in. I walked into this apartment and I'd not seen anything like it in my life before. Apparently what had happened was this: Christine had an Italian boyfriend who was insanely jealous. He had to go away for ten days and he didn't trust her at all. So he locked her up in her own flat. But he first filled it with things from Fortnums. This is what I saw when I first walked in. Cases of champagne stacked halfway to the ceiling, food hampers everywhere. Jars of caviar. Bowls of fruit. It was amazing.

'Anyway, Christine couldn't stand it longer than two days. She felt she was going mental. So she called from the window and someone found the porter to let her out. I met her as she was coming back from buying some clothes. She looked terrific, black gown, big black hat, jewellery. And after showing me all this food and booze, she said, "I've got an idea. Let's have a bath together and drink some champagne."

'I said, "That's a great idea." So she filled the bath and got an ice bucket and put a bottle of champagne in it. Then we went into the bathroom and I started to take my jacket off and she said, "Oh, no. Not like that." And then she jumped into the bath with everything still on, her black hat, her dress, her shoes, everything. And she said, "Anyone can have a bath together in the nude. This is much more fun. Come on."

'Now I had this brand new seventy guinea suit. It was by Colin Fisher, the tailor of that period, and there was no way I was going to get into that bath, even with Christine Keeler, in my brand new Fisher suit. She sat there with water up to her chin and I sat on the edge and we drank this Italian guy's champagne. Christine Keeler was just a bit crazy.'

But still there, lurking in the background, was Lucky Gordon. When later that day Kennedy and some friends decided to take Christine to the River Club, just across the road from Dolphin Square, Gordon confronted them as they were leaving the main entrance. There was a scene and Kennedy and his friends had to smuggle Christine out through the service entrance. When they came back, Kennedy said later, there were three men waiting for Christine. 'She had made dates with all three for the same night.'

The fact that Gordon could frequently be found keeping watch on Christine's flat at this time lends credence to his claim that he knew who her main clients were. For example he has given us the account of the masochistic barrister who was made to clean up the flat. He says that Christine relented and allowed him to watch on other occasions too. Gordon says further that some of Christine's clients were very distinguished people, including several MPs.

Whether Gordon was capable of recognising these 'distinguished people' is debatable, but he could well have learnt their names from Keeler because on at least one occasion he terrorised her to the extent that she would have told him anything he wanted to know, and given his jealousy this could well have included the names of her lovers and clients. This happened after a pub crawl in Chelsea when someone spotted Gordon and invited him to a party in Christine's flat. By this time they were all very drunk. When they arrived back at the flat Gordon was the first to notice a fire-axe attached to the back of the front door. He seized it, brandishing it at anyone who dared approach him and threatening everyone until, one by one, they managed to escape.

Gordon kept Christine and a friend in the flat for two days before the food and cigarettes ran out. When he took the door keys and went out to buy more, Christine rang the police. They arrested Gordon and charged him with assault. Ward bailed him out and when Gordon's brother begged Christine to drop the charge, warning that Gordon, because of his record, would go to jail for a long period, she agreed. The police were angry and Christine must have quickly realised how foolish she had been, for the following day Gordon returned to Dolphin Square. He kept a constant watch on her movements, lurking in the shadows, waiting for her to leave. At this stage, Christine was terrified to be alone in the flat and needed a constant companion. She would not even answer the telephone herself in case it was Gordon wanting to pester her.

In June a chance came to get away from Gordon for good. Mandy Rice-Davies was going through a period of being bored with Rachman and she suggested that they should try their luck in the United States, New York first and then, if all went well, Hollywood. Grand plans were made. Christine had just gone back to living with her old boyfriend, Michael Lambton. He agreed to lend her £500 to get started. He would arrange to transfer some of his publishing business to New York, join Christine as soon as this was done, and they would set up house in America.

The two girls sailed on the Dutch liner, the *Nieue Amsterdam*, which left Southampton on 5 July. They arrived in New York six days later and checked into the Hotel Bedford on East 40th Street, negotiating a special rate of $15.50 a day for a double room on the eighth floor. Then they set out to make New York take notice. They went round all the 'in' clubs showing off their London fashions. Mini-skirts had not yet become the rage in America so the two girls were looked at and admired wherever they went. Their sexy way of dancing, too, was appreciated. They considered they were a hit. But as far as their careers were concerned the trip was a disaster.

Mandy developed a late adverse reaction to her smallpox vaccination and a local doctor, John Maxwell, recommended a weekend's rest. They went to Fire Island, not realising that it was a gay resort: 'The only normal guys there were the three policemen,' Mandy said. They stayed too long in the sun and were badly burnt. Modelling was out until their skin recovered. Back at the Hotel Bedford, they telephoned the Cunard Steamship Company to check fares and sailings and then the British Consulate to see whether they could borrow the money to get back to London.

When told that they could not, Mandy turned to Rachman and Christine to Lambton. They cabled the money and both girls flew back to Britain on BOAC Flight 506 on 18 July. Their American adventure had lasted two weeks. In other circumstances it would have been dismissed as just another typical Christine-Mandy lark, an irresponsible but harmless giggle. But, for reasons which will emerge later, it came to the attention of J. Edgar Hoover, head of the FBI, and a team of FBI officers sought sinister significance in the trip.

# Cooling the Cuban Missile Crisis

In twelve days in October 1962, from the 16th to the 27th, the Soviet Union and the United States took the world to the brink of a nuclear war. The issue was Soviet determination to install missiles in Cuba versus American determination not to tolerate this. The two leaders, Kennedy and Khrushchev were eyeball to eyeball. Khrushchev said that Soviet freighters carrying the missile equipment were on their way to Cuba and would not turn back. Kennedy said that if they did not turn back the U.S. Navy would board them. Both knew that this would mean war and that any such conflict would rapidly become a nuclear one. It was so close at one stage that the White House prepared a list of people who would be allowed into the President's special bunker.

In Britain those who followed events closely enough to understand the stakes watched in fascinated horror. One of these was Stephen Ward. Ward's role over the next few days has been scoffed at as the self-aggrandising fantasies of a political fool. But new information which has slowly emerged since the Cuban missile crisis and new facts we have uncovered show Ward in a different light.

The Soviet approach to diplomacy and intelligence activities is unlike that of the West. In a sense, every Soviet citizen serving his country abroad is a diplomat and an intelligence officer. His duty is to put his country's position in all matters, to project it in the most favourable light, and to gather information that might be useful to his Government. One way of doing this is to identify men and women of power and influence in the West and to cultivate them. Harry Rositzke, one-time head of anti-Soviet operations in the CIA, has said that the Russians are interested in people who can sway decisions on all sorts of matters concerning East-West relations. To identify these people they cultivate friendly contacts with 'persons of influence across the spectrum of private and public élites.'

Ivanov had identified Ward as such a person of influence, not because Ward was a decision-maker himself, but because he could offer Ivanov access to people who were. In this assessment Ivanov

was absolutely correct, as results show. Through Ward Ivanov met
the Secretary of State for War, John Profumo, on a social basis, and
Bill Astor, part of the Astor clan well known as leaders of the
Cliveden Set and its appeasement politics. Through Ward Ivanov met
Lord Mountbatten, a member of the Royal Family, and Paul Getty
and Nubar Gulbenkian, two of the world's richest men. He also
met Sir Godfrey Nicholson, a prominent MP, and dined with him in
the House of Commons. Through Ward he was able to correspond
on an off-the-record basis with the Foreign Office (using Nicholson
as an intermediary), to consolidate his acquaintance with Sir Colin
Coote, an influential newspaper editor, to meet the President of
Pakistan in a relaxed holiday atmosphere, and to open a line to MI5.
So, viewed from the office of Ivanov's GRU boss in Moscow, Ivanov
was doing very well indeed.

Although the main purpose of all Ivanov's manoeuvres was to
further Soviet interests by manipulating what – in modern intelligence
service terms – are called his 'agents of influence' there was another
aim. This was to have available an alternative means of communicating
with the British Government should it ever be needed. The occasion
could arise when Moscow might wish to tell London something it
considered important, but for many reasons it might not wish to do
this through formal diplomatic channels. Such channels involve
letters, proposals, minutes of meetings, historical records. If everything
goes wrong it is then impossible to deny that these events ever
occurred.

Alternative, irregular channels of communication open the possibility
of much more flexible negotiations: 'What would be your attitude
if we were to do this?' And then if the worst happens, both
Governments can plausibly deny that any such negotiations ever took
place. If somehow someone produces proof that they did, then the
Government concerned simply says that this or that junior officer
was acting on his own initiative, entirely beyond his authority, and
that he will now be suitably disciplined. We have seen how this
alternative means of communication between the Kremlin and
Whitehall was used – in a comparatively minor way – over the
Berlin crisis. Now, with the world on the brink of war over Cuba, it
was about to be used again.

Recent evidence suggests that during the Cuban missile crisis there
was a major power split in the Kremlin. The 'doves' in Moscow had
become increasingly worried over Khrushchev's hard line with the
United States and the alarming deterioration in East-West relations –
the U-2 spy plane incident, the collapse of the summit conference in
Paris, the Berlin Wall, the Soviet resumption of nuclear tests in the

atmosphere, and the 'hawks' of both sides arguing for a pre-emptive first strike.

The Soviet doves were deeply concerned by what they called Khrushchev's 'adventurism', his strident tone with President Kennedy, his imposition on the Soviet armed forces of his own personal defence policy and, in particular, his decision to raise the nuclear stakes by putting missiles in Cuba. A nuclear war in defence of the Soviet Union was one thing, but a nuclear war caused by Khrushchev's bluffing was an intolerable and increasingly likely possibility.

The structure of Soviet authority being what it is, there was no way in 1962 that the anti-Khrushchev faction, which included senior military officers, could let the West know, firstly, that there were doves in Russia as anxious as the doves in the West to control the 'first strike' lunatics, and, secondly, that whatever Khrushchev might threaten, he did not have the military capability to carry out that threat.

Here the alternative channels of communication came into play. The main message had to be to the United States, and Penkovsky was the channel. For, in retrospect, Penkovsky's real value to the West was not the secret files he photographed when he was on weekend duty at GRU headquarters, or the clues he gave about Soviet moles in Western services. It was the knowledge he passed on that Khrushchev was bluffing, that the Soviet Union did not have the ability to attack the United States with intercontinental missiles, that the Kremlin did not speak as one voice, and that there were Soviet doves as worried as American doves about the possibility of a nuclear holocaust.

The CIA must have considered at the time the possibility that Penkovsky was not all he appeared to be – in short that he might not be a genuine defector but might be operating with the connivance of some faction within the Soviet intelligence community. But the CIA must have decided that the value of Penkovsky's main message overrode the implications of this collaboration. There are, of course, other variations. Penkovsky could have been genuine, but an unwitting tool of whoever was controlling him. It would not be beyond the KGB to have spotted Penkovsky as a potential defector but to have allowed him to run until the moment came to use him as an 'unconscious' channel of communication during the Cuban missile crisis. If the first hypothesis were true, with Penkovsky party to the Russian scheme, the implication is that he was not executed after his trial in 1963 as reported, but is alive and well and living in Moscow. If the second hypothesis were correct, with Penkovsky a genuine defector but an unwitting medium in a Soviet intelligence operation, the implication is that he was indeed executed. But either way,

Penkovsky's role must have been to act as one channel of communication to the West, because there is no other convincing explanation for his timely arrival on the scene with exactly the sort of information the Americans desperately needed. Nor is there any other explanation why Penkovsky's fellow GRU officer, Yevgeny Ivanov, who came from a similar background, and knew many of the same people in Moscow's ruling circles, was desperately trying to pass important Soviet messages directed at Britain. New information, Ward's recordings, and interviews with people who have not spoken before, make it possible to reconstruct the Soviet plan to pass vital information to the British Government and Ward's role in what occurred.

On 24 October 1962, the ninth day of the crisis, Ivanov telephoned Ward at his consulting rooms and asked him to call at the Soviet Embassy. There, in his office, he made a remarkable offer.

The world, Ivanov said, was on the verge of nuclear war. Kennedy and Khrushchev were locked into a confrontation which no one could win. 'It's like a motor accident,' Ivanov said. 'The two drivers are arguing over who was right and who was wrong while the accident victim, in this case humanity, bleeds to death.' Ivanov said he wanted to get a message to the British Government 'behind the scenes'. Could Ward arrange this? Ward said it might be possible. He returned to his consulting rooms and telephoned Bill Astor. Astor suggested Ward should telephone the Foreign Office and say that Astor had suggested a meeting with the Permanent Under-Secretary, Sir Harold Caccia. Ward did this and spoke with a duty officer who said he would pass on the request.

The following day, Thursday, 25 October, Ivanov telephoned Ward again and said that the matter had now become extremely urgent. Could he come round to Ward's consulting rooms to discuss it? Ward agreed and telephoned his MP friend, Sir Godfrey Nicholson, who had been helpful during the Berlin crisis, and asked him to come to the meeting with Ivanov as well. Ward later described the meeting:

We listened to Ivanov with growing amazement as he unfolded his suggestion. He said he was empowered by his ambassador to speak for the Soviet Government. There is no doubt at all that this was so. No one from the Soviet Embassy would dare to say this unless it was true. The Soviet Government wished to suggest that a summit conference should be called in London. The British Prime Minister, Harold Macmillan, might or might not attend as he saw fit. Once the calling of the conference had been agreed, Moscow would stop their ships, at that moment sailing on a collision course with the US Navy.

Ivanov was very persuasive. He said that if Britain took the initiative in calling the summit conference the world would recognise it as a major contribution to world peace. It would demonstrate that Britain was still an independent power rather than a tool of Washington. If Britain acted now then it would win the trust of the Soviet Union which might want to call on Britain as a peacemaker if further difficulties with the USA arose later.

Nicholson was sufficiently impressed to decide that Ivanov's message should be passed to the Foreign Office immediately and he hurried off to Whitehall to do so. From there he telephoned Ward to say that he had passed on the gist of Ivanov's offer to someone he knew at the Foreign Office. This was the Deputy Under-Secretary, Sir Hugh Stephenson. Stephenson was an old boy of Winchester — as was Nicholson — and had been to Christ Church, Oxford — as had Nicholson — so Ivanov was right to think that the 'old boy' network could still be useful in Britain. He was also right in telling Ward that his unofficial approach could sometimes achieve things that a formal one could not.

For, at almost the same time that Nicholson was passing on Ivanov's proposals, the Soviet chargé d'affaires, N. A. Loginov, was trying to convince the Foreign Secretary, Lord Home, that Britain should use its influence with the United States to stop the Cuban missile crisis from developing into a nuclear war. When Ivanov and Ward met the following morning, Friday, Ivanov relayed Loginov's report of the abortive meeting: 'Page after page of shorthand notebooks had been filled with mutual recrimination about past events but nothing positive was achieved.' Ivanov said that Home was probably blocking higher discussion of the Soviet offer.

There was every likelihood that this was so. Home thought that the whole Soviet approach — Loginov's general suggestion and Ivanov's specific proposals — were classic Soviet subversion tactics. He later wrote: 'I think that the Soviet intention was two-fold. First, it was to drive a wedge between ourselves and our American Allies. Second, it was to test our resolve and to lay a bait to our vanity.' This remained his opinion throughout the crisis and, as a result, he did not take Ivanov's overtures very seriously. Ivanov realised this and told Ward that they would have to go higher — if possible directly to the Prime Minister himself.

So Ward telephoned Bill Astor and asked his advice: how could Ivanov get a message to Macmillan? Astor's answer was to suggest a meeting with the Earl of Arran, Arthur Kattendyke Strange David Archibald Gore, known to his friends as 'Boofy Gore' and to his enemies as 'Goofy Bore'. Ward was sceptical but Astor convinced him. True, Arran was eccentric – he once informed the House of Lords during a debate on drunken driving that he had tested his own reactions at the wheel by a series of experiments in which he drank increasingly large quantities of alcohol, thus winning himself another title, 'The Plastered Peer'. But he had marvellous contacts, either through his very large family, through a network of old boys from Eton, or from his own time in the diplomatic corps. He had easy access to Lord Home – when they wrote they addressed each other as 'Dear Alec' and 'My dear Boofy' – and, whatever one thought of Arran's lifestyle, no one would question his motives in a diplomatic démarche like this. So Astor telephoned Arran to introduce Ward, and when Ward himself telephoned on Friday, Arran suggested that he bring Ivanov over to Arran's home in Hertfordshire for a drink on Saturday morning.

Ward still felt they were not doing enough, so after fixing the appointment with Arran he had lunch with Ivanov at the Kenya Coffee House in Marylebone High Street and decided to try another direct approach to the Foreign Office – this time on his own. He telephoned and was quickly granted an interview with Sir Harold Caccia's private secretary. To him Ward repeated his understanding of the Soviet offer on the crisis. Although the Foreign Office later said they had not taken Ward seriously, this meeting suggests otherwise. The fact that an ordinary citizen could telephone the Foreign Office, say that he wanted to discuss the Cuban missile crisis and soon afterwards be in the office of the private secretary to the top-ranking mandarin in the department, suggests that Ward was being taken very seriously indeed.

The next day, Saturday, with the world one step closer to the brink, there were two developments in London. One official, one irregular. At 10.30 a.m. Lord Home again met the Soviet chargé d'affaires, Mr Loginov. Ivanov later reported to Ward what had happened. Loginov had gone to the Foreign Office in an optimistic mood. Why would Lord Home summon him on a Saturday unless the Soviet backstairs manoeuvres had been successful. Instead Home was firm and unfriendly: Britain would stand by the Anglo-American accord; there could be no negotiations.

The other meeting was at least more convivial. As Ward described it: 'We drove out into the country near King's Langley and eventually located Lord Arran's charming house. Lord Arran greeted us in the drive and then we sat down to talk with some excellent rosé for myself and a bottle of vodka for Ivanov. Ivanov put the Soviet position and Moscow's offer once again.'

The meeting took an hour and three quarters. As soon as Ward and Ivanov left, Arran sat down and wrote a memorandum on what had been discussed. He made an assessment of Ivanov, 'a pleasant fellow who gives the impression that he must have been at the Leningrad Charm School.' He set out his impressions as to why Ivanov had come to him: 'Throughout our conversation, Ivanov kept stressing the major role still played by the British aristocracy. To him the mere fact of being a Lord meant that one was in a position to influence events.' And Arran made a concise and fair summary of the Soviet proposals. By late that afternoon the memorandum had reached the Prime Minister's office.

Whether Macmillan read it before the crisis had reached its climax the next day is not clear. If he did, he certainly did not have time to act on it. The world went to bed on Saturday night wondering if there would be a Sunday. A few hours later the Cuban missile crisis was over. Khrushchev agreed to dismantle and withdraw the missiles from Cuba under adequate supervision and inspection. Kennedy called off his plans for a military invasion of Cuba and tacitly agreed to leave Cuba alone. The leaders of both countries had been educated into the realities of the nuclear age, and from this was to grow the improved East-West relationship that marked the next ten to fifteen years.

Ward and Ivanov heard the news at a dinner party that night in the main house at Cliveden. The other guests included Arran, who had planned to continue his discussion with Ivanov, and the Labour politician Lord Longford. Ward later wrote: 'We were in the long drawing room overlooking the Thames, probably the finest view from a country house in the south of England. We were agog to hear the television news, but when it was switched on there was only vision, no sound. To our bafflement and dismay, we saw first Khrushchev's face and then Kennedy's. Until we got the news a bit later from the other channel we did not know that a settlement had been reached. Ivanov looked stunned. "A mistake," he said.' Arran's picture of Ivanov is harsher: 'It was a very chagrined comrade who met us that evening. He kept on saying that he couldn't believe it and that he was sure that Mr Khrushchev had some counter-demand to make on the Americans. We all felt embarrassed by the man's humiliation.'

With Ivanov humiliated and Ward written off as being under Ivanov's influence and allowing himself to be carried away by spy fantasies, the affair would appear to have been a disaster, especially as it was to arouse intense suspicions about Ward's loyalty. Even Ward himself told Lord Denning later that although he felt at the time he was doing something momentous, he afterwards realised that it was of little significance.

But, with the benefit of hindsight and new information, we can see that this assessment was wrong. The principal piece of new information is that Ward was working as an agent for MI5. This was not admitted at the time and even Denning did not mention it in his report. This gives Ward's role in the Cuban crisis a different perspective: he was acting in a semi-official capacity. It was only *after* the crisis that MI5 began to reassess Ward's activities and not until 2 November that it decided that he might have come too deeply under Ivanov's influence.

Next, the plan that Ward was pushing on Ivanov's behalf, a summit conference in London called by Britain, was not such a hare-brained idea. Khrushchev himself had suggested a summit meeting in a telegram to Kennedy on 24 October and Kennedy had replied that he would be willing to meet – once the missiles had been removed from Cuba. The variation – that Britain should make an intervention by calling the meeting – was being canvassed openly by press and parliamentary circles at the same time that Ivanov and Ward were pushing it privately.

The fact that so many Russians were using every means at their disposal – diplomatic, agents of influence, and through Penkovsky and Ivanov – to tell the West that there were doves in the Kremlin and that they needed a gesture to strengthen their hand seems a more likely explanation of the affair than Lord Home's simplistic 'drive-a-wedge-into-the-Anglo-American-Alliance' one. Ivanov's approaches added weight to the information the West was receiving from Penkovsky – Khrushchev was bluffing, he did not have the wholehearted support of his colleagues, there was a powerful faction in Moscow prepared for concessions. All this strengthened the voice of those Americans who did not want war.

The real message was not the Soviet call for a summit meeting in London. It was the sentiments that prompted the suggestion that were important, the fact that the offer was made, not that it did not eventuate. That the message reached the right ears was largely due to the efforts of Dr Stephen Ward. He had been able to open lines to the people in power.

# 19 | *Problems with Profumo*

In the middle of the Cuban missile crisis, on Thursday, 25 October, Ward was lunching alone at his usual haunt, the Kenya Coffee House in Marylebone High Street. At a nearby table, William Shepherd, Conservative MP for Cheadle, Cheshire, was entertaining three doctors, all Hungarian refugees. Their talk, as did that of most people at the time, concentrated on the crisis. The Hungarians attacked Khrushchev and the Soviet attitude and praised the American stance.

Shepherd and his guests were startled when Ward suddenly turned in his chair and joined the conversation. Shepherd remembers: 'He began to put a pro-Russian view, mildly pro-Russian admittedly, but sufficient to anger my Hungarian guests. Things began to get a bit heated and I had to smooth things over. Ward may have interpreted this as a sign of sympathy because when I left the restaurant he was waiting for me.'

Shepherd says that Ward then tried to impress him by name-dropping, casually referring to his weekends at Cliveden and his friendship with a senior Cabinet Minister. Shepherd says that he took an instant dislike to Ward because of this but could not resist the opportunity Ward then offered him – a chance to meet the Soviet assistant naval attaché, Yevgeny Ivanov, and hear the Soviet view of the crisis. They exchanged telephone numbers and Ward agreed to make the arrangements. Before they parted Shepherd asked Ward how he was involved. According to Shepherd Ward replied, 'I'm just an honest broker. I simply want to see countries brought together.'

Ward duly fixed a meeting – drinks at his flat on Wednesday, 31 October. By then the crisis was over but Ward saw no need to cancel the appointment, a major mistake on his part. When Shepherd arrived, Ward, Ivanov, Christine Keeler and Mandy Rice-Davies were waiting for him. At this stage, according to Shepherd, the others had no idea that he was an MP. But this seems unlikely. Ward knew most of the regulars at the Kenya Coffee House and may well have learnt who Shepherd was even before the incident with the Hungarian doctors. Would Ward have gone to the lengths of inviting

Shepherd to meet Ivanov if he thought that Shepherd was an ordinary citizen with no influence? Besides, Shepherd knew Percy Murray and frequented his club. It is likely, therefore, that Christine and Mandy knew he was an MP.

Nevertheless, Ivanov began the conversation by asking if Shepherd was connected with politics. When Shepherd, still determined to conceal his identity, said no, Ivanov replied, 'Well, then, we can talk freely.' He then gave his views on the Cuban crisis, attacking his own Government vigorously. 'His attitudes were those of a big-fisted Stalinist,' Shepherd says. 'When I mentioned the merits of a free society, he got wilder and wilder. He seemed to want to turn the conversation into a shouting match. I didn't want to get involved, so I shut up; then he angrily accused me of behaving in a superior manner. So we started off again. He was making statements that were totally unjustified. I should have let him go on and have encouraged him to make more, because my job was to find out all I could about him. But I got rather annoyed by this truculent fellow, so I slipped him a thing about our knowing about the Bison bomber which they thought was super secret, and in the end to finish him off I said, "We didn't enter into a squalid pact in 1939 to share the milk with Hitler." That blew the whole show up. When I left Ward came out with me and apologised for Ivanov's behaviour.'

There the clash might have ended had Shepherd been nothing more than an MP. But, like so many characters in this story, he too had a secret side. He had close links with MI5 and some officers of Scotland Yard. The basis of these relationships was a two-way flow of information: Shepherd told his friend in MI5 items of news and gossip he picked up in the course of his duties as an MP and MI5 gave Shepherd information it wanted him to use. (A similar arrangement existed with Shepherd's police contacts.) Occasionally Shepherd's MI5 friend would ask him to do some small job, hence Shepherd's revealing remark about his meeting with Ivanov – 'My job was to find out all I could about him.'

Shepherd now decided that it was his job to discover all he could about everyone present in Ward's flat at that meeting, and how they tied in with Ivanov. Who *was* Ward anyway? How were Christine Keeler and Mandy Rice-Davies involved? What was Ward's relationship with them? They had hardly spoken during the meeting but when they had it was to defend and support Ivanov. What was Ivanov's relationship with them?

Shepherd began by making inquiries about Christine at Murray's Club. Not only had Shepherd recognised Christine as a one-time Murray showgirl when he had seen her at Ward's flat, but according to him he had already heard stories linking Christine with Profumo. In fact Shepherd to this day does not subscribe to the accepted account that has Profumo and Keeler meeting for the first time at Cliveden that hot summer's Sunday in July.

'Jack Profumo and another Minister were regulars at Murray's and I think it was highly probable that there was a meeting there . . . The Minister was very keen on Mandy Rice-Davies. He once started physical trouble with the staff of Murray's over Mandy being with another man and had to be thrown out. Well, you see, this sort of behaviour would have been acceptable at a slightly earlier period, but not really very acceptable then for Secretaries of State. As for Jack, he was almost as regular at Murray's as I was. I would say Jack knew Christine Keeler through Murray's Club.' (Profumo has denied this.)

Shepherd says that none of this concerned him until, through Ward, he met Ivanov, and Christine and Mandy were present. 'Until Jack got into office, the fact that he was one of those people who went around to nightclubs would not have been regarded as untoward. As Mosley says in the book about his father, the life of these people revolved around clubs like the Embassy and the Four Hundred. After Jack became Secretary of State for War everybody expected him to be more discreet, but he wasn't.

'Other members of the House would not necessarily have known what was going on because not many of them went to Murray's. I did, because I wanted to be up late at night and I liked dancing, so I was really one of the people who could be found at the nightclubs fairly regularly. Those MPs who would be doing it like me wouldn't say anything. We wouldn't discuss it with anybody. We wouldn't think of saying one saw Jack last night and Mandy Rice-Davies.'

Shepherd says that meeting Christine and Mandy with Ivanov, 'a Russian spy', changed his attitude. 'If it had been any other department; if Jack had been − he ought to have been, perhaps − Minister of Public Works, it wouldn't have mattered. But for Christine Keeler to be involved with a Secretary of State for War and for her to have an association with a Russian spy!'

Shepherd felt obliged to do something and acted on several fronts. First he spoke the next day to Iain Macleod, Leader of the House of Commons. The reason for this was a remark of Ward's when Shepherd was leaving Ward's flat: 'We must go too,' Ward had said, referring to himself and Ivanov. 'We're going to have dinner with Iain Macleod.' This was typical of Ward's tendency to exaggerate. There was a drinks party at Macleod's flat and Ward had wangled an invitation for himself and Ivanov by getting another guest to telephone and ask if it would be all right if he were to bring them, too.

Shepherd told Macleod about his meeting with Ward and Ivanov, 'the Russian spy', and warned him that Ward had given the impression that he knew Macleod well. 'I had to tell Iain this because he was being implicated,' Shepherd recalls. 'Well, Iain had a very strong sense of self-preservation, so that night he wrote a letter to the Home Secretary, who was responsible for certain elements of the Security Service, explaining what it was all about.' Macleod also spoke to the Foreign Secretary, Lord Home.

Next, Shepherd arranged to meet his friend in MI5 and told him not only that Ward and Ivanov appeared close friends but that Christine Keeler also knew Ivanov and that Profumo knew Christine Keeler. And finally Shepherd wrote a letter to Harold Macmillan himself. 'I said, look, I'm sick of the bad behaviour and immorality of your ministers. You've had public exposures, two or three narrow escapes, and you've got other risks which are being run. And he wrote to me and said, "I don't accept what you say, but will you go and see Martin [Redmayne] the Chief Whip and discuss." '

So Shepherd met Brigadier Redmayne and gave him the names of half-a-dozen ministers who, in Shepherd's eyes, constituted a risk to the Government 'in moral/political terms'. The main weight of Shepherd's accusations did not concern Profumo but were linked with homosexuality. They came on top of other accusations made in the *Sunday Pictorial* which was serialising Vassall's story. The newspaper, which had paid £7,000 to Vassall, said that letters and a postcard in his possession 'appear to give a clear picture of the friendly relations between an Admiralty junior clerk [Vassall] and some high officials for whom he worked'. The *Sunday Pictorial*, introducing Vassall's story, said: 'Before Vassall was sentenced for spying he talked of the urgent need for an inquiry into sex blackmail of high people who work for government departments. But he warned that such an inquiry, to weed out homosexuals in high office, would be unlikely to succeed. Many of the types who would be vetted are respectable married men holding senior posts.'

So it was with some trepidation that Redmayne listened to what Shepherd had to say. 'I told Martin that he ought to know what I knew about these men . . . including one very high minister who was involved with young boys. I said that he ought to have access to what they know across the road, which was then Scotland Yard.' And at the end of this amazing interview, which must have caused Redmayne some embarrassment, Shepherd dropped his bombshell. He simply said, 'And there's a problem with Jack Profumo, and you'd better be very careful.'

# 20 | *A Knife Fight in Soho*

Fights were not unusual in Soho, but one that broke out in the All-Nighter's Club late on Saturday, 27 October 1962 was something special. It involved Lucky Gordon and another West Indian, Johnny Edgecombe, and it was over Christine Keeler.

Christine had met Edgecombe earlier that year and had lived with him for a while at Boston Manor Road, Brentford. According to Edgecombe, when he was out working Christine took other lovers. But if Christine imagined Edgecombe's presence had at least scared off Lucky Gordon, she was wrong. Coming out of the hairdresser's one afternoon, Lucky sprang on her, knocking her to the ground and bruising her badly. When she told Edgecombe he insisted that the only way to be rid of Lucky Gordon was to confront him together. Then Christine could say that she was living with Edgecombe and was finished with Gordon for ever.

When they finally found Gordon in the All-Nighter's Club, he was in no mood for a reasonable conversation. He immediately picked up a chair and swung it at Christine. In seconds there was pandemonium. As customers struggled to reach the exits, Gordon and Edgecombe smashed their way around the club. The fight ended as suddenly as it had begun. Edgecombe whipped a knife from his pocket, flicked it open and slashed at Gordon's face. The tip of the blade caught him high on his forehead and as Edgecombe's arm came down, the knife edge opened Gordon's cheek to the chin, exposing for a brief second the wet whiteness of the cheekbone. Then, as the blood poured forth and Gordon screamed, Edgecombe grabbed Christine and they fled into the night.

Mandy Rice-Davies provided the postscript a few weeks later. She answered a knock at the door of Ward's flat. 'I was confronted by a diminutive West Indian asking to see Christine. When I said that she was not at home, he replied, "Give her these with my love," and put something in my hand. At first I did not recognise the tiny black scraps and when I did I let out a scream. They were stitches! Souvenirs of a fight between Lucky and Johnny, removed at the hospital that day. I thought I would faint with revulsion. Christine agreed it was all very sordid and nasty, and that she was finished with that side of her life.'

Mandy, too, was having ups and downs in her love life. Rachman clearly had no intention of leaving his wife, so Mandy saw no reason why she should not have the occasional affair herself. There was, for example, a rich American who visited London just after the Cuban missile crisis. He met Mandy at a private party and during his three-week stay he took her out to dinner six times. On five of these occasions he picked Mandy up at Ward's flat where Ward made a good impression on him: 'financially well off, a man of prominence, with a good practice in osteopathy.'

The American liked Mandy a lot. He said later that although she was only 18, 'she conversed like a woman of thirty'. He found her 'a very charming young lady, who appeared to have a good background.' She was cultured, refined and a pleasure to be with. This man, whose identity remains a mystery, is significant only because he later went voluntarily to the FBI to say that he could not reconcile what he was reading in the newspapers about Ward and Mandy Rice-Davies with the people he had met, albeit briefly, during his visit to London.

Later that same month, on 29 November 1962, Peter Rachman died of a sudden heart attack. Mandy had been in Paris to attend a wedding with Center Hitchcock, relative of Mrs David Bruce, the American ambassador's first wife. When Mandy arrived back in London, Ward broke the news to her. She collapsed to the floor in a flood of hysterical tears. (Ward, never one to miss a good story, insisted later that Mandy recovered briefly, opened one eye and asked, 'Did he leave a will?'). The following day Mandy persuaded Ivanov to drive her to Rachman's house in Hampstead Garden Suburb:

The front door was open, in the Jewish custom of a sitting *shivas*, with friends calling to pay their respects to the bereaved . . . the room was full of people, many of whom I had been in the habit of dining with over the past eighteen months. Nobody acknowledged me. Audrey came towards me. I think that this was the moment I knew that Audrey was his wife, and not just the woman he had lived with for years . . . [But] some masochistic urge drove me to Somerset House [then the Register Office for births, deaths and marriages] to prove to myself that Peter and Audrey were married. Perhaps it had happened years and years before, I hoped. To

discover that they had been married only a short time, their
wedding was in March 1960, was salt in the wound.'

Mandy's grief at the loss of Rachman was genuine because two
days later she took 30 sleeping pills. Christine found her with her face
turning black and called an ambulance. She recovered in hospital and
went back to Ward's flat to convalesce. He invited her parents to stay
there as well until Mandy could cope. 'Once again they asked me to
go home with them, but I had grown too far away for that. I
preferred to stay with Stephen, at least for the time being. At
Stephen's there were always people coming and going and this
created a feeling of bonhomie.'

Ward saw no reason why Mandy should not stay as long as she
wished but he also saw no reason why she should not contribute to
the cost of running the flat. They agreed on £6 a week rent and a half
share of food, electricity and telephone. Ward even suggested that a
simpler arrangement would be that they marry. 'Possibly Stephen
was getting to like our domestic partnership and found it comfortable
to come home to,' Mandy said later. 'He was by then in his late
forties, a bit of a cynic, basically lonely. Approaching old age many
people in similar circumstances elect for a marriage of convenience.'
And to illustrate the undemanding nature of the marriage, Ward told
Mandy that she could continue with her own life; she could
concentrate on modelling, extend her acting. Ward said he had
influential friends in many places and he could ask them to help her.
Mandy showed scant interest and the matter was dropped — only to
resurface in court later with a sinister twist.

What Mandy was probably looking for was another Peter
Rachman, and she soon thought she had found him in the person of
Emil Savundra, a self-styled 'doctor', confidence trickster, and later
notorious for swindling 40,000 British motorists out of their
insurance premiums when his company, Fire Auto and Marine,
collapsed. When Ward, who knew him casually, introduced him to
Mandy, Savundra was an unknown, middle-aged, silver-haired
Sinhalese; married, reasonably rich, and with a taste for young girls
and high life.

The day after Ward had introduced them, Savundra sent Mandy
roses and two days later he invited Ward and Mandy for a drink, then
Mandy alone for lunch. This turned out to be an hour-long drive
around London in a black taxi while they ate a huge Fortnum and
Mason picnic hamper — smoked salmon, caviar, cold chicken and
vintage champagne. Ward watched the progress of the relationship
with interest. 'Emil would like to rent your room,' he told Mandy.

'He needs a place to take his girlfriends.' Mandy said she did not believe Savundra could be serious: he had enough money to rent a permanent suite in a hotel. But Ward said Savundra wanted something more discreet and if Mandy agreed she could charge Savundra £6 a week, which would cover her rent. According to Mandy, she was persuaded. She had, she explained, in any case, planned to move out. 'I had no strongly possessive feelings about the room.' When she agreed, Ward, she said, then added, 'Anyway, if you two get together he won't have to bring outsiders in' — a casual joking remark which was to cost him dearly. The truth was, as we shall see, very different.

Mandy and Savundra did get together. 'He was fun, he was almost mad. He did not send me flowers, he had whole carloads delivered to the door. When I was with him I felt happy and alive and, most of all, secure. I remained close to him long after I left Wimpole Mews.' Savundra, always the gentleman, did not make Mandy an allowance. Instead, he asked her how much her drama lessons cost and when she replied twenty-five pounds a week, he insisted that he be allowed to pay. This, too, was to rebound adversely on Ward.

# 21 | A Shooting in Marylebone

At one o'clock on the afternoon of Friday, 14 December 1962, a minicab drew up outside Ward's flat at 17 Wimpole Mews, Marylebone, and Johnny Edgecombe got out. He had telephoned half an hour earlier, had spoken to Christine, and had begged to see her. Christine, who was going through a period when she was 'off' Edgecombe, had said no. He had come anyway, and was now furiously ringing the doorbell. Mandy, who was still staying with Ward after her suicide attempt, looked out of the upstairs window, saw Edgecombe and asked Christine if she should let him in. Christine, too, peeped out of the window, saw Edgecombe's rage and warned Mandy not to give her away.

Mandy told Edgecombe that Christine had gone to the hairdressers. Edgecombe's reaction was to take a handgun out of his pocket and fire it at the door lock. 'Oh my God,' Mandy said. 'He's got a gun.' Christine went back to the window and told Edgecombe to cool down and go away. Edgecombe pointed the gun at the window and fired two more shots. One hit the brickwork, the other went through the window and into the wall. Then he went round to the back of the flat and tried to climb up the drainpipe. Mandy telephoned Ward and he told her to call the police. They had already been alerted by neighbours who had heard the shots, but by the time they arrived Edgecombe, who had cunningly kept the minicab waiting, had gone.

The story of the shooting made little impact in the papers the next day. Both girls had allowed their ambitions to override the truth in describing themselves to the Press: 'Miss Keeler, twenty, a freelance model, was visiting Miss Marilyn Davies, an actress, at Dr Ward's home when . . .' The gun Edgecombe had used was found at the back of Ward's flat, and Edgecombe was quickly picked up and charged. There seemed some confusion as to whose gun it was. Christine told the police it was hers; that she had bought it and seven rounds of ammunition for £25 from a respectable gentleman she had met in a club. She told them she wanted the gun because she was afraid of Lucky Gordon, and if he showed up again she was prepared to kill him. The story sounds improbable for the simple reason that Christine was unlikely to have had £25 to spare at that time. Another account says that the gun had been bought from a criminal when Christine and Edgecombe were living together in Brentford and that it had earlier been used in a hold-up at Queen's Park; but the same doubt applies here, too.

A third version is that the gun belonged to Profumo, and that he had given it to Christine for her protection. William Shepherd, the former MP, believes this version. 'Jack gave Christine this revolver because there had been some trouble somewhere. When I left the army I had two guns and I didn't know what to do with the damned things. I finally gave them up when we had an amnesty. Probably Jack had the same sort of thing.' But Profumo has denied that he ever had a gun.

If, and it seems unlikely, the gun did belong to Profumo, it would have been only one more thing for him to worry about. His main cause of concern was that Christine would be questioned by the police about her association with Edgecombe and that this questioning could well expand to include her other liaisons. She could well be a witness at Edgecombe's trial. Although the Press had taken scant notice of the shooting itself, there was no guarantee that the trial would not receive sensationalist coverage – the combination of a black man, white girls, violence, and the fact that it had happened at the home of a society osteopath, would be an irresistible combination. And would Christine be able to keep her mouth shut in the witness box? Profumo would have been even more concerned had he known that, within hours of the shooting, Christine was telling all to a man fascinated by conspiracy theories, particularly involving espionage or political assassinations.

This was Michael Eddowes, a London solicitor, a tall, distinguished, middle-aged man, who was a patient of Ward and a casual friend. Eddowes had met Christine with Ward and would occasionally drive her back from the West End to Brentford when she was still living with Edgecombe. He warned her of the dangers of playing around with the affections of two men. 'One of them will try to kill you one day!' he predicted.

On 24 October Eddowes had agreed to meet Ward and Ivanov at the Coffee Bean in Marylebone High Street to discuss the Cuban missile crisis. 'Ivanov began by trying to recruit me,' Eddowes said later, 'telling me that rich people were far better off in the Soviet Union.' After a heated debate in which Ivanov became very threatening, Eddowes decided that Ward was entirely dominated by the young Russian. Later when Eddowes asked Ward if Keeler knew

Ivanov, he replied, 'Oh, yes and Profumo too.' Ward added that MI5 knew about this and were watching his flat. Eddowes then decided that Ward and Ivanov had embarked on a major conspiracy to compromise not only Profumo but several other cabinet ministers as well. However, he felt satisfied that, if Ward was telling the truth about MI5, the matter was under control.

Immediately after the shooting Christine telephoned Eddowes to tell him that his prediction had come true. 'Lucky attacked me with an axe and now Johnny has tried to kill me!' Eddowes suggested a meeting. Under his skilful, sympathetic questioning, Christine not only poured out details of her friendships with Profumo and Ivanov but embellished them. She told Eddowes what he wanted to hear: Ivanov was a spy (true); he had specifically asked her to find out when the United States was going to supply West Germany with nuclear warheads (highly unlikely). The idea that Ivanov would compromise himself by asking such an incriminating favour from Christine, a girl notorious for her indiscretions, simply does not ring true. (Eddowes later extracted a signed statement from Christine's manager, Robin Drury, that she had confessed on tape to passing on this, and other bits of information she had gleaned from Profumo, to Ivanov.)

Christine had probably overheard Ward and Ivanov discussing when Germany would receive nuclear warheads. (We have Ward's account of this conversation, which Ward repeated to MI5 at his very first meeting with Woods.) Now she remembered it when Eddowes quizzed her on Ivanov's area of interest. We have seen that Christine's affair with Profumo was simply not the type of relationship where she would be able to raise, subtly or otherwise, a matter like nuclear warheads for West Germany without making Profumo instantly suspicious. Christine was not the sort of girl to want to discuss such a subject, in or out of bed; it would have been completely out of character for her to have done so.

In fact by the time Eddowes had finished questioning her, Christine was already bored with her own fantasy and when Eddowes put the clinching question – so what information did you manage to get out of Profumo? – she told the truth: 'Nothing really.' And then, realising that the Edgecombe shooting and now her confessions to Eddowes would finally cut her off from Profumo, she said wistfully: 'I don't suppose I'll be seeing Jack again.'

Eddowes's intense interest in the Ward-Ivanov-Profumo triangle made Christine realise that she had been leading a much more fascinating life than she had thought. A week later she had another chance to talk about it to an audience which was even more captivated by her story than Eddowes. It consisted of a casual friend, Paul Mann, journalist and racing driver, two girls from Murray's Club, and John Lewis, the former Labour MP who had vowed to ruin Ward for taking Mrs Lewis's side in a rather sordid divorce action. Christine's story was much the same as she had told to Eddowes, a little more polished perhaps, but, probably realising that her former colleagues from Murray's Club would be reluctant to believe her claim to have had an affair with Profumo, she added the startling and vital proof: 'I've kept two letters from him.'

Of all the group, no one listened more attentively to this than John Lewis. At this stage all he saw was a chance to embarrass the Government. But he knew that Christine lived off and on with Ward and he must have hoped that somehow an opportunity would arise to embarrass Ward as well. The essential thing was to get what Christine had said written down before she changed her mind and shut up, so he impressed on her that to protect her own interests she should repeat everything she had said to a solicitor as soon as possible, and he recommended one: David Lee, of Tringhams, Portman Square.

A week later Lewis rang Christine and invited her to come to his house to discuss her problems. There followed an amazing pas-de-deux with a gun. Lewis, who was secretly tape-recording their conversation, asked Christine a lot of questions about Profumo, Ivanov and Ward. This time Christine changed her story slightly: it was now Stephen Ward who had first made the suggestion that Christine try to find out when West Germany would get nuclear warheads. Later Christine, still insisting it was Ward who raised the matter, made it clear that it was Ward's idea of a joke. Ward had himself joked to several friends, 'Christine's a powerful lady. She can change the world. She's got the British War Minister and the Russian naval attaché eating out of the palm of her hand!'

This is a convenient moment to suggest reasons why Christine's accounts of events at the time changed frequently. Firstly, she often saw life through a marijuana haze. According to her butler, John Hogan, she spent most of her nights 'in smoke-filled "pot" dens'. Next, she was only 20, a girl always anxious to please whichever man she happened to be with, so she tended to tell older men of powerful personality, like Eddowes and Lewis, what she believed they wanted to hear. As well, although she knew Ward well, his sense of humour was frequently over her head and, often to his delight, she would take seriously, and repeat in good faith some outrageous remark he had made. Later, there was to be another, more worrying factor – Christine would take to repeating, almost parrot-fashion, lines that other people had reason to feed her.

When Lewis heard, as he had hoped, Ward's name brought into Christine's story, he must have been delighted. He already had plans for using Christine's information to best advantage and Ward would fit in nicely. Mullally heard a story that was going around at the time, that Lewis was so pleased he decided to celebrate: he too would have Christine. His first approach was to try to buy her. She rejected him. Lewis was unabashed. There was no way he would allow Christine to leave until she had made love to him. He handed her the gun and challenged her to shoot him. Christine outbluffed him. She pointed the gun directly at him and pulled the trigger. There was a loud click. Lewis went white when he realised Christine really would have killed him, and he let her go. Not surprisingly she never saw him again.

As 1962 drew to a close even the most loyal Tories agreed that the Macmillan Government was in trouble. The Vassall scandal rumbled on. After the *Sunday Pictorial* allegations were reinforced by the official release of 25 letters, cables and postcards from Galbraith, the Civil Lord of the Admiralty and his wife to Vassall, Galbraith resigned. Macmillan accepted the resignation with bad grace: 'I believe in the long run this will help you but it will not help me.'

The newspapers, dissatisfied with Galbraith's scalp, kept hammering away over the failure of MI5 to detect Vassall sooner. Even the most dedicated Conservative newspapers joined this chorus, until, on 13 November, Macmillan announced the setting up of a Tribunal. But its terms of reference made it clear that it would be as much an inquiry into the conduct of Fleet Street as into the efficiency of MI5. The gap between the Prime Minister and the Press had never been wider.

This was not all that Macmillan had to weather. The economic climate was bad, with unemployment rising, and Britain's negotiations over the Common Market causing such uncertainty that the economy appeared to be running rapidly down. Public dissatisfaction was expressed in the by-election results of 24 November. The Conservatives held three of the five seats but were crushed in the other two. Macmillan's response to the crisis was to leave London for Lanarkshire to go pheasant shooting with Lord Home. The hit tune of the day was 'Beautiful Dreamer' but many MPs were wondering if the man living in a dream world was the Prime Minister.

For already London was buzzing with rumours of yet another scandal. It had not taken long for the initiated to work out from the clues in the article in *Queen*, 'Sentences I'd Like to Hear the End Of', that the men involved were Profumo and Ivanov. For evidence of this, consider what took place at a party to mark the opening of John Aspinall's Clermont Club on 5 November. At one table were businessman James Goldsmith, Churchill's son-in-law Christopher Soames, at that time Minister of Agriculture, Fisheries and Food, Benjamin Fisz, the film producer, businessmen Gordon White and James Hanson, Alfred Wells, secretary to the US ambassador, David Bruce, and Stephen Ward. Ward and Wells had attended the same dinner before the party and over the dinner table Ward had told part of the story of his role during the Cuban missile crisis. Wells asked another dinner guest who Ward was and the man whispered the reply: 'He's an osteopath who procures girls for his wealthy clients.' This set the tone for the exchange which took place at the party. Someone said something that linked the names Profumo and Keeler. Soames overheard the two names and burst out: 'So what? At least it's a girl. You too could have her for five pounds a go.' If a senior Minister in Macmillan's Government knew of Profumo's relationship with Christine Keeler, how much longer could it be kept from the public?

Before putting the Cuban missile crisis behind him, Ward sat at his desk in his consulting rooms and between seeing patients wrote a long letter to the Leader of the Opposition, Harold Wilson. It set out the efforts he had made to get the Soviet message through to the British Government and then went on to give his analysis of the events leading to the crisis and the state of East/West relations after it. One sentence read, 'I was an intermediary between the British and Soviet governments in this matter.' Wilson, who had never heard of Ward, must have thought that the whole letter was an airing of someone's fantasies, not unlike other letters which MPs sometimes receive. He told his secretary to send off a standard 'thank you' letter and to file Ward's analysis. He then forgot all about it.

The letter to Wilson acted as something of a catharsis for Ward. The Cuban crisis was over, the world had survived, he could get on with enjoying his life. He even found he could enjoy a joke about it all. When a Sunday newspaper published an artist's impression of how a British submarine could take secret photographs of a Russian cruiser's hull, Ward cut out the drawings, pinned a note to them saying, 'The last remaining secret in the British Admiralty' and posted it to Ivanov at the Soviet Embassy. As Ward probably expected, the letter never arrived; no doubt it had been intercepted by

MI5. Ward and Ivanov considered this a great joke and told it around London dinner tables with delight.

MI5 was not amused. Its leading agent in the 'honey-trap' operation against Ivanov was, on the one hand, taking the matter too lightly; and on the other − as his interventions in the Cuban missile crisis showed − was getting delusions about his importance. The service was being flooded with reports about Ward. He was being seen so often around town with Ivanov that the MI5 informants, not knowing about the 'honey-trap', thought that Ivanov must have recruited him, and could not wait to tell their masters.

MI5 assessed the situation. Ward's case officer, Woods, was asked for his view. He wrote: 'It is not easy to assess Ward's reliability but we believe he is probably not a man who would be actively disloyal, but that he is so under the influence of Ivanov that it would be most unwise to trust him.' By any reckoning this was a negative report. As sometimes happens with a 'honey-trap' operation, the agent who is supposed to bait the trap gets so close to his target that normal, human emotions take over. At this stage Ward had grown to like Ivanov. Their joint efforts, misconceived or not, to help save the world from a nuclear war had brought them closer together. If Woods had suddenly told Ward that the time had come to spring the trap on Ivanov, it is doubtful if Ward would have been able to bring himself to do it.


Ivanov spent his last Christmas in Britain with Lord and Lady Ednam at their country house, Great Hundridge Manor, Great Missenden, Buckinghamshire. Ednam, the eldest son of the third Earl of Dudley, had married the actress Maureen Swanson a year earlier. Maureen had been a close friend of Ward for years and, according to the show-business writer Logan Gourlay, Ward's introductions helped set Maureen on the path to stardom.

Ward had introduced Ivanov to Lord and Lady Ednam and they had taken a liking to the charming Russian. They played bridge together, dined together, and, at this Christmas house party of 1962, they worked off their Christmas dinner with a brisk ride together. Ward was there too, having driven down for the day. It seems reasonable to assume that Ward and Ivanov discussed Christine's problems, the pending court case and what it might mean for them both.

In the light of subsequent events Ivanov must have reported to his GRU bosses that he might be dragged into a British courtroom drama. Over the next few weeks they probably gave serious consideration to his position. On the one hand Ivanov had achieved a place in British life that had great potential. It is fair to say that no other Soviet diplomat since has managed to cultivate such a wide range of friends and acquaintances of influence as did Ivanov. On the other hand for a Soviet assistant naval attaché to be involved, however peripherally, in a sordid shooting case would gain no credit for the Soviet diplomatic corps. The uncertainty worried the Russians and after a few weeks' bureaucratic delay, Moscow decided to pull Ivanov out. Once the decision was taken, it happened very quickly. From its intercepts of Soviet radio and telephone traffic, MI5 knew that the order recalling Ivanov was received at the Soviet Embassy on 22 January. Ivanov was given seven days to wind up his duties and he left, on schedule, for Moscow on 29 January.

Did he and Ward meet one last time? There is a contradiction here. Lord Denning states categorically that Ward saw Ivanov on 18 January and warned him that the story might break soon. But two of Ward's closest friends, Noel Howard-Jones and John Zieger both swear that Ward last saw Ivanov at Christmas and was very hurt not to have received even a telephone call from Ivanov to say goodbye. Mandy Rice-Davies, too, says that Ward was puzzled by Ivanov's silence and 'hurt at not having had the chance to say goodbye'. In his recording Ward said philosophically: 'Anyway, whatever else happened, Ivanov's bridge improved remarkably while he was over here and I hope that he profited from the book I gave him, *Bridge is an Easy Game*.' Later, however, he added rather regretfully, 'I wonder what happened to Eugene.'

January 1963 was a month of great activity for the cast in what was soon to become known as 'The Profumo Affair'. In the simplest terms, Christine spent the month trying to get her 'memoirs' published while virtually everyone else spent the time trying to stop her. It all began with a quarrel between Christine and Ward. Ward said it was a petty one. They were driving home from a New Year's Eve party with a girlfriend of Christine's crammed into the tiny back seat of his Jaguar sports car. The roads were icy and he was having trouble controlling the car. He suggested that the girl get out and take a taxi. Christine protested that if her friend was made to get out, she would get out too. So Ward drove off leaving both girls on the street.

But the flashpoint, stupid though it was, could have been indicative of some more serious change in the Ward/Keeler relationship. There had been signs that Ward was growing tired of Christine's comings and goings — his efforts to persuade Mandy to live permanently with him, for example — and his realisation that however hard he might work at turning Christine into another Vickie Martin, he was not going to succeed; the raw material was simply not there. The trouble with Lucky Gordon and then Johnny Edgecombe had impressed on Ward that his professional practice might suffer; his patients might be reluctant to entrust their backaches to a man whose residence was the scene of a shooting. On Christine's side, too, there had been a still unexpressed resentment at Ward's domination of her personality and her life. She needed Ward, but resented that need. When she got out of his car on New Year's Eve she was, perhaps, getting out of Ward's life as well.

If Christine, without fully formulating her decision, had taken the first step in breaking with Ward for good, then this would go a long way toward explaining her subsequent behaviour. For without Ward to fall back on when she was 'skitters' she would need some sort of financial security. So she now became obsessed with getting her hands on some money. She said that she needed this to get her mother out of Wraysbury because West Indians were calling there seeking Christine and scaring her mother; because Lucky Gordon was still pestering her and she wanted to get away from him; because she needed money for her lawyers; and because she had a dream that once the Edgecombe trial was out of the way, she would go off to the United States with Mandy and try again to get into the big time. Add to this the fact that she had lost her base with Ward, that she was only 20, a bit of a scatterbrain, and easily influenced, and her behaviour in those January weeks is more easily understood.

Christine knew nothing of 'cheque book journalism', but she had friends who did: Paul Mann, the racing driver/journalist and Nina Gadd, a freelance writer. Together they convinced her that, if she listened to them, she could make a small fortune. They reminded her that she was constantly broke and that Lucky Gordon was still making her life miserable. They told her they had been in touch with certain newspapers in Fleet Street which were prepared to offer her a great deal of money. This was true. Several newspapers were interested in Christine Keeler, especially when her appearance at the committal hearings of the Edgecombe shooting case at Marlborough Street Court reminded editors of the rumour floating around Fleet Street about her: that she was having an affair with Profumo.

There were problems, of course. The first was the English contempt law. No newspapers could publish anything about Christine's relationship with Edgecombe until his trial was over because the details of it were central to the charge. Next, there were the libel laws. If Christine's memoirs named other lovers, unless there was solid proof that what she said was true, they might sue for defamation. On the other hand most of the news at that time was bad, and a light sexy story of an English suburban girl who could arouse such passions – 'I love the girl,' Edgecombe had said, 'I was sick in the stomach over her' – would certainly appeal to the readers of the Sunday sensational press.

Nina Gadd knew a reporter on the *Sunday Pictorial*, so on 22 January, with Mandy along to steady her resolve, Christine walked into the newspaper office carrying Profumo's farewell letter in her handbag. The newspaper's executives heard her out, looked at the letter, photographed it and offered her £1,000 (about £10,000 at today's values) for the right to publish it. Christine said she would think it over. She left the offices of the *Sunday Pictorial* and went straight to those of the *News of the World*, off Fleet Street. There she saw the paper's crime reporter, Peter Earle. Earle was desperate to have the story – for reasons that will emerge – but Christine made the mistake of telling him that his offer would have to be better than

£1,000 because she had been offered that by another newspaper. Earle, who had had long experience of cheque book journalism, told Christine bluntly that she could go to the devil; he was not joining any auction.

So Christine went back to the *Sunday Pictorial*, accepted its offer and was paid £200 in advance. Over the next two days she told her entire life story to two *Sunday Pictorial* reporters. They soon saw that the nub of any newspaper article was her relationship with Profumo and Ivanov. It is easy to imagine how the story emerged. Christine was being paid £1,000 for her memoirs. The second slice, £800, was due only on publication. If the story did not reach the newspaper's expectations, Christine would not get it. She was anxious therefore to please the *Sunday Pictorial* reporters and dredged her memory for items that interested them. The trend of their questions would soon have indicated what items these were.

What started out then as an article about Christine's double life — with Ward's rich friends in high places and her own West Indian friends in low — soon changed tack. Christine knew a Russian diplomat; had she slept with him? Had she been sleeping with him at the same time as she was sleeping with Profumo? Was the hint given in the *Queen* article true — that one left the flat as the other arrived? Gradually the story built up. But it was still only a young girl of loose morals sharing her favours with a British Cabinet Minister and a Soviet diplomat, and one of the leading characters, the diplomat, had already gone back to Moscow. It was not much use naming him as the guilty man. And there remained great legal doubt whether it would be safe to name Profumo, either. The paper could make out a case that the triangle posed a security threat, that Profumo had left himself open to blackmail. But readers are not gripped by stories full of 'ifs'.

Then Christine gave the story that extra lift that it needed. Remembering the interest shown by the solicitor Michael Eddowes and by John Lewis when she had said that she had been asked to find out from Profumo when West Germany would get atomic warheads, Christine now told the *Sunday Pictorial* this ludicrous tale. Christine's first version — the one told to Eddowes — was that Ivanov had asked her to get this information. Her second version was that it had been Ward, but that he was joking. Now, perhaps realising that since Ivanov was gone he was of lesser interest to the paper, Christine insisted that it was Ward who had put the idea to her — and that he had been serious. In the paper's most unChristine-like words: 'I did find it worrying when someone asked me to try to get from Profumo the answer to a certain question. That question was: "When, if ever, are the Americans going to give nuclear weapons to Germany?" I am not prepared to say in public who asked me to find out the answer to that question. I am prepared to give it to the security officials. In fact I believe now that I have a duty to do so.' Christine clearly tailored this story to suit her audience. (For what it is worth, twenty years later she had reverted to its being a Ward joke and claimed that when she had first told it to the *Sunday Pictorial* reporters, they had also understood it to be his idea of a joke.)

The story was now a very attractive one indeed. As Lord Denning later said, 'The newspaper reporters saw how greatly the "spy interest" heightened the story.' They set about writing the new version, and on 8 February Christine signed every page as being true and correct. But in between there had been prolonged and vigorous efforts to persuade her not to do so. These came from two main sources – Ward and Astor. Ward heard about Christine's plans from Peter Earle, the *News of the World* crime reporter who had refused to bid for the story against the *Sunday Pictorial*. Deprived of the main event, Earle was looking for a way to recoup for his paper by finding a subsidiary story that would take some of the sheen from the *Sunday Pictorial* scoop. Perhaps Ward would provide it.

Ward immediately telephoned Astor and on 28 January they met in the chambers of Ward's counsel, William Rees-Davies, MP. For Astor, the meeting was very short. Rees-Davies stood on legal protocol. He had not received a brief from Astor's solicitor to act for him. Astor went off to instruct his solicitor while Ward settled down to tell Rees-Davies the problem: Christine Keeler had sold her memoirs to the *Sunday Pictorial*; Ward did not know what they contained but he was worried that his name, and Astor's and Profumo's might be mentioned. Further, he suspected that Christine might try to give her memoirs a boost in advance by using the three names in evidence when she was called as a witness in the Edgecombe trial due to start the following week.

The rest of that day became very busy. Rees-Davies saw the possibility of handling the matter on a political-legal level. The *Sunday Pictorial* was operating in a grey area of the law. It could be argued that, by selling her memoirs *before* she gave evidence in the Edgecombe trial, Christine had compromised her integrity as a witness. And the *Sunday Pictorial*, by offering her money, might well be in danger of the accusation that it had interfered with a witness in a criminal trial. This was the legal side and justified Rees-Davies's next move. He went to see the Solicitor-General, Sir Peter Rawlinson, repeated what Ward had told him, and offered his views on the matter. But Rees-Davies knew that Rawlinson would also be interested in the political angle – Profumo's name might be dragged into a criminal trial and splashed over the Sunday sensational press. Rawlinson wasted no time. Within half an hour of seeing Rees-Davies he had located the Attorney-General, Sir John Hobson, who had just finished a hard afternoon's cross-examination at the Vassall Tribunal, and had briefed him on the affair.

Hobson did not like what he heard. The simplest way of stopping the *Sunday Pictorial*, he decided, would be for Profumo to warn the paper that if it published he would sue for libel. Would Profumo be prepared to do that? Rawlinson did not know, so Hobson scribbled a quick note to Profumo asking him to meet him later that evening. The note was no surprise to Profumo, because at 5.30 p.m. Astor had called on him to report the day's events. Profumo moved immediately to put the lid on the whole business before it got out of hand. He thought he knew exactly how to do it.

MI5 had told him about the 'honey-trap' operation against Ivanov. That had gone sour; Ivanov had returned to the Soviet Union and the operation had been abandoned. But Profumo did not know this. He thought it was possible that Ivanov had been 'turned' before he left and that he might now be a 'double', working in the Soviet Union for British Intelligence. If this were the case, any mention of Ivanov in Christine Keeler's newspaper article might endanger him. Therefore it would be logical for MI5 to approach the *Sunday Pictorial* discreetly and ask, on grounds of national security, for it to drop the article. So Profumo asked the Director-General of MI5 to come to see him.

There is some conflict as to whether Hollis himself went to the meeting or whether he sent a deputy in his place. Denning, using an MI5 brief provided for him, says categorically that Profumo met 'the Director-General of the Security Service'. But Profumo, although he does not deny that the meeting took place, has said that he never met Hollis. Whichever senior MI5 officer attended the meeting is not as important as what was said.

The meeting began at 6.45 p.m. and lasted only 15 minutes. Profumo gave the MI5 officer an account of his relationship with Ward, Christine Keeler, and Ivanov which was true — as far as it went. He described the bathing party at Cliveden, visits to Ward's flat in Wimpole Mews, usually when there had been parties, but once or twice when he had found Christine there alone. He said that he had written one or two notes to Christine but insisted that they were harmless. He referred to the Edgecombe shooting and added that he had heard that Christine was a drug addict. He said he had been warned that the *Sunday Pictorial* story included a section in which Christine claimed to have had an affair with him and that it might also mention an affair with Ivanov, 'a Russian spy'.

We can imagine the MI5 officer's reaction as he listened to this. Most of it was not new to him. He knew that Ivanov was a Russian spy. He knew that Profumo, Ivanov and Keeler were all acquainted with each other — because Ward had told his MI5 case officer, Woods, and Woods had reported this to his superiors. He knew that Christine Keeler might have slept with Ivanov; after all, that was what a 'honey-trap' was all about. He suspected that Profumo had slept with Christine because, again, Ward had also told Woods this, although Woods was uncertain whether to believe Ward on this point. The MI5 officer gave Profumo no indication that he was either surprised or worried about what he had heard. He simply said that he would consult his fellow officers on the matter but he doubted that there was anything the security services could do to stop the *Sunday Pictorial* from publishing.

At 11 p.m. Profumo called on the Attorney-General at his house in Hereford Square, London SW7. The two men were friends. They had been in the same school (Harrow), the same college (Brasenose) and the same regiment (Northampton Yeomanry). But Hobson at this stage was inclined to think that the rumours about Profumo and Christine were true, so he began the interview fairly aggressively. He said he could probably help Profumo but he needed a full and frank account. Unless he was going to tell the truth then they might as well end the meeting immediately. Profumo insisted that he *had* been telling the truth and he went over the story once again, adding a little more detail — he said his note to Christine might have begun with the word 'Darling'. But Profumo insisted on the innocence of his friendship with Christine, denied that there had been any adultery or sexual impropriety and explained his use of 'darling' as a habit which was quite meaningless.

Partly to test Profumo's truthfulness, Hobson said that Profumo's only course would be to issue a libel writ the moment any newspaper published anything suggesting that he had had an affair with Christine Keeler. He suggested that Profumo should consult Derek Clogg, a senior partner in Theodore Goddard and Company, a firm of solicitors with wide experience in libel matters, so as to be ready to act the moment anyone published. When Profumo readily agreed to do this, Hobson's doubts about Profumo began to fade.

Over the next few days Profumo put up equally convincing performances before other senior Government officers. The Solicitor-General, Sir Peter Rawlinson, heard Profumo's denial and his vehemently expressed intention to take action for libel — 'even against a friend or colleague' — if anyone published the rumours. He went through the whole story again for the Chief Whip, Martin

Redmayne, who, like the others, was impressed by Profumo's willingness to sue. Yet, in retrospect, all these worldly men must have wanted desperately to believe Profumo because each time he told his story he revealed something a little more incriminating than before.

When he told MI5 about his relationship with Christine Keeler, Profumo said he had written one or two letters but they were harmless. When he came to repeat the story to Hobson, Profumo admitted that the letters began with 'Darling'. By the time he told the story to Hobson and Rawlinson, the letters began with 'Darling' and he had given Christine a gift of a cigarette lighter. And when he went through it all again for Redmayne, Profumo said that he had seen Christine in Ward's flat and that 'most of the young ladies to be found at this flat were not the sort of people one would wish to accompany one to a constituency meeting'. Certainly Profumo had explanations for these admissions − 'Darling' was a habit picked up from his wife's theatrical friends and did not mean anything; the cigarette lighter was not at all valuable, and − again because of his wife's theatrical friends − he was used to relaxing in a galère of people who were not the sort to take to constituency meetings.

That men of the world like Hobson, Rawlinson and Redmayne should so easily be prepared to believe that nothing had occurred between Profumo and Christine seems, at this remove, incredible. (Redmayne seems to have harboured the deepest doubts. He said to Profumo, 'Well, look Jack, nobody would believe that you didn't sleep with her.' To which Profumo replied, 'Yes, I know they wouldn't believe it, but it happens to be true.') The only explanation is that these three senior Government officers did not fully trust Profumo's denials, but because of the convention that no Tory gentleman would lie to a colleague and because of their ardent wish to save their Government from yet another scandal, all three willed themselves to accept Profumo's account and to act accordingly.


At this stage − the last days of January and early February, the interests of the Government, Profumo, Ward and Astor all coincided. But the most active initiative to stop Christine from publishing her story was mounted by Ward. Ward's counsel, Rees-Davies, and Profumo's solicitor, Derek Clogg, decided that there were two possible ways of stopping the articles. One was to issue a writ against Christine for slander − she had told her story to the newspaper reporters − and then to warn the *Sunday Pictorial* that if it printed the article before the slander action it risked being in contempt of court. But judges are reluctant to enforce this sort of 'gagging writ' and if the *Sunday Pictorial* called their bluff and went ahead, then the damage would have been done anyway. A better tactic, they decided, would be to approach Christine and try to persuade her to withdraw the article. There was some delay while Christine found a solicitor of her own through whom they could negotiate and who could protect her interests, but at 4.30 p.m. on 4 February in the offices of Christine's solicitor, Gerald Black, the discussions began.

It is important that the nature of such negotiations be clearly defined. Christine had entered into a contract with the *Sunday Pictorial* to publish her story. The newspaper was to pay her a total of £1,000. Legal advisers acting for Ward and Profumo wanted to persuade her not to go ahead with this deal. There would be nothing wrong in English law for Christine to say, 'Very well. But by breaking my contract with the *Sunday Pictorial* I will be losing £1,000. So you must compensate me for that loss.' But if the compensation sought was clearly much more than Christine's *actual* loss – plus, say, reasonable expenses – then the parties would enter a dangerous area. The demand for a large sum over and above compensation could be called blackmail.

Well aware of this, Ward's counsel, Rees-Davies, was not surprised when he heard Christine's solicitor say to him on the telephone, 'She says she would like to have five.' That accorded with his own calculations which he had worked out like this: Christine had already received £200 from the *Sunday Pictorial*. If she withdrew from her arrangement with the newspaper she would have to repay this. She needed accommodation during the Edgecombe trial, say another £100. And so that she would not be pestered – or tempted – by other newspapers after the trial, she would need to get away from London for a fortnight. This would cost another £200, making £500 in all. So Rees-Davies replied that he was certain that this would be acceptable. He paid out £50 in advance and the next day handed over the balance, £450, to Christine's solicitor.

It then dawned on both men that there had been a monumental misunderstanding. When Christine's solicitor had said, 'She says she would like to have five', he had meant £5,000, not £500. So he now told Rees-Davies that he could not accept the £450. He went back and told Christine what had happened. She was furious. She felt that she had been tricked. She stormed out of his office and he never saw her again.

But the same offer to settle the matter had been made to Profumo's solicitors as well, and they heard and understood the figure — £5,000. They regarded it as so outrageously high that it could not possibly be regarded as legitimate compensation and within hours they had taken an opinion of a Queen's Counsel, Mark Littman. He, too, considered that there might be grounds for a criminal prosecution and he, Profumo, and Profumo's solicitors, all went immediately to see the Attorney-General, Sir John Hobson. He suggested that the details be placed before the Director of Public Prosecutions. This was done the following morning, but he advised against a prosecution, arguing that its success would depend on proving Christine's *intention* to extort money and that this might be difficult to do.

He was probably right. Christine's own version to Lord Denning was that someone else at the many legal conferences that were going on at this time had mentioned £3,000 as possible compensation and all she had done was to try to increase it to £5,000. She admitted to Denning that she had turned down the original offer of £3,000 and had held out for £5,000 because she wanted to move her parents into a house. She managed to convince Denning that this was not blackmail. If she had wished to blackmail anyone, she told him, she would have asked a much higher price. Lord Denning agreed. He decided that Christine only desired a fair recompense and had no intention to extort. But whether this was really fair recompense remains debatable.

In the end it proved surprisingly easy to stop Christine's article in the *Sunday Pictorial*. Ward telephoned an assistant editor on the newspaper and later wrote to him saying that certain major facts in Christine's story were wrong and that he, Profumo, Astor and possibly others would take legal action if the article were published. The newspaper began to back away. Christine had dithered about signing the proof pages and although she had eventually done so, all this did was make it impossible for *her* to sue the paper for libel. It did not rule out writs from other people. The whole story was becoming too much bother. Ward clinched matters by offering an article to replace Christine's. When the Edgecombe trial was over, the *Sunday Pictorial* could publish a description by Ward of 'the real Christine Keeler'. The newspaper took the easy way out. There were dangers in publishing Christine's story; none in publishing Ward's. Christine's contract was torn up but she was allowed to keep the £200 advance. Profumo's letter to her − Christine's proof that she had been telling the truth about her relationship with Profumo − was returned to his solicitor. The *Sunday Pictorial* had missed the scoop of the decade.

Profumo's reprieve was only temporary. Christine Keeler's amazing article had been stopped — largely due, it must be said, to Stephen Ward. But now so many people knew the thrust of Christine's story — that she had had an affair with Profumo — that the fact the *Sunday Pictorial* had not published hardly seemed to matter. Firstly, the police now knew, because Christine had told them. On Saturday, 26 January, Detective Sergeant John Burrows, who was soon to figure prominently in the affair, made a routine call on Christine and Mandy to warn them that they would be required as prosecution witnesses at the Edgecombe trial at the Old Bailey.

From the police point of view he could not have arrived at a more opportune moment. Christine was smarting at Ward's efforts to stop her collecting £1,000 from the *Sunday Pictorial*. Her friends had convinced her that Ward had dumped her because she had become an embarrassment to him and that now it was each one for himself. Mandy had a different grudge. Ward had persuaded Audrey Rachman to allow him to rent Rachman's old flat in Bryanston Mews, the one in which Rachman had kept Mandy. Mandy, who had furnished the place herself, still regarded it as hers and bitterly resented Ward's action.

Burrows stayed for a cup of tea, and, experienced policeman that he was, he allowed the girls' indignation to run its course, prompting them occasionally with a sympathetic nod, or a leading question. It was Stephen Ward's fault that Lucky Gordon was pestering her, Christine said, because he had taken her to Notting Hill to buy pot. Ward was a very wicked influence on young girls, Mandy said, because he picked them up and then dropped them. He had thrown her out of his place after the shooting and now he had taken her flat.

Burrows turned to Christine again. By now Christine understood what Burrows was interested in hearing. She filled in details of how Dr Ward enjoyed using whips and collecting high heeled shoes. She told him how Ward picked up young girls in coffee bars and restaurants and took them down to Cliveden for sex orgies. She even told him how she had heard that Ward had become thoroughly dissipated and now only had sex with filthy prostitutes.

Christine told Burrows everything that was in her newspaper story and some that was not. Burrows must have wondered what he had stumbled upon, but because he was a good detective and accustomed to acting by the rule book, he simply went back to the station, wrote his report and gave it to his superior officer. Since this report was the origin of police interest in Ward it is instructive to reproduce its main paragraph and then to see what happened to it.

> She [Christine] said that Dr Ward was a procurer of women for gentlemen in high places and was sexually perverted; that he had a country cottage at Cliveden to which some of these women were taken to meet important men − the cottage was on the estate of Lord Astor; that he had introduced her to Mr John Profumo and that she had had an association with him; that Mr Profumo had written her a number of letters on War Office notepaper and that she was still in possession of one of these letters which was being considered for publication in the *Sunday Pictorial* to whom she had sold her life story for £1,000. She also said that on one occasion when she was going to meet Mr Profumo, Ward had asked her to discover for him the date on which certain atomic secrets were to be handed to West Germany by the Americans and that this was at the time of the Cuba crisis. She also said that she had been introduced by Ward to the Naval Attaché of the Soviet Embassy and had met him on a number of occasions.

Although some of the phraseology is clearly that of Burrows − one cannot imagine Christine using the expression 'procurer of women for gentlemen in high places' − the accusations had definitely come from Christine, with some help from Mandy. So it is important to note that Burrows's superior officer dismissed the first part of the report out of hand. He rightly concluded that the sexual behaviour of Ward, Profumo and Christine was a private matter of no concern to the police; it was 'outside the field of crime'. The references to certain atomic secrets and the Soviet naval attaché [sic] might, however, interest the Special Branch, the executive arm of MI5, and Burrows's report was duly sent there.

At first Special Branch was keen to follow up, and arrangements were made for three officers to interview Christine on Friday, 1 February. The officers were to be Burrows (since he knew her); a Special Branch inspector, and a Sergeant from the Drug Squad (because Christine had complained that Ward was trying to have her 'put away' as a drug addict). But at the last minute the Commander of Special Branch cancelled the meeting. He later explained that his reason for doing this was that he thought Christine would tell the Press and that this would cause a lot of speculation.

There is a much more convincing explanation. Special Branch liaises closely with MI5. In a matter as delicate as this appeared to be Special Branch would not have dreamed of opening an investigation without first checking with MI5, otherwise it might well accidentally sabotage some secret MI5 operation. So on the morning before the interview, the Commander of Special Branch checked with MI5 and was asked to desist. It was left to the CID to decide whether it wanted to see Christine again on any criminal matter arising out of her interview with Burrows, with the suggestion that if anything came to light of interest to Special Branch then the CID officers could pass it on.

The significance of all this can be swiftly stated: Christine's interview with Burrows contains one of the principal accusations eventually made against Ward at his trial – that he was a procurer of women. Yet not only did Marylebone CID when it first heard the allegation decide it was not worth investigating, but when given a second opportunity to do so, it still took no action. For the Chief Superintendent of the CID, asked on 4 February whether he intended to have Christine Keeler interviewed again, said he did not. In his report Denning puts this down to several failures of co-ordination. The real explanation is: at the time the police considered Christine's allegation to be so absurd that they decided any further investigation would be a waste of time.

MI5, too, wanted to drop the whole matter. Throughout the last days of January MI5 was being bombarded with reports, official and otherwise, about Profumo and Christine Keeler. There were police reports passed to them via Special Branch. One of these was Christine's interview with Burrows. Another was an extract from a complaint Ward had made to Marylebone police about the theft of some photographs of Profumo and Christine from Ward's flat. In the course of the complaint, probably to impress on the police the importance of the photographs, Ward said that if the association between Christine and Profumo became public it would 'bring down the Government'. And Ward, probably because he could not resist the chance, said that he was a close friend of a Soviet diplomat and that MI5 knew about it because Ward had told his MI5 case officer.

There were reports to MI5 from its informants in Fleet Street. One journalist telephoned his MI5 case officer to say that there was a story around Fleet Street that Profumo had been having an affair with a call girl. The case officer asked for more details and the following day the journalist telephoned to say that he had learnt that the *Sunday Pictorial* had two letters from Profumo and would soon be publishing the call girl's memoirs. Reports from other informants at about the same time stressed Christine Keeler's friendship with Ivanov. Ward's case officer, Woods, was working on a final report on the Ivanov 'honey-trap' operation, and it seemed an appropriate moment for a conference to discuss what should be done next.

Accordingly, MI5's Director-General, Roger Hollis, called his deputy, Graham Mitchell, and a group of about eight senior officers to a meeting on Friday morning, 1 February. Hollis said that the main question now was whether the service should continue to be involved or whether it should withdraw. His view was that it was safer to withdraw. If the service were to be seen as willing to probe into a Minister's private life this would leave it open to criticism. There was no reason to believe that Profumo had ever told Keeler anything secret that she could have passed to Ivanov. Anyway since Ivanov had left the country, even if there had been a risk of this happening, it had now passed. As far as Ward was concerned, Profumo had been warned of a possible leakage of information to Ivanov via Ward. Further, Ward's case officer, Woods, had given his view that Ward would not be disloyal to his country. In short, MI5 was in the clear so long as it now did nothing. The meeting agreed and Hollis immediately issued this instruction to his officers: 'Until further notice, no approach should be made to anyone in the Ward galère, or to any other outside contact in respect of it. If we are approached, we listen only.' Then, after lunch, Hollis left early for the week-end.

Two hours later there was a telephone call for him from the Prime Minister's office, at that time temporarily accommodated in Admiralty House. Hollis's deputy, Mitchell, took it. The Prime Minister's Principal Private Secretary, Sir Timothy Bligh, would like to see him immediately. Could he come round? There now occurred a scene which, if written into a spy thriller, would evoke amused disbelief. Mitchell took the deputy director's car from the service pool and drove off towards Admiralty House. Behind him, discreetly following, were two 'watchers' from Mitchell's own service. They were under orders to keep Mitchell under surveillance 24 hours a day — because there was circumstantial evidence that Mitchell was a KGB penetration agent! Nothing was ever proved against him and later suspicion shifted to Hollis himself. (Currently suspicion has reverted to Mitchell.) But the internal investigation into Mitchell meant that, on this occasion, the Prime Minister's office was about to discuss a

security matter with the deputy director of its Security Service who
was under surveillance as a suspected Soviet spy!

For what Sir Timothy Bligh had to say to Mitchell was this. Earlier
that afternoon the Prime Minister's private secretary, John Wyndham,
had met a friend, Mark Chapman Walker, general manager of the
*News of the World* and a former director of research at the
Conservative Central Office, at Chapman Walker's request. Chapman
Walker had revealed what he had learned of the Profumo affair from
the *News of the World* crime reporter, Peter Earle. This was that
Keeler had slept with Profumo and Ivanov and that Ward was
somehow involved, although MI5 had warned him about his
association with the Russian. Wyndham had passed this information
to Bligh and now Bligh told Mitchell.

Like so much in this affair, the story had passed through so many
people that it had become somewhat garbled, so what Mitchell
actually heard was: 'Mr Profumo had compromised himself with a
girl who was involved with a negro in a case of attempted murder. Mr
Profumo is alleged to have met this girl, Kolania [*sic*] through Lord
Astor at Cliveden where they chased her naked around the bathing
pool. It is also alleged that Kolania got into this company through the
agency of a Mr Ward who was a psychopathetic specialist [*sic*] of
Wimpole Street. Mr Profumo visiting Kolania in Mr Ward's house
passed in the passage the Russian naval attaché [*sic*] on his way out
from Kolania . . .'

Mitchell said that MI5 was well aware of the rumours and that
recently Profumo himself had told the Director-General a story that
was obviously the same one, despite some differences in names and
details. Mitchell knew of Hollis's suspicions that the story might be
true, so he readily agreed with Bligh's suggestion that the first step
was to tell Profumo what had been said and to ask him point blank if
there was any truth in it. In accordance with Hollis's instruction that
MI5 should keep out of the affair, Mitchell said that it would not be
part of MI5's duties to ask this question of Profumo.

Mitchell thought that after his meeting with Bligh, MI5 was shot of
the whole business but he was premature in this conclusion. On
Sunday, 3 February, the *News of the World* published a picture of
Christine Keeler, saying that she was to be a witness in the
forthcoming Edgecombe shooting case. The newspaper had chosen
the picture with care; Lord Denning said of it: 'Most people seeing
this photograph would readily infer the avocation of Christine
Keeler.' One of those who saw it was Ward's case officer, Woods.
Woods, of course knew of Profumo's real relationship with Christine
and it seems to have dawned on him for the first time that a scandal

might be brewing. So when he arrived at his office on Monday morning he wrote a short memo to his Director-General, Hollis.

If a scandal results from Mr Profumo's association with Christine Keeler, there is likely to be a considerable political rumpus in the present climate produced by the Radcliffe Tribunal [which examined the Vassall case]. If in any subsequent enquiries *we were found to have been in possession of this information about Profumo* and to have taken no action on it, we would, I am sure, be subject to much criticism for failing to bring it to light. I suggest that this information be passed to the Prime Minister and you might like also to consider whether or not, before doing so, we should interview Miss Keeler. [Emphasis added.]

Hollis and Mitchell discussed Woods's memo. They realised that Woods was right to say that MI5 would be criticised for not bringing up the matter earlier. But one sure way of provoking this criticism would be to bring it up *now*, because one of the first questions the Prime Minister would be certain to ask would be: how long have you known about this? At the moment the Prime Minister's private secretary believed that MI5 had learnt about Profumo's affair only recently – when Profumo had seen Hollis. But if MI5 was forced to admit that it had known for 18 months, then Macmillan might be very angry. As well, some critics of the service might view the whole Ivanov entrapment as a disaster, arguing that it had led directly to Profumo's current situation.

With that instinct for self-preservation that characterises most secret services, Hollis and Mitchell decided that MI5's best course was to declare that the affair was a political matter, and that it was now in the hands of politicians, and that it was not the concern of the security services. Hollis's reply to Woods was: 'The allegations there referred to are known to Admiralty House. No inquiries on this subject should be made by us.' As far as MI5 was concerned, the Profumo case, like that of Ivanov, was now most definitely closed.

# 24 | *The Scandal Begins to Break*

With MI5 out of the picture – but, as it turned out, only temporarily – the scandal now moved towards its dénouement. Three separate strands were about to join: the legal, the political and the journalistic. On 4 February the Prime Minister, Harold Macmillan, returned from his visit to Italy. The very next day, Redmayne, the Chief Whip, went to see him and told him of the rumours about Profumo and about Profumo's denials. Macmillan took the news calmly, mainly because it did not come as a total surprise to him. The story about Profumo and Keeler had been around Westminster for months and it is inconceivable that the Prime Minister had not heard them. The MP, Shepherd, had written to him in November mentioning scandals that were brewing. Shepherd had also met Redmayne and had specifically mentioned Profumo. It seems highly unlikely that Redmayne had failed to tell Macmillan this.

But now the substance of Redmayne's report was more than just further confirmation of Profumo's affair. It was the warning that its revelation was likely to produce another political scandal and to inquire what Macmillan was going to do about it. The Prime Minister was in a fix. His instinct told him to leave Profumo alone. The Vassall Tribunal, then in its second week, had been steadily knocking down all the rumours which had been published about Vassall's relations with Ministers, including the one that the First Lord of the Admiralty, Lord Carrington, had been warned 18 months earlier that there was a spy in the Admiralty.

On the other hand, the Government and Fleet Street had never been farther apart. That very day two journalists, Brendan Mulholland and Reginald Foster, respectively of the *Daily Mail* and the *Daily Sketch*, had been sent to jail, Foster for three months, Mulholland for six, for refusing to tell the Vassall Tribunal the sources for stories they had written about Vassall and Galbraith. Would Fleet Street seek revenge by pursuing Macmillan if he did nothing about Profumo? On the other hand this was no time to undermine another Minister's career. Profumo had denied the allegations. He had said he would sue if they were published. At this stage, Macmillan decided he would do and say nothing. When and if the rumours took a tangible form, then they would be challenged and discredited.

This did not happen until the beginning of March. The last weeks of February saw practically every newspaper in Fleet Street desperately seeking confirmation of the story sufficiently trustworthy to enable them to publish. In the end they were scooped. Andrew Roth, an American journalist who had settled in Britain, ran a very successful weekly newsletter called *Westminster Confidential*. This specialised in political gossip and inside information and Roth was skilful at digging out scandal. Sold mainly to MPs, journalists and embassies, it was available only on subscription.

In the first week of March Roth was working on a story about foreign exchange rates. At the last minute this collapsed. His production method, in those days before personal computers or modern photocopying machines were in use, involved typing the story direct on to a stencil from which his whole print run would then be produced. With time short, Roth had to find a replacement story which he knew sufficiently well to type on to the stencil without alterations, because they were difficult to make. Only one filled the requirements – the Profumo rumour. Roth says that he had first heard it from the Tass correspondent, who had no doubt heard it from Ivanov. Roth had discounted the story as malicious gossip, but a few days later he had heard a much more detailed version from Henry Kerby, a right-wing Tory MP, who had once been a member of the Secret Intelligence Service. Kerby had probably heard it from his Intelligence Service contacts. This version rang true and now, desperately racing against his deadline, Roth typed the story for his newsletter. He says that the pressure and the inability to correct or change anything explains the rather dramatic style.

' "That is certain to bring down the Government," a Tory MP wailed – "and what will my wife say?" This combination of tragedy and tragi-comedy came from the efforts of this MP to check with a newspaperman on the story which has run like wildfire through Parliament.' The story went on to spell out the rumours, mentioned the Edgecombe case, and Christine's efforts to sell her story to the *Sunday Pictorial* and the *News of the World*. Then it continued: 'One of the choicest bits in the story was a letter, apparently signed "Jack", on the stationery of the Secretary for W-r. The allegation by this girl was not only was this Minister, who has a famous actress as his wife, her client, but also the Soviet military attaché, apparently a Colonel Ivanov. The famous actress wife, of course, would sue for divorce, the scandal ran. Who was using the girl to "milk" whom of information – the W-r Secretary, or the Soviet military attaché – ran in the minds of those primarily interested in security. It was probably knowledge about this story . . . which led the Chief Whip, Brigadier Redmayne, to tell a correspondent with resignation: "We have all the luck." '

Here, at last, was the story out in the open. Despite its obvious errors and exaggerations, the kernel of the account was true. Fleet Street was certain that Profumo would sue and that Roth would be taken to the legal cleaners, but nothing happened. Profumo sought the advice of his solicitor and also of the Attorney-General. Both told him to do nothing. The newsletter had too small a circulation to justify issuing a libel writ. To do so would only draw further attention to the rumours. But Roth's article would give Fleet Street a push towards publication. When a major newspaper carried the allegations that would be the moment to strike.

On the political front the mud was being stirred by George Wigg, Profumo's one-time friend, now an enemy. He was being primed by John Lewis, one-time friend of Ward and now his enemy. The two made a powerful combination. They had started working together on 2 January, when Lewis called on Wigg and told him all he had managed to squeeze out of Christine Keeler. Wigg was intrigued but had reservations. He did not see how he could make it a political issue.

But five days later Lewis came back to him with a new item he had learnt from Christine, suitably twisted to serve Lewis's ends. Ward had asked Christine to find out from Profumo when Germany would get nuclear warheads from the United States. Wigg saw the opportunity this offered him. What had been a private affair could be turned into a matter of public interest because national security was involved. Wigg opened a file on Profumo, Christine Keeler, Ward and Ivanov. He asked Lewis to find out all he could and to report to him regularly. In the meantime he raised the matter with some of his parliamentary colleagues to enlist their support.

To his chagrin, they wanted nothing to do with it. One of them was Richard Crossman. He said later that Wigg had told him of his plans on the way to a party which Barbara Castle had arranged for Harold Wilson. 'When we arrived at the party George outlined the story to us and we emphatically and unanimously repudiated it. We all felt that even if it was true and Profumo was having an affair with a call girl and that some Russian diplomat had been mixed up in it, the Labour Party simply should not touch it. I remember that we all advised Harold very strongly against it and in a way rather squashed George.

'Why were we so sensitive about the whole thing? The Vassall affair was still hanging over us, when we'd had the experience of the effect on the Labour front bench of George Brown's trying to exploit the charge that Thomas Galbraith had had homosexual relations with George Vassall. We had seen how unfortunate this was. As we left the party at the end of the evening, George deliberately stayed behind to brief Harold even more fully on what he kept repeating was the security aspect of the affair.'

Despite the fact that his colleagues had squashed Wigg he was determined not to give up, 'not to allow the honour of the army to go undefended'. When he was alone with Wilson he suggested that one way of making the matter public would be to use the forthcoming debate on the army to question Profumo in the Commons. Wilson was as keen as any of his colleagues to bring down Macmillan's Government but he was not certain that this was the best way to do it. In the end he opted for a political compromise – he advised Wigg against questioning Profumo but said that this was advice only, and that Wigg should feel free to act as he thought best.

Wigg was in a quandary. If he confronted Profumo and Profumo outsmarted him again, then Wigg's own position would be endangered. His colleagues would say that they had warned him. His leader could abandon him because he had made it clear he did not want to be too closely associated with whatever steps Wigg took. Wigg pondered for 24 hours and then consulted his friend, the lawyer Arnold Goodman. He, too, advised against direct confrontation. After long discussion with Goodman and a review of his file on the matter, Wigg decided that what he needed was an incident to bring the rumours to public attention. He could then step in and use Parliamentary privilege to name all the parties concerned, including Profumo. Wigg curbed his impatience and settled down to wait.

# 25 | *The Boil is Lanced*

Nine days before the trial of Johnny Edgecombe on the charges arising from the shooting at Wimpole Mews, Ward and Profumo met in the Dorchester Hotel. Ward said that he arranged the meeting. Profumo said that it was his idea. Its purpose was plain – to discuss how to keep Christine quiet. Ward said that unless Christine could be persuaded not to publish her memoirs, then sooner or later there would be a headline reading 'Christine Keeler's Affair with Minister'. Profumo tapped his forehead with his finger and said, 'Christine Keeler; who's she?' This annoyed Ward because he felt he was doing his best to help Profumo, so he replied with some anger, 'Go and ask MI5 who she is. They can tell you. They can tell you when you visited my flat and saw her there.'

Both men then calmed down and agreed that there was little that they could do. A lot would depend on what Christine said when she was in the witness box at the Edgecombe trial. If, for example, she were to say, 'Johnny Edgecombe shot at me because he was jealous that I was having an affair with Jack Profumo', then the newspapers would be able to print this with no fear of libel because it would be a fair and accurate report.

But when the trial opened on 14 March it did so with a sensation. Christine Keeler had disappeared. At first, for obvious reasons, the rumours – and there was absolutely no substance in them – said that Profumo had had a hand in spiriting her away. The *Daily Express* carried on its front page a story about Christine's failure to turn up at the trial with a large picture of her headlined 'Vanished'. This was separated by only one column from an even larger story headlined 'War Minister Shock'. Written by the paper's political correspondent, Ian Aitken, it said that Profumo had offered the Prime Minister his resignation on the grounds of the coming reorganisation of the defence departments. The juxtaposition of two stories to carry the implication that they are somehow linked is an old newspaper trick, although, on this occasion, the *Daily Express* swore that it was accidental – and Lord Denning believed it! Intentional or not, the effect was the same: it reinforced the rumours that Profumo was responsible for Christine's failure to turn up at the Old Bailey. The Attorney-General was sufficiently concerned to interview Profumo and ask him point blank whether he had spirited Christine away. Profumo denied that he had, and the Attorney-General believed him.

Over the years the details of Christine's disappearance have emerged in some detail. But even today it is not 100 per cent clear who was behind it. There are, however, some clues. As far back as early February, Ward had had discussions about Christine's getting out of London for a while. These had been mainly with Paul Mann, Christine's racing driver/journalist friend. Ward's idea was that Christine be persuaded to bring forward her plans to visit the United States. Since Ward and Christine were not on speaking terms, Mann was to act as go-between for the arrangements. What inducement was to be offered to Christine was not mentioned, but since Ward knew Christine he realised that she would not agree to leave with nothing. All the indications are that when Ward was negotiating through his lawyers for Christine to withdraw her article from the *Sunday Pictorial*, one of the conditions for the payment of the £500 (or £5,000, depending on whether you were Ward's lawyer or Christine's) was that Christine would disappear for a time.

The important point, as far as the law is concerned, is: was Christine to vanish before or after the trial. If it was before, then all the parties involved would be guilty of a conspiracy to defeat the ends of justice in that they had removed a material witness from a criminal trial. Mann is vague on the matter – understandably because he could be considered one of the conspirators if such charges were brought. He said that he had suggested to Ward's counsel, Rees-Davies, that he would be prepared to help Christine go away. 'I said I would be only too willing to take her away after the trial and to keep the Press away from her. I remember saying too that I certainly could not do it all on my own funds . . . ' But when Denning asked Mann: 'They wanted her to disappear *after* the trial?' Mann replied: 'No, this was purely a suggestion that she should disappear; nobody said, "Yes, we want her to go *after* the trial." '

The lawyers involved were certainly very edgy themselves, in case they were dragged into the matter. Ward's counsel said, 'The only thing I was afraid of was that Christine Keeler . . . would be spirited out of the country.' Worried about this because of things Ward had said to him, he advised Ward: 'On no account must any of us be party to that thing.' Yet, on the night of Friday, 8 March, Christine, Paul Mann and their friend, Kim Proctor, left London by car for the

Continent. They drove across France, crossed the border into Spain and vanished.

Without the principal Crown witness, the Edgecombe case was over in only two days. Since Christine's evidence on the knife fight in the All-Nighters' club was central to the charge that Edgecombe had wounded Lucky Gordon, and Christine was not there to give it, Edgecombe had to be acquitted. On the Wimpole Mews shooting charge, he was acquitted of shooting with intent to do grievous bodily harm but convicted of possessing a firearm with intent to endanger life. He was sentenced to seven years' imprisonment.


All this time Mandy Rice-Davies had been watching Christine's act with some envy. Christine had become a media star. Her photographs, despite Denning's statement that they left no doubt about her 'avocation', were glamorous and exciting. Christine was in negotiations with newspapers for her life story; she was busy with her lawyer discussing contracts; she was thinking about buying her mother a house; she was planning a modelling career in the United States. Mandy felt that she was rapidly being out-distanced by her friend. On Saturday, 16 March she made her bid to join the cast of this drama. That day's issue of the *Daily Sketch* carried Mandy's ghosted story of her life with Christine and Stephen Ward.

Mandy knew better than Christine what would sell papers and she had fed her ghost writer so much hot material that the newspaper's libel lawyers wore out the points of their blue pencils bowdlerising the story. It was safe to mention Ivanov; he had gone home to Moscow and was unlikely to return to sue. 'Of course Christine and I thought Eugene may have been a spy; but we would never have told him anything even if we *had* any information.' But Profumo had threatened to sue, so he became 'one well-known man' who bought Christine 'a huge bottle of perfume, swathed in wrappers, from Fortnum and Mason's'. It was all sensational 'top-drawer life among the Peers and the VIPs' and all quickly forgettable. But for the first time in a national newspaper Ivanov had been introduced as one of the players in the Christine Keeler/John Profumo saga.

The top people's paper, *The Times*, like Mandy, was also feeling rather left out. It, too, had heard all the rumours and was torn between dismissing the whole thing as sordid, suitable only for the sensational press, and its desire to live up to its reputation as a newspaper of record. It compromised by approaching the subject obliquely. Earlier the paper had carried a fiery editorial about the jailing of the two journalists Foster and Mulholland for refusing to disclose their sources to the Vassall Tribunal, arguing that they were right to defy the law. The paper's readers were appalled at such irresponsibility from an establishment organ and wrote in droves to say so.

At this point the editor, Sir William Haley, struck back. He wrote of the ignorance, complacency and apathy towards dangers threatening a free society which now stood revealed. 'There really are people who believe that the encroachments of authority, the corruption of society, and maladministration can safely be left to the powers-that-be to put right . . . The truth is that in a quiet way very much is going seriously wrong . . . Journalists . . . have in their hands an instrument which, when courageously and responsibly used has so far proved in free societies to be the most effective in informing, in promoting discussion, in exposing error and malpractice, and in preserving liberties . . . '

No one heeded this clarion call, least of all *The Times*, even though Haley had been privately briefed on the affair by *The Times* defence correspondent, Arthur Gwynne Jones (later Lord Chalfont). No editor was prepared to call Profumo's bluff, to take Christine Keeler's word, supported by Profumo's letters to her, against the word of Profumo himself. 'Models' lied; Secretaries of State for War did not. The *Daily Mail* made a half-hearted effort to stir some action by floating the resignation of Profumo again: 'Continuous speculation about possible resignation is always irritating for a government, and naturally embarrassing for the Minister concerned.'

What Fleet Street wanted, of course, was cast-iron evidence of the Profumo–Keeler affair and, preferably cast-iron evidence of orgies, witchcraft, black magic, call-girl rackets, and evidence supporting any of the other worthless rumours circulating at the time. Where could such evidence be found, the sleuths from the Street of Adventure asked themselves, and came up with several possibilities. On 21 March Ward's cottage at Cliveden was ransacked. Trevor Kempson of the *News of the World* later said he had entered the cottage accompanied by a photographer but found nothing of interest except a roll of film which, when developed, turned out to be passport-type shots of Christine Keeler. The day before, someone broke into Lord Astor's house in Upper Grosvenor Street. Was this, too, a journalistic foray? It would appear so because the culprit took nothing except a bundle of uninformative letters.

Fleet Street may have found itself stalled, but on the political front things were moving. On the afternoon of Thursday, 21 March the House of Commons was due to debate the case of the two imprisoned journalists. George Wigg had decided that this would be the moment to reveal all he knew about Profumo and Christine Keeler. But Parliament being the eccentric place that it is, some of Wigg's glory at being the first MP to do so was stolen from him by Ben Parkin, the Labour MP for Paddington North. Parkin took advantage of a tradition that allows MPs to wander quite some way off a subject without interruption. Parkin was speaking to Standing Committee F on the subject of the London sewage system. In the middle of his speech he suddenly made the other committee members sit up by saying, 'Then there is the case of the missing model. We understand that a model can quite easily be obtained for the convenience of a Minister of the Crown.' This seemed somewhat remote from the London sewage system, so the committee Chairman, Sir Samuel Storey did interrupt. 'I do not think that there is anything about a missing model in this schedule.' Parkin was not fazed. 'No, Sir Samuel,' he said, 'but at the beginning of our discussions there was a *model* just outside this room and I admired its gracious *curves*. It was provided by the Ministry of Transport to make it possible for us to understand the complicated proposals for London traffic. I have looked in vain for a similar *model* showing me the Minister's vision of the future when the new type of drainage is installed in London.'

When the Press Association report of Parkin's speech hit the news desks of Fleet Street there was a buzz of excitement, and by the time Parkin left the committee there was a pile of message cards in the lobby asking him to telephone various newspapers, all no doubt hopeful that Parkin would expand on his model speech. But it was another six hours before they got the headline they were seeking.

At 11 p.m. George Wigg rose in the House of Commons to speak on the debate about the two jailed journalists. He began by examining the relationship between the Government and the Press. He said he felt that the Vassall Tribunal had treated the Press as kindly as possible, but that the investigative machinery of the tribunal was the wrong kind of machinery and that the worst of the British system of concealment was that rumours were spread by it. Then, having introduced the key word, 'rumours', Wigg carefully set the scene. 'So far, so good. Here was a set of rumours that gained and gained in strength, consumed men's reputations – might, in fact, have destroyed them – and which here infringed on the security of the State.' Wigg paused, then pressed the bomb release.

But are we quite sure that the same thing is not happening again? There is not an hon. Member in the House, nor a journalist in the Press Gallery, nor, do I believe there is a person in the Public Gallery who, in the last few days, has not heard rumour upon rumour involving a member of the Government front bench. The Press has got as near as it could – it has shown itself willing to wound but afraid to strike. This all comes about because of the Vassall Tribunal. In actual fact these great Press lords, these men who control great instruments of public opinion and of power, do not have the guts to discharge the duty that they are now claiming for themselves. That being the case, I rightly use the Privilege of the House of Commons – *that is what it is given to me for* – to ask the Home Secretary, who is the senior member of the Government on the Treasury Bench now, to go to the Despatch Box – he knows that the rumour to which I refer relates to Miss Christine Keeler and Miss Davies and a shooting by a West Indian – and, on behalf of the Government categorically deny these rumours.'

Wigg's speech had occupied barely five minues. His place was taken by Richard Crossman, who had abandoned his earlier stance that the Labour Party should stay out of the affair. Crossman said that a Paris newspaper had by that time probably published the whole story anyway. He said he agreed with Wigg. 'It would have been infinitely wiser if we had established a Select Committee ten days ago to go into the rumours.' Another Labour Member, Reginald Paget, intervened: 'What do these rumours amount to?' he said. 'They amount to the fact that a Minister is said to be acquainted with an extremely pretty girl. As far as I am concerned, I should have thought that that was a matter for congratulation rather than inquiry.' This brought a chorus of 'hear-hear' from the Government benches.

Another forty minutes passed before the debate again turned to the affair. This time the speaker was Barbara Castle, who had also changed her mind about Labour having nothing to do with it all. She went further than either of her colleagues had been prepared to go. She said:

It would suit the book of many people, no doubt, to deplore the avidity with which the Press is at this moment pursuing the question of where Miss Christine Keeler has gone – the missing 'call girl', the vanished witness. Is it the pursuit of sensationalism for its own sake, or could it be that there is a public interest at the back of the agitation by the Press. My hon. and learned Friend, the Member for Northampton, said that if it is just a case of a Minister having been found with a pretty girl, good luck to him. But what if there is something else of much greater importance? What if it is a question of the perversion of justice that is at stake? . . . If accusations are made that there are people in high places who do know [Keeler's whereabouts] and who are not informing the police, is it not a matter of public interest?

Reginald Paget got up again. 'Surely the hon. Lady should tell us from whom and where the rumour has come – other than from herself – that people in high places have been in any way responsible for the disappearance of Miss Keeler. I have seen that stated in no newspaper. I have seen it suggested nowhere until this evening.' To this Barbara Castle replied: 'All I can say is that my hon. and learned Friend must be the only person in this House who has not heard it mentioned.'

Paget was quite correct. The rumour may have started elsewhere, but Barbara Castle was disseminating it under parliamentary privilege, a fact that did not escape MPs' notice. Even at this stage Wigg's bomb risked turning out to be a dud. Barbara Castle's unplanned intervention had switched Fleet Street's interest away from the security angle which Wigg had stressed in his own speech, to the disappearance of Christine Keeler, an issue he rightly considered a red herring. And although Wigg, Crossman and Castle had made a strong impression on the debate, not all their Labour colleagues thought that they were doing the right thing. Crossman noted in his diary: 'I think the people on our own side much disliked what we had done.'

But the Government wanted to squash the accusation once and for all and this seemed the moment to do it. The two law officers, the Attorney-General, Hobson, and the Solicitor-General, Rawlinson, conferred with the Chief Whip, Redmayne, on how best to proceed. They decided that the right tactics would be for Profumo to make a personal statement to the House of Commons as soon as possible. The Prime Minister's approval was needed for this so he was telephoned, told what had happened in the House and what form it was proposed the answer should take. He gave his approval.

Speed was now essential. The House would resume at 11 a.m. on Friday and Macmillan wanted Profumo to make his statement before the weekend. It would have to be written that night. Profumo had taken a sleeping pill and did not hear his telephone. Redmayne's assistant had to take a car, drive to Profumo's house and bang on the door. Even then Profumo was slow to wake up. His wife says, 'I remember Jack groping his way round saying, "I must have a clean shirt" and trying to push the cuff links through.' Sleepy-eyed, Profumo reached the Commons just before 3 a.m. His solicitor, Derek Clogg, brought along at the Attorney-General's suggestion, was none too happy at being dragged out in the early hours. But both came suddenly alert when they saw not just the two law officers waiting for them in the Chief Whip's room, but three other Ministers as well – the Leader of the House, Iain Macleod, the Chief Whip, Redmayne, and William Deedes, Minister without Portfolio who advised the Government on its public relations.

There are two versions of this meeting. The official one is that it was not an interrogation of Profumo to discover the truth before proceeding further; because everyone present was already convinced by Profumo's earlier denials. The line-up of Ministers is explained by the need to have the two law officers to draft the statement, the Chief Whip because of his earlier involvement, the Leader of the House because he is especially concerned when a special statement is made, and William Deedes because he had been in the Commons when Wigg, Crossman and Castle made their speeches and could give a first-hand account of the debate. The length of the meeting, nearly three hours, is explained by the fact that they had to wait for Profumo and his solicitor to arrive.

The official version is that the meeting split into two parts. In one room were the Attorney-General, the Solicitor-General and Profumo's solicitor. They did the drafting of the statement. In the other were Macleod, Redmayne, Deedes and Profumo. At about 4 a.m. a draft of the statement was ready and this was brought in and read out by the Solicitor-General. This was approved, then typed, and Profumo read it through and said that he was happy with it. Then at 4.30 a.m. they all went home.

The other version is that the official one is to explain in retrospect how five presumably highly-sophisticated politicians either fell for Profumo's lies or willed themselves into believing his account to be true. Or – and it must be stressed that there is no evidence for this assertion – they suspected that Profumo was lying but, for political and social reasons (Hobson and Deedes had both been at school with Profumo), they wanted to help him do the best possible job of denying Labour's allegations. Either way, Profumo's statement, read to a packed House at 11 a.m. on that Friday, 22 March 1963, is a remarkable one. As Wigg had feared, the five ministers had latched on to the one main point which Profumo could convincingly deny – his knowledge of Christine Keeler's disappearance. In fact every point in the statement is true – as far as it goes – except one. It reads:

I understand that in the debate on the Consolidated Fund Bill last night, under protection of Parliamentary privilege the Honourable gentlemen, the Members for Dudley [Mr Wigg] and for Coventry East [Mr Crossman] and the Honourable Lady, the Member for

Blackburn [Mrs Castle], opposite, spoke of the rumours connecting a Minister with a Miss Keeler and a recent trial at the Central Criminal Court. It was alleged that people in high places might have been responsible for concealing information concerning the disappearance of a witness and the perversion of justice.

I understand that my name has been connected with the rumours about the disappearance of Miss Keeler. I would like to take this opportunity of making a personal statement about these matters. I last saw Miss Keeler in December 1961, and I have not seen her since. I have no idea where she is now. Any suggestion that I was in any way connected with or responsible for her absence from the trial at the Old Bailey is wholly and completely untrue. My wife and I first met Miss Keeler at a house party in July 1961 at Cliveden. Among a number of people there was Dr Stephen Ward, whom we already knew slightly, and a Mr Ivanov, who was an attaché at the Russian Embassy. The only other occasion that my wife or I met Mr Ivanov was for a moment at the official reception for Major Gagarin at the Soviet Embassy. My wife and I had a standing invitation to visit Dr Ward. Between July and December 1961 I met Miss Keeler on about half a dozen occasions when I called to see him and his friends. Miss Keeler and I were on friendly terms. There was no impropriety whatsoever in my acquaintanceship with Miss Keeler. Mr Speaker, I have made this personal statement because of what was said in the House last evening by the three hon. Members, and which, of course, was protected by privilege. I shall not hesitate to issue writs for libel and slander if scandalous allegations are made or repeated outside the House.

With hindsight it is easy to see where the legal minds occupied in drafting the statement realised that their case was weak. The disarming phrase 'my wife and I first met Miss Keeler at a house party' – although strictly true, hardly accurately reflects the actual meeting. Again, 'My wife and I had a standing invitation to visit Dr Ward' suggested that if the Profumos visited Ward it would be as a couple. Yet in the very next sentence, Mrs Profumo has vanished, and Profumo is going alone to Ward's flat where he meets Miss Keeler on about 'half a dozen occasions'. They are on 'friendly terms'. But, and here there had to be a direct lie, otherwise the statement would have totally lacked conviction – 'There was no impropriety whatsoever in my acquaintanceship with Miss Keeler.' Since it was widely known at that time that Fleet Street had seen one of Profumo's letters to Christine Keeler – and had considered publishing it; something a newspaper would not do unless it suggested a close relationship – this denial of any impropriety seems foolhardy at best.

By convention a personal statement to the House of Commons cannot be debated or challenged because the honour, truth and integrity of the Member making the statement is accepted absolutely. Yet what Profumo had to say reeked of omission, inconsistency and unanswered questions. Why did his wife not accompany him on the occasions he saw Christine Keeler at Ward's flat? Exactly how friendly was he with Keeler? For example, did he ever see her alone? Take her out? Give her any gifts? Write her any letters? If the House of Commons had known about the outings, the gifts, the letters and the use of the endearment, 'Darling', it is inconceivable that anyone who heard Profumo's denial of any impropriety in his relationship with Christine Keeler would have believed him for an instant.

But the convention was observed. The establishment backed its beleaguered Member. The Prime Minister gave his support by sitting alongside Profumo on the Government front bench, and when Profumo had finished speaking Macmillan clapped him on the shoulder, a public gesture of warmth and confidence. Yet we have discovered that Macmillan had every reason to believe that Profumo was lying.

One of Macmillan's closest American friends was the ambassador, David Bruce, a great Anglophile, with whom he lunched regularly at Bucks Club. Macmillan had been hearing rumours about Profumo and Keeler since November the previous year. He had begun to suspect that his own advisers were not telling him the truth about the affair, either because they were involved in it themselves, or they were trying to cover up to avoid a scandal. So at one of his lunches with Bruce, the Prime Minister asked the ambassador to make discreet inquiries to see what he could discover.

Bruce went to Thomas Corbally, the American businessman who was a friend of Ward. Bruce knew of this friendship from his nephew, Billy Mellon Hitchock, the cousin of Center Hitchcock, the American who had taken Mandy Rice-Davies to Paris three months earlier. Corbally recalls, 'Ambassador Bruce asked me to find out what was going on and to let him know as quickly as possible. I telephoned Ward from Bruce's office and arranged a lunch – Ward, me, the ambassador's secretary Alfred Wells, and Billy Hitchcock.

'The lunch was held upstairs at Simpson's in Piccadilly in a booth where, we hoped, none of us would be recognised. There Ward told Wells the fully story, including Christine's dealings with the newspapers and the letter from Profumo she had kept which made clear her relationship with him.'

On 29 January, in Wells's office in the American Embassy in Grosvenor Square, Corbally filled in the details while Wells made a note of them. The substance of this note is now in the FBI files in Washington. The FBI got some of Corbally's details wrong – they said, for instance that it was Profumo who had taken Christine Keeler (and Mandy) to Astor's swimming party – but the thrust of their account was correct: Profumo had definitely had an affair with Christine; Ivanov may have done so. And the FBI version added some new information. They insisted that Macmillan had been informed of the scandal the day before by 'a British newspaper' and that an official letter had been sent to this newspaper warning it of the dangers of publishing anything until the trial of Johnny Edgecombe was over.

Wells passed his note to Bruce. Bruce in turn passed the information to Macmillan. (Foolishly, Bruce failed to tell as well his employers, the State Department, and this was later to cause him a lot of trouble.) So Macmillan, with every reason to believe that Profumo was lying over the main point in his statement, must have had some uneasy moments as Profumo read his way through it. But the reaction from the Government benches quickly reassured him – they had got away with it; Labour's attack had been routed. 'The atmosphere in the House was icy,' Crossman wrote in his diary. 'We were extremely isolated . . . We had made ourselves unpopular.' Wigg was furious; Profumo had beaten him again. 'I left with black rage in my heart because I knew what the facts were. I knew the truth . . . I had been trussed up and done again.'

Profumo gloated over his victory. That afternoon he went to Sandown Park races with his wife and the Queen Mother and in the evening he appeared at Quaglino's for a fund-raising dance given by the Hatch End Conservative Party. He received a rousing reception. All this was reflected in the newspapers the following day. Most reported Profumo's statement in full and with sympathy. (But the *Daily Sketch* called Profumo 'lucky' and said that 'the spectacle of a Minister of the Crown having to get up to explain his acquaintance with a 21-year-old girl is, to say the least, unedifying.') When the European press – *Paris Match* in France and *Il Tempo* in Italy – failed to follow Fleet Street's lead and instead said that Profumo's name continued to be linked with Christine Keeler, Profumo sued. *Paris Match* published a retraction and *Il Tempo* paid Profumo's costs and damages of £50 which he gave to an army charity.

Robbed of Profumo as the main target for their stories, the Press turned instead to the other players. Reporters had been scouring Spain for Christine Keeler and they finally found her in Madrid on 25

March. Mann quickly did a deal for her with the *Daily Express*. She was to get £2,000 immediately, of which a quarter would go to Mann. This was for a statement about Profumo, and photographs which showed her as a sex goddess. The statement was short and false: 'What Mr Profumo said is quite correct. I have not been in his company since 1961.' The *Express* then flew her back to London.

The following Sunday, in an interview with the *News of the World*, Christine repeated her line on Profumo. 'Certainly both he and his wife were friends of mine. But it was a friendship no one can criticise.' Ward supported her. Interviewed on television he said, 'I was there when the meetings took place, and there is absolutely nothing of a sinister nature to these occasions.' In this welter of denials, the one point Fleet Street failed to probe was: who was behind Christine's disappearance?

It is possible, knowing how impulsive and irresponsible Christine could be, that she just decided on the spur of the moment to run away from all the fuss and the pressures around her. It is also possible that she was manipulated by one or more of those with an interest in seeing that she was out of the country. As her manager, Mann would expect to see publicity and money in her disappearance. Wigg and Lewis might have wanted to exploit her absence to highlight the security risk of her association with Profumo. Astor or Ward could have been trying a desperate exercise in damage limitation.

Lord Denning went to some lengths to find an answer. He reasoned that whoever wanted Christine out of the way would have had to pay for it. True, the trio did not have much money in Spain and it would appear that all Christine got out of the trip was her £2,000 contract with the *Daily Express*. But that does not rule out a payment to, say, Mann, for organising the disappearance. Denning followed up this line. When he asked about Mann's bank account Mann said he had a couple of safe deposit boxes that were not in his name and were 'entirely secret'. But he strongly denied that they contained any money given to him for organising Keeler's disappearance or, indeed, that he had received any such sums.

Next, Denning checked the bank accounts of Profumo and Lord Astor and could find nothing to indicate that they had made payments to anyone to further Christine Keeler's disappearance. Both denied making any such payments. But what little evidence there is points to a joint effort by Ward and Astor, motivated by a desire to save themselves – and Profumo – from a scandal. As we have seen, Ward first suggested the idea that Christine should go away as early as February. His solicitor warned him of the dangers of being seen to be involved in such a scheme.

But Ward went ahead with negotiations to pay Christine compensation for her loss of the contract with the *Sunday Pictorial*. This appeared legally acceptable, and if there was a secret clause to the arrangement – that, after getting the cash Christine, aided by Mann, would disappear, then who was to know about it? All that went wrong was the sum of money. Ward offered £500; Christine wanted £5,000. But even if the £500 had been acceptable, Ward was in trouble. He did not have £500 to hand. Who 'lent' it to him? Bill Astor. Although the loan was supposed to be for 'legal expenses' it is inconceivable that, with the main characters and their lawyers in almost constant touch over this period, Astor did not know what the money was for.

So Astor becomes the most likely source of further funds when Ward persists with his scheme to get Christine out of London before the trial. Conveniently, Astor had left for a visit to the United States on 27 February and it would not only have been simple for him to have transferred funds from there to Spain, but it would be untraceable in any examination of his British bank accounts. We believe that Astor financed Christine Keeler's disappearance and that Ward arranged it (Ward said at the time that he knew where she was) but that he did so with the impression, justified or not, that not too much fuss would be made officially over her failure to appear in court. As evidence that this was Ward's impression, there is the fact that when the newspapers headlined Christine's vanishing act Ward voluntarily went to the police and told them where she was – hardly the act of a man who knew he would be liable to prosecution himself. When questioned on television on 22 March about Christine, Ward implied that he was in touch with the runaway group, probably with Mann. 'The impression I got this morning was that she was blissfully unaware about all the furore she had caused by her disappearance.'

In the end, all the effort to get Christine out of the way only postponed the reckoning. In the short term, however, it looked as if the scandal was over. As the *Sunday Telegraph*, a staunch supporter of the Conservative Party put it, 'The boil is lanced.'

# 26

# *The Move to Silence Ward*

Just when George Wigg imagined that Profumo had escaped him, he had a stroke of luck. On 25 March, three days after Profumo's statement to the Commons denying any impropriety with Christine Keeler, the BBC's leading current affairs programme, 'Panorama', invited Wigg to appear to discuss the whole issue. Wigg seized the opportunity to stress that he was concerned with the security aspects of the affair, and that none of his doubts had been answered in Profumo's statement. Wigg said that he wanted to learn more about Ivanov. Who was this junior naval officer who drove expensive sports cars, wore Savile Row suits and went frequently to West End nightclubs?

Ward was watching the programme and Wigg's description of Ivanov annoyed him, so he telephoned Wigg at the House of Commons the next day and left a message asking Wigg to return his call. Wigg, who knew who Ward was, took the precaution of getting a friend to listen to the call on a separate earpiece. Ward said Wigg was totally wrong about Ivanov. Ivanov drove an Austin A40 or a Humber Snipe, his suits came from John Barker's, and Ward had seen him at a nightclub only once. Most interesting, Wigg said. Why not meet to discuss the matter? Could Ward come to the House at 6 p.m?

The only account of the meeting, which lasted three hours, is that of Wigg, who was unsympathetic to Ward. Yet even in Wigg's version it is clear that Ward's main aim was to defuse the scandal and clear himself and that to do this he was frank and truthful with Wigg. Ward said that Ivanov had visited his flat only for social purposes, mainly to play bridge and meet girls. This was true but did omit the occasion that Ivanov met Shepherd at Ward's flat when the discussion on the Cuban missile crisis took place. Ward said that he had helped Ivanov get across the Soviet message during the crisis, acting as an intermediary, and that he had put this in a letter to Wilson. Ward pointed out that MI5 would surely have Ivanov under surveillance most of the time and that Profumo could not be considered a security risk because he would never have allowed himself to be put in such a position. Anyway, Ward added, MI5 already knew all about Profumo and Christine Keeler because he, Ward, had told them. Ward said that he was worried about Christine Keeler's determination to sell her story. 'I questioned Ward closely about what exactly Christine Keeler and her new friend, Paul Mann, were offering for sale,' Wigg wrote later. 'Ward was positive that Mann had taken the photograph of Profumo and the girl [from Ward's flat] and he suspected that Mann also held the Profumo letters. Ward said that he was deeply upset by it all, especially by Keeler's efforts to sell her story to the newspapers and by the way she had played off one West Indian lover against the other.'

What Ward had to say must have been music to Wigg's ears. It confirmed all that he knew to be true about Profumo – that he had had an affair with Christine Keeler, that he had written her compromising letters (otherwise why would the newspapers be so intensely interested in Keeler's story) and that he had lied to the House. Wigg went immediately to see his leader, Harold Wilson. He told him of his conversation with Ward, reminded him of Ward's letter and asked what he should now do. First, Wilson went to his files and found and re-read Ward's letter. Then he asked Wigg to write a full report on his meeting with Ward as soon as possible.

Wilson was in Washington when Wigg finished the report the next day so Wigg showed it to the Labour Party's lawyer, Sir Frank Soskice. Wigg had gone beyond Wilson's brief. Using information about Christine Keeler and her friends, including Ward, which had been given to him by Lewis, Wigg had highlighted the underworld aspects of Keeler's life. Soskice was deeply shocked by the company Profumo had been keeping and at a meeting with Wilson on his return from the United States it was decided that only an edited version should be shown to the Conservatives, and then only to Macmillan and some of his senior advisers. (One of the paragraphs which was edited out was Lewis's statement that Ward had asked Keeler to get information from Profumo about nuclear warheads for Germany. Wilson considered the idea preposterous.) Macmillan did not see the report until nearly two weeks later. In the meantime, however, one of his Ministers, the Home Secretary, Henry Brooke, had taken a decision that led directly to Ward's ruin.

A Member of Parliament since 1938, Brooke had represented Hampstead for twelve years. A large man, not easily flustered, he held very conservative political views and since he had become Home Secretary only the previous year he was fresh to the ways of MI5. When he heard, therefore, a rumour that the service had been sending anonymous letters to Mrs Profumo – to what supposed end the rumour did not say – he was upset and annoyed. On 27 March, he summoned the head of MI5, Roger Hollis, to see him and asked the Permanent Under-Secretary at the Home Office, Sir Charles Cunningham, and the Commissioner of the Metropolitan Police, Sir Joseph Simpson, to attend the meeting. All these people are now dead and the only account of what took place is a semi-official one leaked in 1982 by MI5.

According to this account, when Brooke tackled Hollis on the rumour that MI5 had been sending anonymous letters to Mrs Profumo, Hollis vigorously denied it. He said his service had ceased to take any interest in the affair once Ivanov had left Britain. The question of Ward's role then came up, but the MI5 account fails to explain why Ward's name was mentioned at all. Hollis then explained to Brooke the allegations that had been made against Ward. The only one that might have concerned MI5 was Christine Keeler's statement to the police that Ward had asked her to find out from Profumo when Germany would receive nuclear warheads. But, said Hollis, in any court case that might be brought against Ward over this accusation all the witnesses would be completely unreliable.

According to the MI5 account, Brooke then asked the Police Commissioner's view on this. Simpson agreed with Hollis but then gratuitously added that it might be possible to get a conviction against Ward with a charge of living off immoral earnings. But, he said, even this seemed unlikely. The MI5 account says nothing of Brooke's reaction to this but he must have shown his dissatisfaction in some way because the meeting ended with Hollis agreeing to have a second look at the possibility of prosecuting Ward under the Official Secrets Act.

What are we to make of this amazing meeting? Brooke called it with one express purpose – to discover whether MI5 officers had been harassing the Profumos and to put a stop to it if they had. But the meeting quickly moved on to Ward, and the Home Secretary and his three distinguished civil servants began to hunt about for some crime with which to prosecute him. The initiative clearly came from Brooke; the two service heads, Hollis and Simpson, were pessimistic about successfully prosecuting Ward for anything. They went away reluctantly agreeing to see if they could come up with a charge that might stick.

Brooke's motives might become a little clearer if we go back to the rumour about MI5 and the anonymous letters to Mrs Profumo. It is now clear that what Brooke had heard was a garbled version of an actual incident. Soon after Profumo had made his statement to the

House denying any impropriety with Keeler, he received letters threatening him with exposure. Profumo told the police. They intercepted his mail, hoping to identify the blackmailer, and discovered that some of the letters were addressed to Mrs Profumo. (The blackmailer was never caught.)

When Brooke heard the garbled version of this – the one incorrectly involving MI5 – his annoyance must have been due to two considerations. Firstly, it looked as if MI5, on its own initiative, was ignoring the Government view that the scandal had ended with Profumo's statement and was playing some deep game of its own. Secondly, Brooke realised that if the newspapers got hold of any version of the rumour that they could print then the scandal would indeed drag on. This explains why he summoned Hollis. But there can be only one explanation of why, when Hollis satisfactorily killed the rumour, Brooke quickly turned to Ward.

This is that Brooke had somehow learned of Wigg's report to Wilson and that the source of much of the information in the report was Ward. Brooke's fear that the scandal would not be allowed to die, that the boil had not been lanced, was heightened by his knowledge of Wigg's report and his apprehension as to what use Labour would make of it. So when Hollis told Brooke all about Ward it was because Brooke asked him to. And Brooke at that moment made up his mind that the Profumo affair would not end until Ward was somehow made to shut up.

Five days later Brooke's decision was confirmed for him when a statement by solicitor Michael Eddowes landed on Brooke's desk. It was a long and detailed account of Eddowes's investigation of the security aspects of the Profumo affair, complete with Eddowes's own conclusions. A firm believer in the KGB international conspiracy theory, Eddowes set out his reasons for believing that Ward and Rachman had been running an espionage call girl ring in London and New York. Some of the wilder accusations – Rachman was a member of the Italian mafia and involved in the as yet-unreported disappearance the world's first nuclear submarine – must have made Brooke wary of of Eddowes's views, but Eddowes was a solicitor, he had advised Christine Keeler at one stage, and he did seem to know a great deal about Stephen Ward.

Brooke's subsequent actions give some indication of his thinking on the Ward matter. There was always the possibility that if Ward were given a bad fright then this would make him realise that he had been interfering in delicate matters and that his only hope of survival would be to withdraw and shut up. On the other hand, if Ward persisted, then there was still nothing to be lost by prosecuting him.

Conviction on a criminal offence would largely discredit what he had to say and there would be the added benefit of allaying public disquiet. There had been a scandal, but the Government was acting, someone was being prosecuted over it, and it could soon be disposed of and forgotten. Brooke decided to try to find grounds to bring Ward before the courts.

MI5 disappointed him. Hollis reported that same day that any prosecution against Ward under the Official Secrets Act would fail. So Brooke turned instead to the Metropolitan Police and within hours the Commissioner had authorised a full scale investigation into Ward's activities. At first there was some argument over whether the Special Branch or the CID should run the operation. In the end the CID got the job. A team was hastily assembled: Chief Inspector Samuel Herbert and Detective Sergeant John Burrows were to run the investigation and to handle the interviewing; Sergeants Arthur Eustace and Mike Glasse were to be the 'hunters' – they would carry out the surveillance of Ward and try to identify suspects and witnesses. When the team assembled it was briefed by Commander Fred C. Pennington. He let the team know exactly how he felt about the investigation by opening with the amazing remark: 'We've received this tip-off, but there'll be nothing in it.' At least one of the team, Mike Glasse took this as a hint not to try too hard.

But the pressure the Commissioner must have been under soon filtered its way down to the investigators. Glasse and Eustace were ordered to file a progress report every day which they were told would be forwarded to 'relevant interested parties'. At first only one or two copies of these reports were all that were needed. But this soon increased to ten. Glasse remembers, 'I'd not experienced anything like this before and I queried it. I was told that the reports were going to the Prime Minister, the Leader of the Opposition and other prominent people in and out of Parliament. I was told this was because of the many names which were being mentioned during the investigation, some of whom were Members of Parliament, judges and churchmen, and so the Prime Minister had to be kept informed.'

This was not the only unusual aspect of the investigation. Its very nature was a departure from ordinary British police practice. Police normally launch an investigation when a specific crime has been committed with the aim of discovering who committed the crime and of gathering evidence to convict that person. Less frequently they investigate a complaint about a possible specific crime to establish whether such a crime has indeed been committed. What police seldom do is to carry out an investigation of a specific person in order to establish if he has committed any crime at all. The reasons are obvious – such investigations would impose too heavy a workload to make them worthwhile. They would also encourage malicious complaints and lead to justifiable charges against the police force of harassment. Yet the investigation of Ward's social and business activities was just such a 'fishing expedition' – as the wide variety of charges eventually brought against Ward confirms. It was as if someone had said, 'We want to prosecute Stephen Ward for a criminal offence. Go and find one that has a chance of sticking.'

The police team lost no time in getting to work. Each officer was excused all other duties and told to concentrate on the Ward investigation. Herbert and Burrows began with Christine Keeler and three days after the team had been assembled the two senior detectives called on her. At this stage it is clear that the police did not know what they were looking for because we have established that they told Christine that they were carrying out an investigation into a possible case of espionage and warned her that if she did not co-operate she might face charges herself under the Official Secrets Act. They began with nuclear warheads for Germany and made her repeat the suggestion that it was Ward who had told her to ask Profumo about the bomb. The police made it clear that, unlike her, they did not consider it amusing.

Christine apparently felt sufficiently alarmed by the interview, brief though it had been, to contact Ward, even though they had not been on good terms for some weeks. He invited her to come round to discuss it. A journalist acquaintance of Ward, Warwick Charlton of *Today* magazine, was present. Ward thought that Christine was exaggerating the significance of the police interview. Throughout the evening he sensed that their relationship had changed and that there was now a lack of trust that could not be restored.

But Charlton said that Christine had admitted that she had seldom brought Ward anything but trouble, despite all the help he had given her. According to Charlton, the conversation went like this:

'Keeler's problem,' said Stephen, speaking as though she was not present, 'is that she is essentially a good girl, too easily led. She will insist on listening to the last person who speaks to her. If she'd listened to me none of this business would have happened.' Suddenly, he turned to her and asked: 'Isn't that true, baby?' Christine smiled and nodded . . . Later on, when she had gone, Stephen said, 'You see, I really do like helping people. I know Christine has said things that have been harmful to me, but I know that she hasn't meant them. I have forgiven her now as I have forgiven her in the past.'

On Friday 5 April, Herbert and Burrows interviewed Christine Keeler again, and yet again the following morning. The interviews were now at Marylebone Police Station. They sat Christine down on a hard chair facing an empty wall. The officers alternated their questioning. Herbert's style was sharp, abrupt and uncompassionate, while Burrows was subtler, gentle and probing.

Their questions still concentrated on security matters but they had a hidden edge. They showed Christine a plan of Profumo's house and pointed out how easy it would have been for her to enter his office while he was in the bathroom. They wanted to know whose idea it had been for Keeler to go to Profumo's home. Had it been Ivanov's or Ward's? But soon the questions changed. The two detectives, having got Keeler to agree she had been to bed with Profumo, now asked her about Astor. Then they went through the names of every man she might have met through Ward. They asked if she had been to bed with them. They convinced her they had to know the answers because of the espionage angle. They explained to her that they had been informed about Dr Ward's little games several years ago, of how he used girls to wield influence with people in power. They told her they would need a complete list of men with whom she had sex or who had given her money during the time she knew Ward. Before she could retract, they made her sign against each name on the list.

Christine, understandably, made one statement in this list which would later greatly harm Ward. She said that Ward had brought home a friend one evening, 'Charles', that she had liked him and had gone to bed with him and that some time later when they needed money in a hurry, Ward asked her to pop round to 'Charles's' house and borrow some. (We have established that 'Charles' was Charles Clore, the millionaire businessman who lived at 22 Park Street, W1.) By this time Christine was so confused by the police questioning and by the dubious light they had cast on Ward's activities that she began to agree with them that Ward was an evil influence. They managed to convince her that his carefree attitude to life, something which she had always admired and loved about him, hid something sinister.

# 27

*Cooking a Case*

The police had done well with Christine Keeler but elsewhere their investigation was collapsing. Ward was being watched around the clock but had done nothing that even hinted at criminal activities. The only thing that made the detectives suspicious was that Ward seemed to have no set pattern to his life and was eccentric in his choice of parties. 'One evening he would be at a society dinner rubbing shoulders with top people and the next night we'd see him in some café in Notting Hill where his types didn't usually go. We were suspicious as to why he should be roughing it up in Notting Hill when he could have been dining in Belgravia.'

So it soon became obvious that it was unlikely that the police would ever catch Ward doing anything illegal no matter how long they kept him under their surveillance. They would have to rely then on the testimony of the witnesses who could tell a court what illegal acts Ward had carried out in the past. Here the difficulty was that these witnesses would be either friends of Ward in prominent positions, such as Lord Astor, who would not wish to involve themselves, or else girls like Christine and Mandy Rice-Davies, who were so unreliable.

The police realised that testimony from such people would need corroboration if any court were to believe it. They had Christine Keeler's statement. Now they needed other people to back what Christine had said. Mandy Rice-Davies was an obvious choice but when the police approached her she twice refused. Mandy had a boyfriend in Spain at this time and on 23 April she was at London Airport on her way to visit him when two policemen stopped her, took her to a small room and formally charged her with 'possessing a document so closely resembling a driving licence as to be calculated to deceive'. This referred to an incident some months earlier when Mandy had tried to rent a car using the forged licence which Rachman had given her along with his gift of a car. The police had warned her at the time that she had committed an offence but had taken no action against her. Now she was treated in an amazing manner.

The police produced Mandy in court and asked for a remand while they prepared their charge. The magistrate granted the police application and fixed bail for this comparatively minor offence at £2,000 (£20,000 at today's values). In case Mandy had any ideas of finding one of her wealthy friends to put up the money, the police told her that they had numerous other potential charges and would introduce them one at a time if necessary so as to escalate the bail to a level that she would find impossible to meet. So Mandy resigned herself to some days in jail before her case could be heard. 'First there was the depersonalising process of being removed from freedom and locked away. Then came the indignity of the search, the body search, and submitting to the strange ritual of the shaving of pubic hairs . . . I was locked in my cell for twenty out of every twenty-four hours . . . I began my remand fired by indignation at the unfairness of my own plight but also at what I saw as the dreadful indignity of prison life . . . I was ready to kick the system any way I could. But ten days of being locked up alters the perspective. Anger was replaced by fear. I was ready to do anything to get out.'

At this low point in her life Mandy had two visitors – Chief Inspector Herbert and Detective Sergeant Burrows. Herbert opened the conversation. 'Mandy,' he said, 'you don't like it in here very much, do you? So you help us and we'll help you.' They began a series of questions about Mandy's life in London. 'Who I knew, where I went, what I did, who paid for what,' interspersed with an occasional question about Stephen Ward. 'Although I was certain nothing I could say about Stephen could damage him in any way – he was peculiar, certainly, but that doesn't mean criminally so – I felt I was being coerced into something, being pointed in a predetermined direction . . . Whenever I hesitated, Chief Inspector Herbert would say reassuringly, 'Well Christine says . . . ' He told me that they had interviewed Christine numerous times, and that Christine had been most co-operative . . . The prospect of perhaps having to spend a further spell in Holloway over the motoring offence was enough to convince me to keep on the right side of the police. I felt like a cornered animal. I told them all they wanted to know.'

When Mandy's case came up on 1 May, she was fined £42 and was free. She left immediately for Spain. It must now have occurred to the police that having eventually won Mandy's co-operation and having taken a statement from her, they had no guarantee that she would be around to repeat that statement in court. So when Mandy came back briefly from Spain, and was then about to leave again, Burrows arrested her at London Airport and she was charged with the theft of a television set valued at £82.

This turned out to be a set which Mandy had rented for the flat Rachman had given her at Bryanston Mews. After Rachman's death she had not been allowed back into the flat and had not seen the set again. The police drove Mandy to Marylebone Police Station where she was told she would be released if she agreed to enter into a recognisance of £1,000, the only condition to which was that she should appear at the police station – on a date which turned out to be the start of the first court hearing against Ward! In the meantime, of course, the police, as they were entitled to do, took away Mandy's passport. When Mandy duly appeared in court her passport was returned and when she paid the television rental company the price of the missing set, the police dropped the theft charge.

At first it looked as if Lucky Gordon might be a potential witness against Ward. But Gordon was not the sort of man to help the police voluntarily. Fortunately for the police, Christine was staying at that time at the flat of a friend, Paula Hamilton-Marshall, in Devonshire Street. Early on the afternoon of 17 April Christine had a blazing row with Paula's brother, John, in the course of which there was a scuffle. Christine emerged with a black eye and bruises. A few hours later a West Indian called 'Truello' Fenton, Christine's current boyfriend, arrived at the flat to visit her. To cover for John, Christine told Fenton she had received her injuries in a fight with an unnamed girl.

Later still, Keeler made one of her many calls to Herbert and Burrows. (They were now talking on the telephone several times a day.) She told them about her injuries. They suggested that she should try to persuade Lucky Gordon to call at the flat. When he arrived she should call Marylebone Police Station and say that Gordon had assaulted her. Christine, by now totally under the influence of the detectives, telephoned some of Gordon's friends and told them where she was staying knowing full well that word of this would soon reach Gordon himself.

Early in the evening another West Indian arrived. This was Clarence Camacchio, a friend of Paula Hamilton-Marshall. Both Fenton and Camacchio were still present when Lucky Gordon came banging on the door shortly before midnight demanding to see Christine. They let him in but stopped him from getting anywhere near Christine, who screamed, ran to another room and called the police. Fenton and Camacchio told Gordon that he should leave quickly, and he did.

The police arrived sooner than expected, so Christine hid Fenton and Camacchio in the bedroom and persuaded the police not to

enter by saying a child was asleep there. At 1 a.m. Detective Sergeant
Sidney Whitten took a statement from Christine and made one
himself. 'Miss Keeler was in a state of shock and had a slight scratch,
swelling and bruising on the left side of her face . . . We learned from
Inspector Mitackis (who had arrived first) that Miss Keeler had
recently been assaulted on the premises by a coloured man known as
Lucky Gordon.'

Gordon was arrested later that day and charged with having
assaulted Christine Keeler causing her grievous bodily harm. Herbert
and Burrows questioned him. They told him that they were making
inquiries about Stephen Ward on a tip-off that Ward procured young
girls for men well known in London society. If Gordon could help
them, if he could make a statement that would help convict Ward,
then it might be possible for the police to drop the assault charge
against Gordon. Gordon refused to co-operate so the police were
eventually forced to go ahead with a prosecution, a decision that was
to prove very costly to their principal witness, Christine Keeler.

In the meantime the search for more evidence against Ward went
on at a frantic pace. His telephone was tapped and in the 13 weeks
between the beginning of the police investigation and Ward's
appearance at Marylebone Magistrate's Court on 28 June, the police
team located and interviewed between 125 and 140 people in
connection with the case. Christine Keeler was questioned on no
fewer than 24 occasions and came to feel that Herbert and Burrows
were a permanent part of her circle, almost family.

The all-sweeping nature of the investigation is illustrated by the
case of the dirty books. The journalist Warwick Charlton called on
Ward on 22 April. Charlton had originally cultivated Ward so as to
pass information to John Lewis, but he had grown to like Ward and
had become friends with him. However, like other journalists
interested in the affair, he made a point of being friendly with both
the police and Ward and acting as a conduit between the two. He now
told Ward that the police were planning to call on him. Ward,
probably thinking that the police might search his flat, immediately
went into his bedroom and reappeared with an armful of pornographic
books and photographs. Although these were not admitted as
evidence at Ward's trial, the prosecution did show them to the judge
as an example of Ward's depravity. Yet Charlton has described them
as 'the sort of books an adolescent might have tucked away beneath
the bedclothes to read in the furtive reaches of the night'. Most dealt
with bondage and sado-masochism. Sergeant Eustace, who saw them,
has described them as 'very tame . . . today you wouldn't even give
them a second look'.

As well, Ward's statement to the police when they eventually got hold of the material – that the pornography belonged to a friend whom he did not intend to name – turns out to have been true. Ward was protecting an old girlfriend. On a modelling assignment in Paris, she thought it would be a great joke to buy some pornography and bring it back to London where, at the time, she was living with Ward. She told us: 'I dressed up in an overcoat, sunglasses and a headscarf, crept into a sex shop, grabbed a few books, paid for them and carried them out in a brown paper bag. Stephen and I looked at them a few times for a laugh and then I put them away in a drawer and forgot about them. I never remembered them until they were brought up at Stephen's trial. I felt extremely ashamed and guilty but I had just been married and there was no way I could publicly admit to it. Anyway I thought that the whole case was so preposterous that it would be thrown out of court.' Instead the prosecution used it as yet another illustration of Ward's obsession with sexual matters.

But, as Herbert and Burrows worked 18 hours a day and the reports flowed out to Scotland Yard and Whitehall, the chances of establishing a case against Ward still seemed slender. As Sergeant Eustace remembers: 'Ward had no money in his British bank account, no Swiss bank account, no diary, no appointments book (other than for his professional practice), no whips, canes or other instruments that pimps keep in their flats. We had nothing to show that Ward was a pimp or that his flat was a disorderly house or a brothel.' Besides, the investigation was leading the police into dangerous areas.

In the course of interviewing Lord Astor, Herbert and Burrows elicited from him the fact that he had once given Christine Keeler and Mandy Rice-Davies a cheque to cover the rent of their flat in Comeragh Road, Fulham. Since the police had established from Christine and Mandy that they had been to bed with men there and accepted money for sex, the two detectives were elated – they were convinced that Lord Astor was technically guilty of keeping a brothel and they sought permission to develop a case against him. But by this time Mervyn Griffith-Jones had taken the brief to prosecute Ward and he would not hear of it. The police dropped this line of inquiry and continued to concentrate on Ward.

In the last week in April Herbert and Burrows held a series of conferences on the case. They had narrowed down the charges that might possibly succeed against Ward to two main ones – procuring and living on immoral earnings. The evidence on the procuring charge came principally from Christine and Mandy who, in this case, were probably telling the truth. They had told Herbert and Burrows

42, Ward after his release on bail, 3 July 1963

Personalities involved during the Cuban missile crisis: 43, *left*, Michael Eddowes, solicitor; 44, *top*, William Shepherd, MP; 45, *above*, Sir Godfrey Nicholson, MP

46, *above*, scene of the shooting, 14 December 1962: Ward's flat, 17 Wimpole Mews W1; 47 *right*, Paul Mann and Christine Keeler, June 1963; 48, *below*, Lucky Gordon being ejected from the Old Bailey, 1 April 1963

The politicians and the press: 49, *above, left*, Harold Wilson; 50, *above, right*, George Wigg; 51, *below*, Lord Hailsham (right) with the editor of *The Times*, Sir William Haley

A brave face: 52, *right*
Profumo and his wife at the
races after his statement to
Parliament, March 1963
53, *below, left*, Harold
Macmillan with President
Kennedy, 30 June 1963
54, *below, right*, later, out
grouse shooting.

55, *above, left*, William Rees-Davies, QC; 56, *above, right*, Christine's manager, Robin Drury, with the Keeler tape; 57, *below*, Mandy apprehended at London Airport

58, Profumo after his resignation, June 1963

The hearings: 59, *above, left*, Lucky Gordon, with his lawyer, Ellis Lincoln; 60, *above, right*, Rudolph Fenton; 61, *below*, Christine Keeler (left) and Paula Hamilton-Marshall arrive at court

62, *above*, Lucky Gordon (right) and John Hamilton-Marshall celebrate the result of
Gordon's appeal
The policemen: 63, *below* (left to right), Sergeant Mike Glasse, Chief Inspector Samuel
Herbert, and Detective Sergeant John Burrows

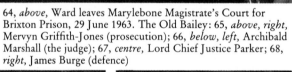

64, *above*, Ward leaves Marylebone Magistrate's Court for Brixton Prison, 29 June 1963. The Old Bailey: 65, *above*, *right*, Mervyn Griffith-Jones (prosecution); 66, *below*, *left*, Archibald Marshall (the judge); 67, *centre*, Lord Chief Justice Parker; 68, *right*, James Burge (defence)

The principals: 69, *above,* Stephen Ward; 70, *right,* Christine Keeler

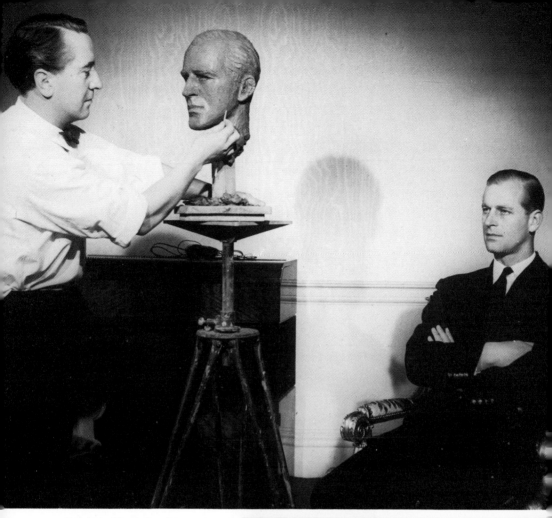

71, *above,* The Duke of
Edinburgh sits for Ward's friend
and defence witness Vasco
Lazzolo; 72, *right,* Noel Howard-
Jones, defence witness

The girls: 73, *above*, Vickie Barrett
(behind the *Guardian*) and Brenda
O'Neil; 74, *right*, Ronna Ricardo; 75,
*below*, two anonymous prosecution
witnesses; 76, *below, right*, Christine
Keeler (right) (with her friend Paula
Hamilton-Marshall)

77, *above,* crowds wait outside the Old Bailey for the verdict; 78, *below left,* meanwhile, Stephen Ward is carried unconscious to hospital; 79, *below right,* an official bulletin says Ward is critically ill

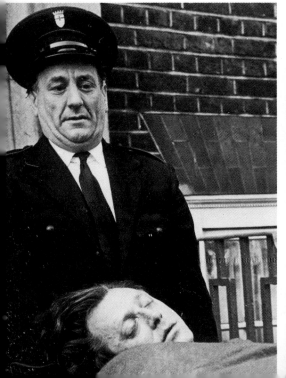

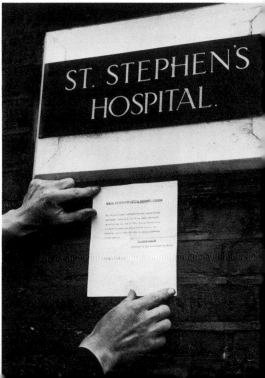

The end: 80, *above*, crowds wait for news while Ward is dying in St Stephen's Hospital; 81, *below*, he is cremated at Mortlake

The postcript: 82, Lord Denning with his files

that they had helped Ward pick up girls. They would be shopping with Ward at say, Selfridges, when a sales assistant would catch Ward's eye. He would send Christine or Mandy to talk to the girl. They would say, 'Dr Stephen Ward noticed you the other day and thought you were extremely beautiful. He's a famous artist, you know, and he would very much like to sketch you. Could you come to a coffee shop after work and let him draw you there?'

Christine and Mandy had told the police that this approach nearly always worked, that the girl would meet Ward, that he would draw her portrait, ask to meet her parents, and receive their permission for her to attend a weekend party at Ward's cottage at Cliveden. There, said Christine and Mandy, Ward's friends would queue to be the first to date Ward's new discovery.

The police were convinced that, technically, this was procuring, even though there was no suggestion of coercion, all the girls were over 16, Ward did not do it for financial gain, and indeed, probably had no knowledge of what the relationship would be between the girl and anyone to whom he introduced her. As Mandy Rice-Davies said later, if this was a criminal offence then just about every bachelor in London was guilty of it. But that was the law at that time – it has since been changed – and the police pressed ahead to get evidence that Ward had broken it.

On the pimping charge there was Christine's statement that she had had intercourse with Charles Clore and that Ward had later asked her to go to his house and borrow money from him. There was a statement from Mandy that Ward had suggested that she should go to bed with Dr Emil Savundra in her room in Ward's flat so as to get money towards her rent for the room. But all this was rather thin stuff, and even if true, hardly pimping in the traditional manner, that is, managing prostitutes and taking a sizeable share of their income.

So to gather this sort of evidence, Herbert and Burrows turned to professionals – prostitutes who worked in that part of London and who, for many reasons, were beholden to the police. Here they were much more successful. Prostitutes, as we have seen, had always held considerable fascination for Ward and there were several in Ward's area who had, in their own phrase 'done business' with him. The police had no difficulty in finding them. One, Vickie Barrett, had been arrested for soliciting, and when the police examined the contents of her handbag they found a diary with Ward's telephone number in it. The arresting officer passed this information to Herbert and he went to see Barrett and asked her what she could tell him about Ward.

We have only Barrett's word for what happened next – Herbert is now dead – but given the relationship between police and prostitutes at that time, we believe her. Barrett said that Ward was a friend, that she had visited him two or three times a week to do business with him, and that she had, on occasions, whipped him at his flat. According to Barrett, Herbert then told her, 'Wouldn't it be better if you said you whipped other men at the flat?' and that when she replied, 'Why should I say that?' he continued, 'if you don't say that you'll never be able to show your face in Notting Hill again.'

Another prostitute who knew Ward was Ronna Ricardo. The police found her because one of her friends had a sketch by Ward on her wall. A police officer interviewing the friend on another matter noticed the sketch and inquired about it. The friend said she knew of Ward through Ricardo who had done business with Ward. Herbert and Burrows soon called on Ricardo. She was a tougher nut than Vickie Barrett and on one occasion when Sergeant Glasse interviewed her she lifted her skirt and pulled down her underwear to reveal on her stomach, written in large, indelible blue letters , the words ALL COPPERS ARE BASTARDS. She flatly refused to co-operate.

But the police persuaded her. Once more, this is the uncorroborated account of Ricardo herself, but again we believe her. She said a police car with two officers took up station outside her flat and was there for days on end, that this was intended to frighten her and that it succeeded. Then Herbert and Burrows interviewed her nine times and put tremendous pressure on her to say that when she had visited Ward at his Bryanston Mews flat Ward had asked her to stay behind to meet men and go to bed with them. Ricardo said that Herbert told her that if she did not agree to help them then the police would take action against her family. Her younger sister, on probation and living with her, would be taken into care. They might even make application to take her baby away from her because she had been an unfit mother. On the other hand, Herbert said, if Ricardo would help them by making a statement, she would not have to appear in court and she would be left alone. Both women had the feeling that the police were out to frame Ward and that they did not care how they did it.

The one thing the police investigating team at this stage did not bother to do was to interview Ward himself. He, of course, was well aware of the police investigation, both from journalists like Charlton who kept him informed, and by what was happening to his professional and social life.

Herbert and Burrows had started to turn up outside Ward's consulting rooms and question his patients as they arrived and left. If the patient was a man they would ask him if Ward had ever introduced him to women. If the patient was a woman then the question was: 'Has Dr Ward ever made an improper suggestion to you?' As a result of this, Ward's patients began to cancel appointments. In addition, his friends began to receive visits from the police. They were asked how they had met Ward, how long had they known him, whether he had introduced them to women and if so, the names of the women concerned. A political element sometimes entered the questioning. Beecher Moore remembers that Herbert and Burrows went through his bookshelves and found some Polish naval books (he sold dinghies to Poland). The two detectives then accused him of being 'one of Ward's Communist friends'.

By mid-April Ward's social diary was becoming as blank as his professional one. His close friends still saw him regularly but acquaintances had started to snub him in public. Ward found this more amusing than upsetting and remained confident that it would soon all be cleared up. He was waiting for his best friend, Lord Astor, to return from the United States. 'When Bill gets back', he told Warwick Charlton, 'everything will be all right. One word from him and this investigation will be dropped.'

Ward now suffered hs first major set-back and for a man who believed in the power of friendship, a deep disillusionment. On Friday, 12 April, Astor arrived back from the United States to find a request from Herbert and Burrows waiting for him; could he agree to see them as soon as possible? They met the following morning. The interview was clearly a traumatic one for Astor. A man in his position had never imagined that one day two detectives would be asking him the names of women he had slept with, whether he had paid them any money, whether he had met them through Stephen Ward, whether he knew that Christine and Mandy had entertained clients at their Fulham flat, the one for which he had on one occasion paid the rent.

We know the effect on Astor because of what he did next. He telephoned Stephen Ward and asked if he could come over to Ward's flat on Tuesday for an urgent talk. Warwick Charlton was there when Ward took Astor's call and remembers how happy Ward was to hear from his friend. But if Ward had thought Astor wanted to discuss the best way of ending the police investigation he was soon disabused. In his account of the meeting which he later gave Charlton, Ward said that Astor quickly dispensed with greetings and went straight to the point. He would like Ward to give up the cottage at Cliveden. Could he return the keys in such a way as to make it appear that the initiative came from Ward himself? This would enable Astor to write him a sympathetic letter saying how sorry he was that Ward wanted to leave. Ward must have been deeply wounded but he kept his dignity by saying that of course he understood and would do this as soon as possible. Astor then said that Ward would clearly need good legal advice in the coming days and that he would like to make £5,000 available for Ward's legal expenses. He suggested that Ward open a special bank account for this purpose and that he would then pay the money into this account.

Charlton visited Ward that evening and remembers that he had never seen him so miserable. He reminisced about the good times he had had at the cottage – the weekend parties, the sparkling conversations over dinner, the quiet days with Margaret Brown when she painted indoors and he reorganised the garden; the lavish evenings at the main house; the unexpected Sunday visitors; the wildlife at twilight. Halcyon days, said Ward, the best years of his life. Now it was all over.

Ward was wounded, but Brooke had underestimated him. Instead of retreating and lying low, he struck back. On Tuesday, 7 May, Ward telephoned the Prime Minister's Parliamentary Private Secretary, Timothy Bligh, and asked for an interview to discuss an important matter. Bligh stalled Ward long enough to ask Macmillan's permission. Macmillan said he saw no reason why Bligh and Ward should not meet, but he thought an MI5 officer should be present as a witness. The meeting was arranged for later that day. An official note was kept of the conversation.

Ward began by saying that the police were conducting an investigation into his affairs. At no stage had they told him why they were doing this but he had, nevertheless, decided to co-operate, and had given them his professional appointments books. This had enabled the police to interview his patients and as a result of these interviews some of his patients were now reluctant to continue being treated by him. He felt this was unfair and that the least the police could do would be to talk to him and give him a chance to clear his name. Bligh replied that he understood Ward's feelings but that there was nothing he could do – the investigation was a police one, not a Government one, and he had no power over the police. Had Ward thought of contacting the Police Commissioner at Scotland Yard?

Ward said that he thought the investigation might be politically motivated and have something to do with his friendship with Christine Keeler and the Soviet diplomat Ivanov, and rumours of Keeler's association with John Profumo. The official note of the conversation then quotes Ward as telling Bligh: 'You see the facts as presented in Parliament were not strictly speaking just like that . . . I feel I should tell you the truth of what really happened. You probably know . . . anyway. He [Profumo] wrote Miss Keeler a series of letters. The attachment was a much deeper one than [has been presented].' Ward said he had defended Profumo even when Profumo had misled the House of Commons but he did not know how much longer he could continue to do so. According to the official note Ward concluded, 'I don't know whether you have any feelings about this, whether there is anything you can do. I know myself here that there is a great deal of potentially extremely explosive material in what I have told you.'

There are two ways of interpreting what Ward said to Bligh. One is that Ward was trying to blackmail the Prime Minister's office into ordering the police – through the Home Secretary, to call off the Ward investigation. If it did not, then Ward would spill all he knew about the Profumo–Keeler relationship. Bligh, and later Macmillan and Lord Denning (in his report) chose the blackmail interpretation. The other interpretation is this: Ward knew he had not broken the law and the desperation with which the police were looking for something with which to charge him confirmed this. Therefore the police investigation must have something to do with the Profumo–Keeler relationship and, possibly, with his, Ward's, involvement with Ivanov. Further, he thought it likely that the police were acting on their own initiative, did not know that he was working as an agent for MI5, and had been fed malicious information by his enemies. So he went to the top to complain that although he had done his best to keep the lid on the scandal he was being harassed by the police because they did not know his true role. Understandably he wanted Bligh to do something to clear up this confusion.

Bligh was technically correct in saying that he could do nothing, but since he interpreted Ward's statements as a blackmail threat, he quickly reported the conversation to Harold Macmillan. Macmillan ordered MI5 to interview Profumo again in case Ward had been telling the truth. This was done but Profumo stuck to his original statement. Ward was lying to save himself, Profumo said. Given the choice between believing his Minister or Ward, well known as a raconteur likely to exaggerate, Macmillan backed Profumo.

Ward continued his fight. First he wrote to Brooke at the Home Office. It is worth quoting the letter in full because it sets out Ward's case succinctly and with force.

It has come to my attention that the Marylebone police are questioning my patients and friends, in a line however tactful which is extremely damaging to me both professionally and socially. This enquiry has been going on day after day for weeks. The instruction to do this must have come from the Home Office. Over the past few weeks I have done what I could to shield Mr Profumo from his indiscretion, about which I complained to the Security Service at the time. When he made a statement in Parliament I backed it up although I knew it to be untrue.

Possibly my efforts to conceal his past and to return to him a letter which Miss Keeler had sold to the *Sunday Pictorial* might make it appear that I have something to conceal. I have not.

The allegations which appear to be the cause of the investigation, and which I only know through the line of questioning repeated to me, are malicious and entirely false. It is an invention of the Press that Miss Keeler knew a lot of important people. It was by accident that she met Mr Profumo and through Lord Astor that she met him again. [Ward's clear implication here is that Keeler and Profumo had met before Astor's swimming party.] I intend to take the blame no longer. That I was against this liaison is a matter of record in the War Office.

Sir Godfrey Nicholson who has been a friend of mine for 25 years is in possession of most of the facts since I consulted him at an early stage. May I ask that the person who has lodged the false information against me should be prosecuted.

This factual and, considering the circumstances, very restrained letter failed to impress Brooke. His office replied the next day, 'The Home Secretary has asked me to explain that the police, in making whatever enquiries they think proper, do not act under his direction.' This was a disingenuous answer. Although the police do not act under the Home Secretary's direction in their day-to-day inquiries, the Ward investigation had started at the initiative of the Home Secretary himself and could have been terminated by him if he had so wished.

Ward was now complaining to everyone he could think of, and sending accounts of his correspondence to Fleet Street editors who, as might be expected, considered any sort of publication too risky. On 20 May he wrote to his local MP, Sir Wavell Wakefield, making much the same case he had made to Henry Brooke but including the sentence, 'Possibly an enquiry may be necessary when a Minister has not told the truth to Parliament.' Wakefield felt the matter beyond him and passed the letter to the Conservative Chief Whip.

The same day Ward also wrote a letter to the Leader of the Opposition, Harold Wilson saying, in part, 'Obviously my efforts to conceal the fact that Mr Profumo had not told the truth in Parliament have made it look as if I myself had something to hide, which I have not. It is quite clear now that they [the Government] must wish the facts to be known, and I shall see that they are.' When Wilson received the letter he immediately sent a copy to the Prime Minister.

All these letters began to have an effect. Two Labour MPs, Ben Parkin and Chuter Ede, put down questions for the Home Secretary asking him what information he had received from Ward in connection with inquiries being carried out by the Metropolitan Police. There was a new burst of speculation in Fleet Street. In his press statement after his letter to the Home Secretary Ward had concluded, 'I have been persecuted in a variety of ways, causing damage not only to myself but also to my friends and patients – a state of affairs which I propose to tolerate no longer.' Since almost every Fleet Street editor now believed that the stories circulating about Keeler and Profumo were true, Ward's statement gave them heart. They need run no risk themselves. All they had to do was wait for Ward to blow the scandal wide open.

But Ward disappointed them. Although he threatened to tell all, he never did. Perhaps he decided it was by now a useless gesture – the damage had been done. His practice had been ruined and he faced financial hardship. His friends, except for a small group who remained loyal to the end, had started to distance themselves from him. He was virtually a prisoner in his flat: if he went to visit anyone he risked being followed by the police who would then interview the person Ward had visited. His journalist friend Warwick Charlton took him out to lunch on Friday, 10 May and made him an attractive offer. If Ward would write a series of articles for *Today* magazine about his life and circle of friends, then the magazine would pay him £5,000; with this he could live abroad for a while. Ward said he still had faith in the British sense of fair play and although the outlook was grim at the moment he was sure that eventually his name would be cleared. (Nevertheless Charlton persuaded him to sign a provisional, non-binding contract.)

Ward would have been less confident had he known that the political side of the affair was rapidly approaching its climax and that when it occurred, far from clearing his name, it would make his position even more intolerable.

*Profumo Confesses*

By now the Leader of the Opposition, Harold Wilson, was not prepared to wait any longer for the Prime Minister to act. No matter what rumours circulated, no matter what Fleet Street thought, no matter how many letters Ward fired off, Macmillan seemed determined to say and do nothing. His last letter to Wilson on 14 May seemed to sum up his attitude: 'I handed all the material to the appropriate authorities who studied it very carefully. There seems to be nothing in the papers you sent which requires me to take action.' Wilson did not consider this enough, so on Friday 24 May he asked for an appointment to discuss the matter with Macmillan. A meeting was fixed for the following Monday.

It was an unsatisfactory encounter. Macmillan seemed to attach little weight to Wilson's material – even Wigg's dossier left him unmoved. But before the meeting broke up Wilson made one point which must have stuck in Macmillan's mind. Wilson recalled the case of John Belcher who had been Parliamentary Secretary at the Board of Trade during Attlee's government. There had been rumours that Belcher had been receiving gifts in return for favours. The moment these rumours reached Attlee he had immediately ordered the Lord Chancellor to conduct an inquiry. There had been a brutal police investigation. The gifts turned out to be trivial – drinks, hospitality, a parcel of food – but Belcher's career had been ruined. And in the Belcher case, Wilson said, there had not been the serious security aspect which existed in the Profumo affair. Although Macmillan appeared unmoved by Wilson's analogy, in the light of what Macmillan soon decided it must have sparked off some response.

It is helpful at this stage to consider what exactly Macmillan knew about the affair. From the American ambassador he had learnt as far back as 28 January of a love affair between Profumo and Christine Keeler and that Fleet Street had a story saying that Keeler was also sharing her favours with a Soviet assistant naval attaché, Yevgeny Ivanov. From 27 March he knew from Ward's letter to Wilson (which

Wilson had passed on) that Ward had acted during the Cuban missile crisis as a go-between in unofficial approaches by Ivanov to the Foreign Office. He knew from 10 April the contents of Wigg's dossier on the affair, with its two main points – Ward claimed to have worked for MI5, and that Profumo had moved for some time in Keeler's rather lurid demi-monde. From 27 May he knew that Ward was sending letters to all and sundry saying that Profumo had lied to the House of Commons in his 22 March statement denying any impropriety with Keeler. And he now knew that Wilson strongly felt that there had been a security risk in Profumo's relationship with Keeler and that Wilson was determined to do something to force all this into the open. Macmillan had consulted MI5 on the matter. What did they know at this stage?

They knew that Profumo had probably had an affair with Keeler because Ward had told them so. They knew that Keeler had said that she had been asked to find out from Profumo when Germany was to get nuclear warheads. This information had come from the police. They knew from Wigg's dossier – which Macmillan had passed to them – that Profumo had been part of Keeler's shady circle of friends.

Why, then, was Macmillan so reluctant to act? If we consider that the affair had two distinctly separate aspects – a security one and a personal one – then we can at least understand Macmillan's attitude. On the security aspect he was obliged to consult MI5, and throughout MI5 maintained that there had been no security risk whatsoever. For one thing they simply did not believe that the relationship between Profumo and Keeler was such that Keeler could ever have posed the nuclear warheads question, or, if she had, that Profumo would have answered it. For another, if the Prime Minister was not satisfied with MI5's assessment of the Profumo–Keeler relationship, there was Keeler's own statement that she had never asked Profumo about nuclear warheads. MI5's last word on the matter was on 29 May when its Director-General, Hollis, told Macmillan that, despite what Harold Wilson claimed, there was no security risk in the affair and an Official Secrets Act prosecution of anyone involved would fail.

That left Macmillan with the personal aspect. Here MI5 was of no help, arguing that what Profumo did or did not do with Christine Keeler was of no concern to the service. So Macmillan had to make up his own mind. He knew of all the rumours and allegations, and he had ambassador Bruce's views. Against them he had to balance Profumo's personal word that there had been no impropriety in the relationship. Years later Macmillan said: 'I consciously felt that it would be a terrible thing if I had told a man that he was a liar and he proved to be true. Even when I have to think it over, I think I would rather carry the burden of having made a mistake and been proved wrong than had it the other way and destroyed a man's life when he was really innocent.'

This is Macmillan the man speaking and behaving according to his code of honour. But there was also Macmillan the politician. The politician had to consider that Profumo had also given his assurance publicly, in the statement to the House of Commons. Macmillan the politician would have felt that he had no choice – he had to back Profumo. Also, he made this decision with the knowledge that the source of most of the continuing allegations about Profumo came from Ward, that there was always the possibility Ward could be wrong, that Ward was under police investigation, and that when this concluded and Ward was prosecuted either he would shut up or his credibility would be so seriously undermined as to make him no longer a threat to Profumo and the Government.

Macmillan must have decided that what he needed was a little time for the police to finish their work, for, on 30 May, he attempted to buy this time by announcing to a surprised Harold Wilson, that he had decided after all to hold an inquiry. 'I am sure in my own mind that the security aspect of the Ward case has been fully and efficiently watched, but I think it important that you should be in no doubt about it,' Macmillan wrote.

This was a carefully worded letter. By referring only to 'the security aspect' of the case Macmillan was turning Wilson's own emphasis back on him. There would be an inquiry, conducted by the Lord Chancellor, Lord Dilhorne, but it would be limited to ascertaining whether national security had been endangered, and to this question Macmillan had already heard the answer from the only body in possession of sufficient facts to form a conclusion – MI5. And MI5 had categorically told Macmillan that there had been no risk. So on 30 May, with Parliament about to go into recess for the Whitsun holiday, Macmillan booked a night sleeper to Inverness believing that he had the Profumo affair under control; he had deflated Wilson by acceding to his demand for an inquiry and had bought time to allow the police to deal with Dr Ward. But there were other forces at work.

One was George Wigg and his obsession with Profumo. Wilson had persuaded Labour MP Ben Parkin to withdraw his question about the Profumo affair because it referred to 'expensive call girl organisations' and this was inconsistent with Wilson's aim to restrict the attack to the security issue. Instead, Wilson suggested, an elder

statesman of the party, Chuter Ede, should table a question. The
question was drafted in Wilson's office: 'To ask the Secretary of State
for the Home Office what information he has received from Dr
Stephen Ward in connection with inquiries carried out by the
Metropolitan Police; and what action he proposes to take.'

Ede was at the races with George Wigg later that afternoon when a
message came from Wilson's office. The question had been ruled out
of order because it referred to an on-going police inquiry. Could Ede
and Wigg redraft the question? They did so and Wigg drove to
Westminster to make certain that the new version was acceptable.
Under Wigg's eager guidance the question now homed in on
Profumo himself: 'To ask the Secretary of State for the Home
Department what information he has received from Dr Stephen Ward
about a Ministerial statement made to the House on 22 March 1963,
and what action he proposes to take thereupon.' The question was
tabled just before the House rose and Macmillan was seen behind the
Speaker's chair in deep conversation with Profumo and the Tory
Whip, Martin Redmayne.

The other factor beyond Macmillan's control was Christine Keeler.
On Wednesday, 22 May her friend Paul Mann had asked Alex
Murray, an author, to write Christine's memoirs. Murray had agreed
and a contract was signed. But Christine had other ideas. She had
decided to replace Mann with businessman Robin Drury, an old
friend from her days at Dolphin Square. Drury told her he had the
necessary contacts and that she should capitalise on her notoriety. As
Drury later stated to the police, he offered to become her business
manager and suggested taping a series of interviews with a view to
writing a book. Christine confessed, 'I've got to admit it, but at the
time the recording was made I was as high as a kite through drink and
a narcotic stimulant . . . I must have unwound and really let my hair
down.' Robin Drury was well satisfied with the result.

How much of what Keeler said on these tapes was truth and how
much was fantasy is impossible to say. A lot of it was certainly true.
She discusses the police investigation of Ward and describes her own
role in it as 'The Home Secretary's Secretary'. She says that if the
police manage to get Ward on a spying charge then she will be all
right. She describes her affair with Profumo, claiming that she had
been to France on several occasions to join him there. (Profumo,
on the other hand, has denied that he ever went to France with
her.) She says that her life had been threatened my MPs from both
parties, that men in high places had used her since she was 14 and
that now she was fed up and was going to tell all. It was time for
her to look after herself and that there was big money to be made.

She says John Lewis had offered her £30,000 to bring down the Government.


John Profumo and his wife had gone to Venice for the Whitsun holiday, intending to return on Wednesday, 5 June. Before they left Lord Dilhorne had told Profumo that he planned to push ahead with his inquiry and would like to see him on Thursday, the day after he got back. The Profumos had barely arrived in Venice when the War Office called to say that Lord Dilhorne wanted to bring the appointment forward a day. This meant that Profumo would have to be back in London by Tuesday night. By now Profumo must have been a worried man. Just when the worst seemed to have passed he now faced the prospect of going through his catalogue of lies again for Dilhorne's benefit. This was becoming increasingly difficult to do because of Ward's intervention. There is, however, no reason to suppose that Profumo suddenly decided to give in because of these two factors – Dilhorne and Ward. He knew he still had his Prime Minister's support: the last-minute conversation at the back of the Speaker's chair before Parliament went into recess had been about how best to handle Chuter Ede's question. All the evidence is that Profumo went off on his holiday determined to stick to his story, confident that he could survive. Yet within 24 hours of arriving in Venice he had made up his mind to return early to London, on Monday, a day earlier than he had planned, to confess that he had lied, resign from Parliament and accept that this would mean his career was finished and his reputation ruined.

The only explanation for this about face that makes sense is that Profumo got to hear of Christine Keeler's tapes, in which Christine not only went through her affair with Profumo in great detail, revealing that it was of longer duration than anyone had imagined, but in which she also named many other prominent people. There are several ways Profumo could have heard of the tapes so quickly. One is that someone who knew what the tapes contained telephoned Profumo in Venice and told him about them, either to warn him or to blackmail him. But Profumo has said that he returned early to London because the Government recalled him.

This cannot have been Lord Dilhorne because Profumo came back on the Monday and Dilhorne was not expecting him until Wednesday. It cannot have been Macmillan because Profumo's sudden return caught his office by surprise. All the evidence points to it being the Home Secretary, Henry Brooke, who told Profumo that he had better get back to London as quickly as possible. The police investigating team knew of the Keeler tapes. They were reporting daily to the Police Commissioner, Sir Joseph Simpson. Simpson would have told Brooke of a matter as important as this, and Brooke, realising that the scandal was about to blow wide open would have warned Profumo.

The Profumos packed their suitcases, left Venice in a hurry, and arrived back in London on the Golden Arrow train service on Whit Monday evening. Profumo immediately telephoned the Prime Minister's Principal Private Secretary, Sir Timothy Bligh, and asked to see Macmillan as soon as possible because there had been 'a serious development'. (The use of this phrase is interesting because it tends to confirm that it was outside pressure that triggered Profumo's decision to confess.) Bligh said that Macmillan was in Scotland and if the matter was urgent then it would be better to deal with it in London. A meeting was fixed for 10.30 a.m. in Bligh's office the next day, Tuesday.

Bligh must have guessed that this was to be no ordinary meeting because when Profumo arrived he found that Bligh had asked the Chief Whip, Martin Redmayne, to be present. The two men listened in stunned silence as Profumo performed his last act as a Minister of the Crown. He told them that his statement to the Commons about his relationship with Christine Keeler had been untrue. His many protestations of innocence to his colleagues and to the law officers of the Crown had been untrue. He tendered his resignation as a Minister and said he would apply for the Chiltern Hundreds, an archaic parliamentary procedure by which Profumo ceased from that moment to be an MP. Then Profumo, his face grim, excused himself and walked out of Bligh's office.

Later that day Bligh told Macmillan of Profumo's confession and resignation. The Prime Minister, shaken by the news, said he did not want the resignation announced yet; he needed time to consider his reply and arranged to dictate it the following morning. This suited Profumo because his solicitors, Theodore Goddard and Company, wanted a say in drafting Profumo's resignation letter so as to absolve themselves from any complicity in his earlier deceptions. The letter was finally agreed the following morning, shortly before Macmillan's reply was dictated from Scotland. Macmillan's press secretary released both letters to the Press at 6 p.m. on Wednesday, 5 June 1963.

Profumo's letter was dated the previous day and sent from his home, 3 Chester Terrace, Regent's Park, London, NW1. It read:

Dear Prime Minister

You will recollect that on March 22 following certain allegations made in Parliament, I made a personal statement.

At that time rumour had charged me with assisting in the disappearance of a witness and with being involved in some possible breach of security.

So serious were these charges that I allowed myself to think that my personal association with that witness, which had also been the subject of rumour, was, by comparison, of minor importance only.

In my statement I said there had been no impropriety in this association. To my very deep regret I have to admit that this was not true, and that I misled you, and my colleagues, and the House.

I ask you to understand that I did this to protect, as I thought, my wife and family, who are equally misled, as were my professional advisers.

I have come to realise that, by this deception, I have been guilty of a grave misdemeanour, and despite the fact there is no truth whatever in the other charges, I cannot remain a member of your Administration, nor of the House of Commons. I cannot tell you of my deep remorse for the embarrassment I have caused to you, to my colleagues in the Government, to my constituents and to the party which I have served for the past 25 years.

Yours sincerely,<br>Jack Profumo

The Prime Minister's reply, dated 5 June, was sent from the home of his hosts, Lieutenant-Colonel and Mrs R. Campbell-Preston, Ardchattan Priory, Connel, Argyll. It was brief and cool and made no mention of Profumo's service to the Government. It read:

Dear Profumo,

The contents of your letter of June 4 have been communicated to me, and I have heard them with deep regret. This is a great tragedy for you, your family, and your friends.

Nevertheless, I am sure you will understand that in the circumstances, I have no alternative but to advise the Queen to accept your resignation.

Yours very sincerely,<br>Harold Macmillan.

The story made headlines all over the world the next day, encompassing as it did, all the ingredients of a typically British scandal – politics, sex, vice, espionage, and hypocrisy. That evening Stephen Ward was interviewed by Desmond Wilcox on 'This Week', commercial television's news-magazine programme. He repeated his statement that he had early on informed MI5 about the liaison between Profumo and Christine Keeler. 'The key point for me to clear my name was to indicate that I had not encouraged the relationship between Miss Keeler and Mr Profumo. I was disturbed by certain parts of it and, as tactfully as possible, I had informed the Security Service. I wanted to make it absolutely clear that I hadn't encouraged it and knowing that I had a friend in the Soviet Embassy I think I was rightly disturbed about it . . . For a while it seemed possible that Mr Profumo's part in this affair could have been concealed altogether. Then the Press flushed him out.'

Wilcox then put to Ward the rumours that he had been running a call girl racket. Ward replied: 'No, indeed I was not. This my friends know and I think that the police will continue their investigation until they are satisfied that I am in the clear.' Two days later the police arrested him.

# The Government Endangered

30 |

The Prime Minister was now fighting for his political life. At first it looked as if he planned to stay in Scotland, play safe and shrug off the whole sordid business. At a Conservative rally at Strathallan Castle near Gleneagles on the Saturday after Profumo's confession he joked with supporters who tried to persuade him to dance. 'They may call me the twister,' he said, 'but I don't do the twist.' But the blast he and his Government received from the Sunday press changed his mind and he left Scotland on Sunday night to return to London.

The *News of the World* led the way with the 'Confessions of Christine', for which they paid her £24,000. Illustrated with a photograph of Christine sitting naked on a wooden chair, the confessions told of how she had met Jack Profumo and his wife at Cliveden and of how she had had an affair with Ivanov – 'a wonderful huggy bear of a man'. Ward was 'extrovert, excitable' and liked to lead her around the streets of Marylebone with a dog collar around her neck and a leash, pretending not to notice when people stared. But regular *News of the World* readers – and probably the extra 250,000 the newspaper attracted that week – knew that this was only the 'warm-up' and the really sensational stuff would come later.

The *Sunday Pictorial* (now called the *Sunday Mirror*) published Profumo's letter to Christine with a rather lame explanation as to why it had not published it earlier. This was illustrated by the same nude photograph of Christine, taken from a slightly different angle. It also had a quote from Mandy Rice-Davies: 'The farcical thing about it all,' she said, 'was that – on more than one occasion – as Jack left Christine at the flat where she stayed, Eugene Ivanov, the handsome young Russian naval attaché, walked in. In fact it was something of a standing joke among us.' (As we have seen, it is highly unlikely that Christine ever slept with Ivanov and there had never been any suggestion that as one lover left the other arrived until the ghost writers of Fleet Street produced their cheque books to two avaricious young girls.)

Macmillan could have lived with this sort of sensational rubbish.

But two serious newspapers, the *Observer* and the *Sunday Times* hit him hard. The *Observer* said that the Labour Party had gained a large electoral advantage from the scandal. The *Sunday Times* said that if the Whips and others who advise the Prime Minister had heard nothing of the stories which had been current in sophisticated circles for some time then they were dangerously remote from life. 'The political waters . . . will be fouled for some time by the mud stirred up by the Profumo scandal,' the paper added.

Macmillan arrived in London on the Monday morning, drove straight to Admiralty House and began a series of meetings with members of his Government. All of them arrived and left looking grim, except the Chief Whip, Martin Redmayne, who smiled broadly at reporters and asked, 'What's all the fuss about?' Macmillan's strategy soon emerged. He was going to bluff it out, confident that the Press and the public would soon tire of the scandal. He announced what had previously been kept secret – that Lord Dilhorne was looking at the security aspects of the affair. There was an element of pre-emptive strategy in the decision to concentrate on the security angle. To add to his other worries, Macmillan had learnt in that first week of June 1963 the whereabouts of H.A.R. ('Kim') Philby, the former high-ranking SIS officer who had vanished from Beirut in January. SIS had confirmed that Philby, long suspected of being a KGB mole, had surfaced in Moscow, crowning a 30-year career as one of the most successful penetration agents in espionage history. Macmillan, already buffeted by the Profumo scandal, decided against making this public. (The full Philby story did not emerge until 1967.) But if Moscow tried to make capital out of Philby, Macmillan at least had an inquiry under way into the security side of the Profumo affair.

Meanwhile he tried to behave as normally as possible. He ignored a mild panic on the stock market as the *Financial Times* Index dropped seven points, its biggest fall since the Cuban missile crisis. He went to Brighton to receive an honorary degree and attend the inauguration ceremony of the new University of Sussex. He had his usual weekly audience with the Queen.

But Macmillan had not taken into account several factors that kept the scandal right before the public eye in the ensuing weeks. One was the desire of just about everyone connected with the affair to have their say, some for money, some for the satisfaction of proving that they had been right all along. Christine Keeler led those who were talking for money. As the *News of the World* continued to serialise her confessions she became the best known young woman in Britain. She turned herself into Christine Keeler Company Limited, rejected an offer of £60,000 to appear in cabaret – a vast improvement on her starting salary at Murrays – and chose instead to play herself in *The Christine Keeler Story* a film to be made in Denmark by two young producers, Nicholas Luard and Dominick Elwes.

And for those who could not wait to see Christine perform, she gave a special show every day at the Central Criminal Court where she was appearing as the star witness in the trial of Lucky Gordon, charged with having assaulted her in the Devonshire Street flat on 17 April. This, as we have seen, was a case trumped up by the police in case they needed Gordon as a witness against Ward.

Christine, stunningly well dressed, arrived at the Old Bailey each day in a Rolls-Royce which her new manager, Robin Drury, hired for the occasion. She insisted in her evidence that it was Gordon who had assaulted her and created an enormous scene in court when Gordon, who was defending himself, made a statement from the dock accusing Christine of having given him venereal disease. Christine had to be removed from the courtroom. Gordon then announced that he wanted to call as witnesses Ward, Profumo, and the two West Indians, Camacchio and Fenton, who had been hiding in the bedroom at the flat when Keeler was supposed to have been assaulted. Ward, Gordon said, had made Keeler work for him as a call girl since the age of 17. The *News of the World* could not have afforded such marvellous promotion for its Christine Keeler series and its readership continued to soar.

The Earl of Arran now spoke out about his role in the Cuban missile crisis when Ward and Ivanov had come to see him to convey Soviet proposals to the British Government. Michael Eddowes, the solicitor preoccupied with the espionage aspects of the scandal, wrote to Macmillan on 13 June saying that as far back as 29 March he had submitted a report to the Special Branch on the relationship between Profumo and Keeler, including the specific statement to him by Keeler 'that Ivanov had asked her to obtain from Mr Profumo the date of delivery of nuclear warheads to West Germany'. After writing his letter, Eddowes released it to the Press. Four days later, accompanied by Michael Marler, a private detective, Eddowes left for the United States 'to continue my investigation on that side of the Atlantic'. Jeremy Thorpe, the Liberal MP, predicted that two other Ministers would soon be forced to resign for 'personal reasons'. Another MP, Conservative Sir Cyril Osborne, spoke of 'too many pimps and prostitutes in high places' and a leading clergyman, Dr Mervyn Stockwood, said it was high places that were giving off 'the unpleasant smell of corruption'.

Names now flew around London like confetti. There was an

atmosphere of fear and apprehension, lightened by occasional flashes of humour. *Private Eye* published a cartoon by Trog, a play on Macmillan's famous electioneering slogan, 'We've never had it so good.' It showed Macmillan pasting up a large billboard reading 'We've never had it so often.' And an anonymous young lady – or young man – from Devon wrote to several Government departments and to one foreign Embassy saying, 'Now that the Profumo case has brought out the question of state security you should probe the affair between --- and ---. She is interested in Minutemen [missiles] and he passes on the info to his Commie pals. Don't trust secrets to --- [a prominent MP]. He talks in his sleep. I know, I slept with him.'

With almost anyone prepared to believe almost anything, this was an ideal moment for Mariella Novotny, the girl who had fled New York to avoid vice charges, to resurrect her partnership with the *News of the World* crime reporter, Peter Earle. London had been buzzing with stories of a dinner party at which the butler was a well known Cabinet Minister (or a minor member of the Royal Family, depending on which rumour you listened to) who wore nothing except a black mask. The story had its origins with Mandy Rice-Davies who had told the *Washington Star* all about London's night

life linked to the Profumo scandal. 'There was a dinner party where a naked man wearing a mask waited at table like a slave. He had to have a mask because he was so well known.' Now Earle and Mariella came out in the *News of the World* with a headline reading 'She knows the Man in the Mask'. Earle wrote, 'In an extraordinary interview in her home in Hyde Park Square, London, Mariella told me of a bizarre "Feast of the Peacocks".' He then quoted Mariella as saying:

In late December 1961 I decided to give a dinner party for about twenty friends ... There was one snag. The man who usually acts as our butler fell sick. It was then that a friend offered to do the job himself. I was surprised because he is a man of substance and birth ... I thought he would dress himself up as a footman, but he had a more startling idea.

I got two peacocks, stuffed them, skewered their necks and replaced the tail feathers. There was a peacock feather for every girl. Just before the guests arrived my footman made his shattering entrance. He wore nothing except a pair of very short, striped pants. He had on a black hangman's type mask.

When we led the guests into the dinner they doubled up with laughter. They thought it was the cleverest stroke . . . That is all there is to the story. All the talk of a masked slave being beaten and reviled by drunken dinner guests is bunkum. I can only suggest that because of the intensive police investigation which followed the Profumo scandal, this incident is but one of many which has been exaggerated and blown up out of all proportion.

The last sentence was probably one of the very few truths Mariella Novotny ever told. We have established that the man in the mask was not one of the famous people it was rumoured to be at the time, but an unimportant Yorkshire businessman.

But it was not the *News of the World*, the *Sunday Mirror*, Christine Keeler, Mandy Rice-Davies, or the man in the mask that sent Macmillan reeling. It was part of his own establishment, *The Times*. On 11 June it published a stinging editorial which had repercussions way beyond the paper's modest circulation. Headed 'It *is* a Moral Issue', the leader said that eleven years of Conservative rule had brought Britain psychologically and spiritually to a low ebb. 'Today [the people] are faced with a flagging economy, an uncertain future, and an end of the illusion that Britain's greatness could be measured by the so-called independence of its so-called deterrent. All this may seem far from Mr Profumo but his admissions could be the last straw.'

*The Times* said that it was strange that not a single member of the Government had resigned when the affair broke in March, including Profumo himself. 'Whether in the next few days some heads fall or none, damage has been done. It may be a caricature for the *Washington Post* to say that "a picture of widespread decadence beneath the glitter of a large segment of stiff-lipped society is emerging". But the essence of caricature is to exaggerate real traits. There are plenty of earnest and serious men in the Conservative party who know well that all is not well. It is time they put things first, stopped weighing electoral chances and returned to the starker truths of an earlier day.'

*The Times* editorial was interpreted as an attack on Macmillan's leadership and the need for 'earnest and serious' men to take over. Other newspapers took up the call and predicted a rash of Cabinet resignations unless Macmillan went. At first the Prime Minister was defiant. There was no obvious successor, and if the hysteria over the scandal continued, he felt that he could benefit from a backlash as the British fondness for an underdog took control. Macmillan told some of his closer friends, 'I will not be brought down by that tart.' He was encouraged when some of his senior colleagues took up this theme. Lord Hailsham, interviewed on the BBC, said, 'A great party is not to be brought down because of a scandal by a woman of easy virtue and a proved liar.' But on 17 June the Commons debate on the issue showed that Macmillan and Hailsham could well be wrong.

Wilson opened the attack. 'This is a debate without precedent in the annals of this House,' he said. 'It arises from disclosures which have shocked the moral conscience of the nation. There is clear evidence of a sordid underworld network, the extent of which cannot yet be measured.' Wilson revealed to a hushed and tense House some of the contents of Wigg's dossier on the scandal, in particular the meeting between Wigg and Ward and the record of it – 'a nauseating document taking the lid off a corner of the London underworld of vice, dope, marijuana, blackmail, counter-blackmail, violence and petty crime.' Wilson put the blame for the lack of early action squarely on the Prime Minister: 'After the Vassall case he felt that he could not stand another security case involving another ministerial resignation, and he gambled desperately and hoped that nothing would ever come out.'

Macmillan replied by emphasising the personal impact of the scandal: 'On me, as head of the Administration, what has happened has inflicted a deep, bitter and lasting wound . . . I could not believe that a man would be so foolish, even if so wicked, not only to lie to colleagues in the House but be prepared to issue a writ in respect of a libel which he must know to be true.' Macmillan's defence was that he had not been told of early suspicions of a security aspect to the scandal. (He omitted to say, however, that the reason that MI5 had not told him of Keeler's accusation to the police – about Ward and nuclear weapons – was because MI5 considered it a ludicrous statement.) Macmillan concluded that what had happened had been unfortunate but that the blame was not his. 'My colleagues have been deceived, and I have been deceived, grossly deceived – and the House has been deceived – but we have not been parties to deception, and I claim that on a fair view of the facts as I have set them out I am entitled to the sympathetic understanding of the House and of the country.'

This was a bold appeal in the light of the fact that – as we have shown – Macmillan had every reason to believe at the time that Profumo's statement in March was a lie. In the event, any chance Macmillan might have had of winning support with this appeal was quickly scuppered by one of his own party, Nigel Birch, the leading spokesman for the critics of the Prime Minister. Why had the House been forced to accept Profumo's personal statement, Birch wanted to know? He had known Profumo for a number of years, as had other MPs. 'I must say that he never struck me as a man at all like a cloistered monk; and Miss Keeler was a professional prostitute,' Birch said. 'There seems to me to be a basic improbability about the proposition that their relationship was purely platonic. What are whores about?'

Birch acquitted Macmillan of any dishonourable act but on the question of competence and good sense he did not see how the verdict could be favourable. He then delivered the *coup de grâce*. 'What is to happen now?' he said. 'We cannot just have business as usual. I myself feel that the time will come very soon when my Right Honourable friend ought to make way for a much younger colleague. I feel that ought to happen. I certainly will not quote at him the savage words of Cromwell but perhaps some words of Browning might be appropriate:

> . . . let him never come back to us!
> There would be doubt, hesitation and pain.
> Forced praise on our part – the glimmer of twilight,
> Never glad confident morning again!'

The Conservative Party Whips shuddered when Birch sat down.

Even George Wigg, who must have still been savouring his victory over Profumo, conceded in an unremarkable speech that he could not hope to emulate Birch's graceful oratory. The vote was, of course, a foregone conclusion – in that the Government would win; no one expected the Conservatives to commit suicide. But every member who abstained from voting for the Government was, in effect, casting a vote against Macmillan's leadership. The Whips had done their figures; 20 abstentions would be bearable; any more would be alarming. There were 27. The Government majority was down to 69 and anything under 70 was considered a threat to the leadership.

There would have to be changes. The *Daily Telegraph*, the most Conservative of papers, headlined the debate 'Premier likely to resign soon'. The *Daily Mail* said, 'Mac: the end'. The *Daily Mirror*'s view was, 'His future, short of a miracle, will be brief.'

Macmillan, who had looked drawn and dejected throughout the debate, confided to a friend, 'My spirit has not broken but my zest has gone.' But he survived. Two factors helped him. He did a deal with some of the more senior Conservatives. He would go, but not yet. It was in the party's interest that he should not be seen to have been forced out of office by the Profumo scandal. He would lead the party into the next election and after victory, bow out. Macmillan took the opportunity of a television interview with Independent Television News to hint at this decision. 'All being well,' he said, 'if I keep my health and strength, I hope to lead the party into the election.' Interpreters of political nuances got the message – Macmillan would resign after the election pleading health reasons, which is exactly what happened.

The other event which gained Macmillan a reprieve was a 24-hour visit to Britain by the President of the United States, John F. Kennedy. The two leaders were photographed together, and the Press announced a tactical victory for Macmillan in persuading the President that NATO should not have a mixed-manned nuclear surface fleet because this would mean the Germans getting near atomic weapons for the first time. Macmillan was seen as a statesman of international stature, on terms of amiability and equality with the American President. What the British public did not know was that the Profumo scandal had created almost as big a stir in the United States as in Britain. But all the American investigations into the affair had been conducted in deep secrecy – because they concerned the President himself.

# 31 | *Save John F. Kennedy*

One of Ward's close friends was Thomas Corbally, the American businessman who had told the US ambassador, David Bruce, about the Profumo affair. They first met at a party. Corbally was in pain from an old knee injury and Ward, noticing this, treated him on the spot. After that they met frequently. 'Ward was a lovely, decent kind human-being,' Corbally recalls. 'He was a fine artist and a brilliant osteopath. He was the most unmaterialistic person I've ever met. There was a period when he was at my flat twice a day to treat me and there was no way I could get him to accept any money at all from me. He would accept dinner. He liked going to the Mirabelle and some other places. And sometimes there he would say, "Tom, can you cash a cheque for me for five pounds?", and I'd say, "Stephen, I haven't got five pounds. Let me give you fifty, I owe you at least that by now." No way. All he would want was five pounds. It gave him a thrill to live on the brink of financial disaster.'

Corbally remembers that all Ward could talk about at this time was the Profumo affair. 'If only Stephen had kept his mouth shut, Profumo would never have been disgraced. But Stephen talked about it and talked about it. At every dinner party he went to and everywhere else. There was no way to shut Stephen up. And he was greatly amused by it all. It was typical of him. He loved being the centre of attention, loved being the one to come out with all the latest gossip. He loved telling stories and taking the establishment apart.'

Corbally's close relationship with Ward had made him the ideal man to gather information for Bruce. But Bruce's mistake was to pass the information to Macmillan and neglect Washington. Perhaps he was worried that he and his staff might be dragged into the scandal. There certainly had been a connection. The US naval attaché in London, Admiral R. B. Lynch, had met Ivanov frequently on the diplomatic party circuit, and when Ivanov had suddenly left London amid rumours that he had been an intelligence officer, Lynch had told many people, 'If he was a spy he certainly fooled me.' The assistant naval attaché, Captain Thomas W. Murphy, had been even friendlier

with Ivanov and there were photographs of Ivanov in a warm
embrace with Mrs Murphy at a party, about to kiss her on the lips.

Unknown to Bruce, someone in the United States Government
was already deeply interested in the Profumo affair and had even been
in touch with the President over it. This was J. Edgar Hoover, head of
the FBI. From the summer of 1962 the FBI had been listening to a
Soviet defector who had agreed to remain in place as an employee of
the United Nations. Codenamed 'Fedora', this would have been
either Victor Lessiovski, a short, plump Russian who worked for the
UN Secretary General, or a lowly press attaché at the Soviet
Embassy. 'Fedora' had been in New York only a short while when he
contacted the FBI, revealed that he was a KGB officer under
diplomatic cover, and offered to work for the United States.

Hoover personally assessed Fedora before accepting him and for
the next twenty years Fedora's reports so intrigued Hoover that often
he passed them direct to the White House. They played a role in the
Kennedy assassination investigation and the 'Pentagon Papers'
controversy. Hardly an intelligence event in the Western world took
place in this period without Hoover seeking Fedora's views on it.
One reason for this was that Fedora confirmed Hoover's worst
prejudice about the UN. It was, Fedora said, a hotbed of espionage.
As well as housing dozens of Communist spies under diplomatic
cover, it provided an easy source of information for Communist call
girl rings who numbered many diplomats, especially black ones,
among their customers.

Hoover was greatly titillated by this because cursory investigation
indicated that call girl rings did indeed operate in the vicinity of the
UN – it would be surprising if they did not – and the link between
sex, espionage and degenerate 'non-Caucasians' was something that
had long intrigued him. It was almost an automatic reaction
therefore, to consult Fedora when the first whispers of another
political sex scandal in Britain reached Hoover. Fedora did not
disappoint him. He said that yes, he had heard of the scandal in
London. Ivanov, a competent GRU officer, had been using a British
call girl ring to collect valuable Western secrets by taping pillow talk
between the girls and their highly-placed political clients. Fedora
knew all this, he said, because Ivanov had boasted about his success,
when on leave in Moscow, to a fellow GRU officer and this officer
had later told Fedora.

All this sounds like a spy fairy tale, especially the route by which
Fedora claimed to have heard of Ivanov's success. Given the Soviet
Intelligence's division of duties and strict application of the 'need-to-
know' principle, it is much more likely that Fedora had heard of the

Profumo scandal from gossip at the United Nations and added the espionage details to intrigue Hoover. But why would Fedora fake a report to the FBI?

It is not unusual for genuine defectors to exaggerate or even invent information to please their employers. But Fedora had an even better reason: he was a KGB plant, a fake defector sent to sow disinformation and dissension in the West, to encourage Western security services to waste energy chasing phantom spies while the real ones worked unimpeded. At the time Fedora was reporting to Hoover no one in the FBI or the CIA knew this – although some suspected it. It was only in 1981, when Fedora's tour of duty in the United States ended, that the FBI became convinced that he was a KGB plant and not a genuine defector. For, with his usefulness as a defector-in-place ended and with him about to be recalled to the Soviet Union, the FBI fully expected Fedora to seek asylum in the United States as any true defector would. Instead Fedora went home to Moscow.

For Hoover in 1962, this was all in the future and Fedora was his pet Russian. Under Fedora's influence Hoover developed a theory of a Soviet conspiracy of international proportions. A call girl ring, secretly controlled by the KGB and made up from girls of many nations, was operating in the major cities of the Western world. The ring was run by local Communists or fellow travellers. It had a dual aim. The first was to gather intelligence from men in important posts – politicians, servicemen, public servants – who used the girls and who could be encouraged to be indiscreet. The second was to create scandals involving Western leaders so as to destroy public confidence in those leaders.

So Hoover had watched the Profumo scandal develop with horrified fascination. All his worst fears about a KGB-controlled international call girl and blackmail ring were being realised. The head of London FBI, Charles W. Bates, was placed on full alert and Hoover sent off an urgent radiogram to the main American stations giving them his version of the background to the scandal. Some of this document remains secret even today but it is worth quoting what is now declassified because it shows both how the conspiracy came together in Hoover's mind and the extent to which he believed the rot had gone.

For information. John Profumo was British Minister of War until his recent resignation following disclosure of his relations with Christine Keeler. Stephen Ward, London osteopath, has been arrested in London charged with living on the earnings of Keeler and Marilyn Rice-Davies, prostitutes. Ward's operations reportedly part of a large vice ring involving many people including many prominent people in the U.S. and England including other Ministers of British Cabinet not yet identified. Other individuals involved include Yevgeny Ivanov, aka [also known as] Eugene Ivanov, former Soviet Naval Attaché, London, who patronised Keeler and who reportedly requested Keeler to obtain information from Profumo; Thomas J. Corbally, U.S. citizen engaged in business in Britain, who reportedly gave wild parties in his flat; Michael H. B. Eddowes, British attorney for Keeler, now in the U.S. representing her interests re sale of her story to publications; Horace Dibben, British citizen, in whose residence sex orgies were held is husband of Maria Novotny; Maria Novotny is prostitute who operated in NYC [New York City], was arrested on March three, one nine six one, and was victim in white slave case involving her procurer, Alan Towers. She fled to England and has participated in orgies at Ward residence. Alan Towers was in NYC for two years prior to his arrest in above white slave case. He jumped bail and is now a bureau fugitive. He is reportedly now permanently residing behind Iron Curtain. Novotny alleges Towers was a Soviet agent and that Soviets wanted information for purposes of compromise of prominent individuals; Lord Astor of England [sic] on whose Cliveden Estate sex orgies reportedly occurred: it was here that Profumo first met Keeler; Douglas Fairbanks, Jnr, movie actor; Earl Felton, American screen writer; and many others also involved.

Early reports from Bates must have made Hoover wonder whether he had badly underestimated the extent of the conspiracy. First, Bates revealed that Admiral R. B. Lynch, the U.S. naval attaché in London, had met Ivanov a number of times on the diplomatic cocktail circuit, and that the scandal was having widespread ramifications. 'Some allege that the Macmillan Government may fall as a result of it.' Then Bates sent a long 'very urgent' message in code. This set out what investigations Bates had been able to carry out at the U.S. Embassy in Grosvenor Square. 'Thomas Corbally told the ambassador's office on January 29 that Keeler and Margaret Davis [sic] had sold article to a Sunday paper listing men with whom they had spent the night. One was Profumo and another was a Russian naval officer.' Bates's message confirmed that the Prime Minister was advised of this on January 28. Then came the sentence that excited Hoover: 'Info received by Embassy from Corbally was not furnished Department of State, Washington, and not known this office.' Bates must have realised how his boss would interpret this because he concluded with : 'Recommend extreme care in handling this.'

Hoover immediately deputed one of his senior officers, William C. Sullivan to look into the Embassy's handling of the matter. As Hoover saw it, the ambassador, David Bruce, had advance knowledge of the scandal and appeared to have kept it to himself. Could Bruce be one of the prominent Americans whom Hoover believed were involved in the international vice ring? Hoover would probably have kept these investigations secret, but a report in the *New York Post* forced him to go public. The report said, wrongly, that 'information had been forwarded to the FBI on the possibility that American diplomats or politicians may have been compromised.'

This brought a flush of inquiries from other U.S. Government departments asking what the FBI knew and Hoover was forced to reveal that the FBI had not received any such information and that he was trying to find out why. In one way the inquiries helped him. He now had the backing of powerful people for his investigations, as an FBI internal memorandum indicates: 'General Joseph Carroll, former Bureau agent and present head of the Defense Intelligence Agency has informed us that Defense Secretary [Robert] McNamara is extremely interested in the Keeler case and has asked to be kept promptly informed of all developments.'

Washington being the town that it is, the State Department quickly learned of Hoover's moves. The last thing it wanted was the FBI investigating the London Embassy. It moved quickly to protect its rights. On 21 June, the FBI recorded: 'Mr Emory Swank who said he was Secretary [Dean] Rusk's special assistant, called at 9.30 a.m. to advise that Secretary Rusk had asked him to check into the report that there were some contacts with the Embassy in London with regard to the Profumo/Keeler matter. Swank said that there is nothing in the State Department files to substantiate that there were such meetings at the London Embassy, but that this, of course, did not mean that the meetings did not take place. Swank said that Secretary Rusk would probably appoint a personal emissary to take this up with the Ambassador in London.'

Two hours later Rusk appointed William C. Burdett, deputy assistant secretary for European Affairs as the emissary. The State Department duly notified the FBI of Burdett's mission and asked, 'in view of the delicacy of the embassy in this matter,' if the FBI wanted a report on the result of the mission. Hoover cunningly replied that the FBI was not investigating the matter in London and it was up to the State Department to decide to whom to distribute Burdett's report. But Hoover immediately alerted Bates in London to watch for Burdett's arrival.

In the meantime Hoover made certain that the Attorney-General, Robert Kennedy, knew what was going on. He did this by sending him a personal letter summarising the case and highlighting the American involvement, both at the US Embassy and at the US Air Force base at Ruislip, West London. 'There is a possibility that some Air Force enlisted personnel may have had relations with Christine Keeler. One airman was reported to have said that Keeler charged 100 pounds a night and gave the impression that he had spent several nights with her. Another enlisted man is said to have referred a coloured airman to Keeler.' Both airmen, said Hoover, had access to classified information.

Hoover's conviction that British society was riddled with whores, pimps, sex maniacs and Soviet agents must have received a boost on Sunday, 16 June when an article by Michael Eddowes appeared in *Journal-American*. In it Eddowes told of his meeting with Ivanov during the Cuban missile crisis. Eddowes described Ivanov as highly aggressive and full of blustering threats to wipe out England and to drop an atomic bomb in the sea 60 miles off New York. According to Eddowes, Hoover immediately 'instructed' him to make further inquiries into the security aspects and report back to him. Washington was now buzzing with as many rumours as had swept London during the height of the scandal, so what happened next was not entirely a surprise. The White House became involved. The most likely explanation for President Kennedy's sudden interest in the affair is that his brother, Robert Kennedy, told him of the long report from Hoover. There were then both political and personal reasons for the President's interest. One was that the scandal could provide Kennedy's opponents in Congress with ammunition to attack his plans for a multi-nation NATO nuclear force. If Britain was so leaky, why should the US share its defence secrets? Another was a call in the *Washington News* for Kennedy to cancel his scheduled visit to London because it would provide 'prestige and moral support for the foundering Government of Prime Minister Macmillan . . . We can think of no better time for an American President to stay as far as possible away from England.' And a third reason, a personal one, was that given Hoover's animosity for the Kennedy family, the President became concerned that Hoover would somehow use the scandal against him. So, on the President's behalf Defense Secretary Robert McNamara telephoned Hoover on 20 June. Hoover was out and his call was returned by one of Hoover's lieutenants, A. H. Belmont.

McNamara said he was concerned about the affair and would like Belmont to come over to his office that very afternoon to meet with him, the director of the CIA, John McCone, and Lieutenant General

Carroll of the DIA, for a conference. What went on at the meeting remains classified, but a note of its discussions made by a CIA officer, was sent off immediately to McGeorge Bundy, the President's special assistant. From what then occurred we can make an informed assessment of what McNamara would have said at the conference. He would have told the FBI that the President wanted any security risk that the United States might have incurred through the Profumo scandal to be identified and investigated without delay. He wanted the whole affair cleared up quickly.

What followed was a rapid acceleration in the FBI investigations. Two FBI agents left for London where they liaised with the Scotland Yard team still gathering evidence against Ward. Sergeant Glasse recalls: 'The two FBI men were here on a fairly permanent basis. Their job was to interview people about possible security leaks because of the Ivanov connection. We would pick the people up and take them to the American Embassy to be questioned. In return the FBI brought two girls over from the United States for the British police to question. The FBI seemed to me to be more interested in the security angle than our own service did.'

At some stage during the FBI investigation the Bureau learnt that Christine Keeler and Mandy Rice-Davies had been in the United States. The resources of the Bureau were then mobilised to find out what the two girls had been up to, whom they had seen, and why? Agents from the Bureau's New York office tramped around the city reconstructing the girls' visit the previous year, checking their telephone calls, questioning hotel staff, and filing minutely-detailed reports. These were then read by Hoover himself who sometimes queried the details and sent the agents back to double check. For example: the FBI agent checking the Hotel Bedford's records reported that the girls had checked out at 3.03 p.m. on 14 July 1962 after paying their bill of $15.50. Hoover queried the date. The chastened agent reported, 'Recheck of Hotel Bedford records discloses the date to be correct. However the bill was $15.50 per day for both rather than a total bill of $15.50.'

The background of everyone who had volunteered information on the affair was checked. Anyone who knew Ward either in Britain or the United States was tracked down and asked to agree to an interview. Some refused. Others, like Margaret Brown, agreed, and said Ward was a wonderful person.

The investigation was not without its funny moments. On 24 June, the *Daily Sketch* said that Ward's former wife, Patricia Baines, had married a lawyer called Charles Hammond, who, the paper said, was the former head of the FBI in London. The Bureau was suitably outraged. 'This is obviously not right . . . The article shows a photo of Hammond and Baines at the time of marriage. He appears to be a lieutenant in the U.S. Navy's uniform.'

The stepped up investigation soon produced results. On 20 June three U.S. airmen, all black, were flown to the United States for interrogation 'to ensure that the thrill-seeking English press does not get their story before the Air Force does'. According to the FBI, 'the three Negroes had met Keeler in low class night clubs, generally frequented by non-Caucasian elements in London . . . The three airmen will be housed at Bolling Air Force Base and the investigation is designed to determine whether Keeler had attempted to pump them for intelligence data which they might have in connection with their Air Force assignments.' The men were given lie detector tests and questioned over a period of days. The results, announced publicly by the Defense Department the following month, was to clear the three men completely. The Department said that the investigation had shown 'none was involved directly or indirectly in any way, or had any knowledge' of the case. Two of the men had met a girl called 'Christine', who was presumed to be Christine Keeler but, the Department added, 'they had no intimate contact with her and didn't even know her last name until they read the publicity concerning her in the newspapers.' As a gesture of confidence in the men, the Department flew them back to Britain to resume their duties.

Meanwhile the State Department's investigation into the London Embassy's knowledge of the affair, the role of Admiral Lynch and Captain Murphy, Ambassador Bruce's possible involvement, and the Embassy's failure to report its knowledge to Washington, had proved equally swift. A search of the Embassy's files produced several memos from Bruce's secretary, Alfred Wells, which showed that apart from Corbally's information, the Embassy did not know any more than Fleet Street as the scandal developed. Wells had either lunched or dined at parties at which Ward had been present, and he had been intrigued at Ward's lack of discretion.

At a dinner party on 5 November 1962, Wells wrote, Ward had made loud statements that he had been the principal liaison between the Soviets and the British Government during the Cuban missile crisis. 'Ward spoke concerning the confidential messages he carried between Ivanov and his friends in the British government.' Wells wrote that he had asked a man sitting next to him who Dr Ward was and the man had replied that he was an osteopath and that he procured girls for wealthy clients.

When the scandal broke, Bruce had asked Wells to put down anything else he remembered of what had occurred in January and

February. Wells now wrote another memo, dated 18 June, saying that apart from his meeting with Corbally on 29 January he had had another meeting with Corbally on 5 February. Corbally had said that he had met Clive Bossom, Parliamentary Private Secretary to Hugh Fraser, the Air Minister, and had told him about Keeler's story naming Profumo. Wells said that while writing the memo on the second meeting, he had telephoned Bossom to learn whether Bossom had actually done anything about Corbally's conversation. Bossom had replied that after hearing Corbally's warning he had passed it to both Fraser and Profumo, and that Profumo had shrugged it off with, 'There are always rumours about men in the limelight'. (Corbally has no recollection of the meeting with Bossom.) Even the FBI saw nothing in this worth pursuing further. It noted, 'While interesting, this does not add anything to the Profumo case.'

Links between a UN call girl and the Profumo affair were now also looking very tenuous. The Office of Special Investigations (OSI) had become interested in the possibility that the Novotny case and the Profumo scandal were linked through an international call girl ring based on the UN – Hoover's original thesis. When the *Journal American* published its own attempts to link the two, the OSI asked the FBI if there was any substance in the report. Three of Hoover's senior men went through the FBI files, talked with agents, and assessed the theory. They had to tell the OSI that there was no evidence whatsoever to establish such a link.

The CIA investigation was the briefest of all. The CIA officer who liaised with the British Secret Intelligence Service, Archie Roosevelt Jnr, was asked to check if Ambassador Bruce knew Ward. Roosevelt adopted the direct method – he asked Bruce. Bruce at first said that he did not. However Bruce later told Roosevelt that when he had checked his diary he had discovered that Ward had called on him to sketch him. Roosevelt passed this news to CIA headquarters, but the agency continued to press Roosevelt and he was ordered to report instantly if any further American connection emerged from the case.

Yet, at the end of the day, the whole American investigation revealed nothing of importance to Washington, there was nothing to substantiate Hoover's thesis – no evidence of treachery or KGB conspiracy. But the extent of the investigation and the high-level interest in Washington in its results cannot be explained solely by Hoover's obsession. The FBI investigation provoked a meeting of three of Washington's most powerful men – Defence Secretary McNamara, CIA director John McCone, and DIA director, Lieutenant General Carroll. The CIA's London liaison officer, Archie Roosevelt was 'constantly badgered by my headquarters and Supreme Boss

personally about an American connection with the Profumo case.'
The President's special assistant, McGeorge Bundy, showed intense
interest in the affair. And the President's brother, the Attorney-
General Robert Kennedy, asked Hoover personally to keep him
informed about the investigation.

The only feasible reason for this widespread fascination is that all
these people feared that the President of the United States was about
to be dragged into the scandal, not on a political level, but on a sexual
one. There is evidence that this fear existed. On 2 July Robert
Kennedy asked Hoover if he could tell him exactly what Christine
Keeler and Mandy Rice-Davies did when they visited New York the
previous year. It seems strange that Robert Kennedy, the Attorney-
General of the United States, a man with enormous issues on his
mind, should have the slightest interest in what two then unknown
English girls had done during a seven-day visit to the United States a
year earlier.

The reason was that Robert Kennedy was worried that one, or
both girls might have slept with his brother, the President of the
United States, during their visit and he needed to know for certain so
that he could protect the President from the scandal that would
follow if the girls blabbed. It would have been simpler for Robert
Kennedy to ask his brother if he had slept with Christine or Mandy
instead of asking Hoover, however indirectly. But, as we now
know, John F. Kennedy's sexual appetite was so prodigious and so
indiscriminate that he would not have been able to remember.

Robert Kennedy was right to be concerned. On 23 July, according
to an FBI internal memorandum, the tape recording which Christine
Keeler had made with her new manager, Robin Drury, mentioned
President Kennedy as one of Keeler's lovers. All that needs to be said
about this allegation is that if Keeler had indeed slept with Kennedy
then it would have been completely out of character for her to have
kept it quiet on her return to London. She would have told everyone.
The fact that she never mentioned it until she was recounting her
memoirs for sale to Fleet Street strongly suggests that she invented it
to make them a more valuable property.

The FBI hastened to tell Robert Kennedy, 'There is attached [to
this memorandum] a letter to the Attorney-General furnishing the
information concerning the allegations about President Kennedy for
his information. It is recommended that this letter be delivered to the
Attorney-General by assistant director Evans.' The letter was never
sent. Hoover considered the information to be too sensitive to come
to rest in the Attorney-General's files. Evans was ordered instead to
contact Kennedy and *tell* him what the FBI had learnt.

We have only the FBI's account of what transpired. This makes Robert Kennedy appear almost pathetically grateful for the FBI's help. According to agent Evans, 'The Attorney-General was appreciative of our bringing this matter to his attention personally. He said that it did seem preposterous that such a story would be circulated when a presidential candidate, during the campaign, travels with scores of newspapermen. He added that with the next Presidential election now less than 18 months away, he anticipated that there would be more similar stories and he would like us to continue to advise him of any such matters coming to our attention on a personal basis, as he could better defend the family if he knew what was being said.'

This, then, was the effect of the Profumo scandal had on the United States. It allowed Hoover to consolidate the hold that he already had over the Kennedy family, by making the FBI appear indispensable in protecting the family name. Stephen Ward would have enjoyed the irony.

Ward had been shocked by his arrest but not too downhearted. When the police had told him of the charges, he had said, 'Oh my God, how dreadful. No one will come forward to say it is true.' But, as the days passed – although he remained confident that everything would eventually turn out all right – he had become concerned about his professional future and was disillusioned with his friends. His arrest had forced some painful decisions on most of his circle as it became clear that they were likely to be called as witnesses for Ward. Some had already fled the country, leaving for summer holidays earlier than they had planned in the hope that if they stayed away until the autumn the scandal would be over by the time they got back.

The police had frightened many of them. They had compiled a list of potential witnesses, largely men who had slept with Christine Keeler or Mandy Rice-Davies, or both. Many of these men had already been interviewed by the police who had made it clear, if the men had not already guessed, that their names had been volunteered by the girls themselves. It did not require a lot of thought to deduce that if the girls had been so free with names when talking to the police, they might be equally free with names in the witness box. This explains why Keeler says that at that time she was receiving death threats, why the police remember that in the investigation 'money passed backwards and forwards like confetti' and why many members of Ward's group were running for cover.

Some extraordinary meetings took place. In the second week in June, not long after Ward's arrest, there was a hastily-arranged dinner at Les Ambassadeurs. No one can now be certain who called it, but among those present were Ward's friends and acquaintances, Sir Colin Coote, the then Earl of Dudley and his brother George Ward, Sir Godfrey Nicholson, Sir Gilbert Laithwaite, Vasco and Leila Lazzolo and Ward's legal adviser, Billy Rees-Davies.

Rees-Davies said that Ward's friends were in a difficult situation. They would all like to help Ward but they should be aware that they would be risking their names and careers by appearing as witnesses.

Rees-Davies said that he had spoken to Lord Astor who had decided not to give evidence. In the light of Astor's decision, Ward's friends would have to consider their position very carefully because this was going to be a very dirty case.

About the same time there was another meeting in a London gentleman's club – the Athenaeum. Those present were mostly patients of Ward and some of them had known him socially as well. All of them held important positions in public life. All of them had been asked by Ward's solicitors if they would be prepared to appear at the Old Bailey to give character evidence for their client. Each wanted to know what the others had decided.

We have spoken with a man who was present at this meeting, a former high-ranking Foreign Office official. He does not want to be identified because, to this day, he remains ashamed of what happened and his part in it. 'We discussed the problem. On the one hand we liked and respected Ward and we wanted to help him. On the other, if we were seen to be involved in such a sordid case in no matter what role, then we would be ruined. We decided that if Bill Astor, Ward's oldest friend and patient, was not going to give evidence on Ward's behalf, then we could also decline.

'Of course, we risked being subpoenaed, but we felt that, on balance, Ward's counsel would not risk this course of action in case, in order to save our own skins, we turned hostile. We've all had to live with our decision. For my part I can't tell you of the moral awfulness of abandoning a friend when he most needs you, and a friend, moreover, who was completely innocent of the charges against him.'

Why did Astor decide not to give evidence? For one thing, since his marriage in October 1960 to his third wife, a former model and television announcer called Bronwen Pugh, the daughter of a county court judge, his relationship with Ward had cooled slightly. Bronwen did not care for Ward. She knew from another model that Ward was frequently seen around London escorting one, sometimes two girls. This model had once given a party, and Ward and Bronwen were among the guests. The model had taken Bronwen aside and warned her, 'Take care with Stephen Ward. If he invites you out, don't accept.'

So it was with some resentment that Bronwen found how close Ward and her husband were. When you add to this the normal suspicions and jealousies that are aroused between a new wife and old friends of the husband, the fact that the Ward–Astor relationship had cooled becomes understandable.

Then there was the advice that Astor received from a family friend who was a solicitor in the City. His brother David remembers, 'This awful lawyer [Bill Mitchell] apparently said to Bill, "Look, you're entirely in the clear. The only way you can get into trouble is by talking, so don't talk. Go around behaving as if it's nothing whatsoever to do with you. That is the proper way for you to behave because you're an innocent person. Don't say anything. Don't be dragged into court. Don't be questioned. You can never tell what nonsense they'll come up with." Bill followed this advice rigidly and as a result did asinine things like going to Ascot and smiling all over when half of his friends were in the dock. He made the most calamitous impression and became the biggest hate figure of the lot because he was following this stupid lawyer's advice and going around smiling as if he hadn't heard of the trouble. I wanted him to take the advice of any of his friends who was not a lawyer. I wanted him to go to Dickie Mountbatten and ask his advice. But I couldn't get through to Bill. He was like a rabbit caught in the headlights of a car.'

Some friends did decide to stick with Ward. Vasco Lazzolo, who had known Ward since 1946, said at the dinner at Les Ambassadeurs that he was going to give evidence on Ward's behalf, come what may. At that time Lazzolo was painting the Duke of Edinburgh's portrait and he realised that when he gave evidence at Ward's trial, Fleet Street might well link the two and drag in Philip's name as someone who had known Ward. So at the next sitting Lazzolo told the Duke what he had decided to do and said that he would understand if the Duke wanted to cancel the portrait. 'Nonsense,' Philip said. 'We carry on.'

The police were less understanding. Herbert told Lazzolo that if he was determined to give evidence on Ward's behalf, then he might have to be discredited; the police might have to 'find' some pornographic material in his studio and prosecute him. Lazzolo called the police bluff and nothing happened.

One of Ward's friends, the Dane Claus von Bulow, made a risky intervention. Von Bulow, who had been Paul Getty's personal assistant, had first met Ward when Ward had treated Getty's back. They got on well together and von Bulow was astonished that more of Ward's friends had not spoken up for him. So when he was lunching at All Souls, Oxford, and happened to meet Lord Hailsham, von Bulow seized the moment to say that Ward had had many an opportunity to offer girls to Getty and enrich himself in doing so, but that he knew for certain that Ward had not. He asked Hailsham to pass this information to the Lord Chancellor, Lord Dilhorne. Since Ward had by that time been charged, or was about to be, Dilhorne could well have considered von Bulow's attempts to help Ward as interfering with the course of justice.

Dr Ellis Stungo, Ward's psychiatrist friend, telephoned Ward's solicitors and said that he would like to give evidence on Ward's behalf. Stungo, at that time Secretary for the Committee on Drug Abuse, wanted to say that Ward, who had always been anti-drugs and anti-alcohol, had approached him to help Christine with her drug problems. This would have been important evidence because of the prosecution's allegations that Ward had introduced Christine to drugs. But about a week later Stungo was telephoned by a man whose name he cannot now remember. The man introduced himself as 'Ward's legal adviser'. He thanked Stungo for his offer to give evidence but said that this would not be necessary. Ward was already sunk. None of Ward's legal advisers made this call and its origins remain a mystery.

At this low point in his life, out on bail after three weeks in Brixton Prison, under siege, dependent on a few remaining friends for accommodation, broke and with little prospect of ever being able to return to his profession, his beloved cottage at Cliveden gone, his best friend Lord Astor gone, his social life gone, his illusions gone and his reputation ruined, Ward accidentally met Christine Keeler.

Herbert and Burrows were still keeping their witnesses in line and frequently reminded Christine during this period that unless her evidence in court matched her statements 'you might well find yourself standing beside Stephen Ward in the dock'. On an impulse, Christine went to Noel Howard-Jones's flat where Ward was staying. She was sitting in her car preparing to go in when Ward drove up, parked, came over to her and suggested that they should have a cup of coffee.

If Christine was expecting to see the old Stephen Ward she must have been disappointed. As Howard-Jones explained, 'Stephen had lost weight in prison and his clothes didn't fit. His face was drawn and the jesting humour had gone. He must have realised it was useless talking to Christine. She left in tears. Battle lines had been drawn. Christine had deserted him.' It was the last time they ever spoke to each other.

# 33 | *The Trial of the Century*

The trial of Stephen Ward opened in the No. 1 court of the Old Bailey on 22 July 1963. The hall of the main court was swarming with journalists, court officials, jurymen, barristers, visiting lawyers, policemen, ushers and witnesses. The crowds outside were ten deep and many people had queued overnight for a place in the tiny public gallery. Touts walked up and down the queue offering to sell seats. Court officials said that they could not remember such widespread interest. Even the distinguished visitors' gallery was full and during the next days reporters noted among others seated there: Lady Plunket, the wife of the Queen's equerry; Lady Parker, wife of the Lord Chief Justice; Lady Dufferin and Ava, wife of Judge Maude; Sir Theobald Mathew, the Director of Public Prosecutions; Sir Frederick Hoare, former Lord Mayor of London, and Lady Hoare; and the television personality Katie Boyle.

Clearly this was going to be *the* trial of the year. (The touts were calling it 'the trial of the century'.) At long last the truth, the whole truth and nothing but the truth would emerge. The innocent would be cleared, the guilty punished. British justice and fair play would triumph. But first there was the ritual which is such an essential part of the English legal system. A door at one end of the judge's bench rattled in warning and then opened. A tall sheriff came in, followed by an alderman. The courtroom rose to its feet and the judge entered, nodded to the lawyers' benches, looked at the crowded courtroom with just a hint of surprise and sat down.

He was Sir Archie Pellow Marshall, 64, a former Liberal parliamentary candidate, one-time President of the Cambridge Union, a lawyer who had spent most of his career doing criminal cases on the Midlands Circuit. A short, tubby figure with a square face set off by horn-rimmed glasses, he seemed almost lost in his billowing grey, scarlet and black robes of office. Marshall was not a well-known judge, a figure of controversy or acclaim. He was a quiet, religious man, a Congregationalist who believed in the sanctity of the family (he wore a wedding ring, unusual at that time), abstinence, discipline and humility, a somewhat fussy, meticulous man known to some of his colleagues as 'The Hen'. Judges are appointed to cases at the Old Bailey by a rota, so it was by chance that Marshall came to the Ward case. Yet it is hard to imagine anyone whose background, inclinations and sympathies could be so different from those of the man who was on trial. The judge obviously felt a personal moral indignation at the lifestyle Ward had adopted. He did not like the idea that women could be susceptible to charm; that Ward could look through a shop window, see a girl he fancied, and within a day or so manage to seduce her. In short, everything about Ward failed to fit Mr Justice Marshall's view on how life should be conducted, and although he did his best to control his feelings, the whole atmosphere of the trial was coloured by his moral outrage.

Barely was the judge seated when, as if on cue, Ward appeared in the dock, soberly dressed in a heather-mixture suit, his shirt crisp and his hair neat. Then, before anyone else could sit, a man in a black gown shouted the time-honoured announcement: 'All persons who have anything to do before my Lady the Queen's Justices of Oyer and Terminer and General Gaol Delivery for the Jurisdiction of the Central Criminal Court draw near and give your attention. God Save the Queen.' The trial had begun.

Criminal trials in English courts start with a speech by the prosecution, in this case led by Mervyn Griffith-Jones. The public had already seen Griffith-Jones in action at Ward's committal proceedings in the Marylebone Magistrate's Court. Griffith-Jones, a tall, good-looking man with a reputation for a ruthless approach to his work, had shown then that he felt the case beneath his dignity. Except in the courtroom he refused to speak directly to prosecution witnesses, even policemen, or to allow them to address him. All communication was carried on through his junior, Michael Corkery. Griffith-Jones represented the worst of the ultra-conservative English bar – arrogant, self-satisfied, out-of-touch with contemporary mores, and given to a pompous mode of speech littered with phrases like 'if so minded . . . it matters not . . . the one with the other . . .' He pronounced words like 'prostitute', 'pimp', and even 'sexual intercourse' with obvious distaste. As Ward's counsel, James Burge, had said at the Marylebone Court, 'My learned friend would make even a honeymoon sound obscene.'

Griffith-Jones had been the morally-outraged prosecutor at the 'Lady Chatterley' obscenity trial. There he had complained to the jury that the word 'fuck' or 'fucking' appeared in Lawrence's novel no fewer than 30 times. He had reserved a place for himself in British social history by appealing to the jurors: 'Frankly, is this a book you'd want your wife and servants to read?'

Now Griffith-Jones began the prosecution of Stephen Ward with a distinct advantage. At the Magistrate's Court Ward had been given the opportunity of having the charges dealt with on the spot by the magistrate, Leo Gradwell. But following his lawyer's advice that he would have a better chance of being acquitted if his case went before a jury, Ward had elected to be tried by a higher court. As a result a peculiarly English legal procedure had swung into action. The magistrate had to hear the prosecution case – and only the prosecution case – and decide whether it was strong enough to justify sending Ward for trial. Ward's defence would not be heard until then.

This system of a public preliminary hearing has many disadvantages. It gives the prosecution a chance to rehearse its case, test its weaknesses, and strengthen them before the main trial. It adds to the emotional strain that the accused person is already suffering – in effect he hears himself tried twice. And, most important, since at that time virtually everything that took place in the Magistrate's Court could be reported, wide newspaper coverage would be given to the hearing of only one side of the case, the prosecution's.

This was bound to create a public climate against the accused and make it almost impossible to find for the main trial a jury that was unprejudiced. Although the judge in the higher court usually reminded the jurors to put out of their minds all that they had read of the prosecution's case, few were capable of such voluntary brain-washing. (Since the Ward trial the law has been changed to limit what can be reported of committal proceedings in magistrates' courts.)

The Magistrate's Court hearing had also caused such public interest, even outrage, that the authorities had little choice on the venue for the main trial – normally such minor charges would never have been heard at the nation's central criminal court, the Old Bailey. But there had been demonstrations outside the Marylebone Court after Christine Keeler and Mandy Rice-Davies, both already in the pay of newspapers, had shamelessly described in evidence their busy sex lives. Mandy, for instance, had created a sensation in court when she said that she had slept with Ward, Douglas Fairbanks Jnr and Lord Astor. When told that Lord Astor had made a statement to the police saying that this was untrue, she had giggled and replied, 'Well, he would, wouldn't he?', a remark that was to find a place in modern English usage. When she and Keeler left the court crowds of women had hissed, booed, and banged with their umbrellas on the top of the girls' car.

Another point for the prosecution was that the magistrate had fixed

Ward's bail at such a high figure. After police had objected to Ward's release, saying that they felt that he would vanish or would interfere with witnesses, the magistrate said that he would allow bail at £2,000 (£20,000 at today's values).

This was widely reported and conveyed the impression that if the police and the magistrate considered Ward so important, then there must be more to the charges than had been revealed. All this had given Griffith-Jones a considerable edge even before the Old Bailey trial had started. As one juror said later, 'Griffith-Jones conducted the whole affair as if he had already won, but had come back for an action replay.' Now he was about to use his opening speech to consolidate this advantage.

The aim of the opening speech is to set out for the judge and jury the nature of the charges and to explain how the prosecution will go about proving them. But it is also an opportunity for the lawyer to create the atmosphere for the trial and since this is a speech, and not evidence on oath, a measure of exaggeration, hyperbole and theatrics is customary. In this latter area, Griffith-Jones excelled. The author Ludovic Kennedy, at the trial to write a book, said, 'Somehow or other, Mr Griffith-Jones managed to make everything seem so very much worse than it could have been. One realised that however badly Ward had behaved, it could hardly have been as bad as this.'

But Griffith-Jones did more. He made assertions in his opening speech that either went further than the evidence subsequently introduced to support them or, on the contrary, they were completely let down by it. Sometimes he even made assertions about matters that were not contained in the indictment. It was as if he were determined to paint Ward as evilly as possible, so that when the jury came to hear the actual evidence they would be better prepared to believe it. He also deliberately set out to persuade the jury that Ward was a thoroughly undesirable character and that with this man they should not bother to draw the line between criminal behaviour and sinful behaviour. The noted jurist, Louis Blom-Cooper has said that the English legal system tends to arrive at a verdict not by scrupulous examination of the evidence but by way of general impressions, and when the jury takes its seats in the jurybox, the first words of the trial are likely to make the most lasting impression.

The danger is easily discerned. Jury members are often unaware that it is the style of some advocates to do what Griffith-Jones did in his opening speech – treat it as a means of engaging their emotions against the accused person. These jurors see prosecution counsel as an officer of the court and it would not occur to them that such a person would exaggerate, dramatise, stretch the truth and introduce extraneous and irrelevant matter as a tactic to help obtain a conviction. And even if they did, at the end of a long case how many would be able to distinguish between what Griffith-Jones told them in his opening address he would prove against Ward, and what he actually did prove during the trial?

To check whether this had occurred during the Ward trial we tracked down a juror and on the promise of anonymity he recalled how he had felt. 'I can't begin to emphasise the power of Griffith-Jones,' he said. 'He called Stephen Ward a thoroughly filthy fellow and we all knew he must be a thoroughly filthy fellow. Then a string of girls was paraded through the court and we really didn't know who was going to come next and, quite frankly it didn't matter.'

There were five counts against Ward. The first three concerned living on the earnings of prostitution – of Christine Keeler at Wimpole Mews during a 15-month period between June 1961 and August 1962; of Mandy Rice-Davies at Wimpole Mews during a four-month period between September and December 1962; and of Ronna Ricardo and Vickie Barrett at Bryanston Mews during a five-month period between January and June 1963. The two other counts were that Ward incited Christine Keeler to procure a girl under 21 to have intercourse with him; on one occasion a girl called Sally Norie and on another occasion a girl called only Miss R. Two other charges, that Ward had helped procure an abortion were on a separate indictment which meant that they would not be heard until this case was over.

The prosecution told the jury it would show that Keeler and Rice-Davies were prostitutes and that Ward was living with them. The law was that it then became Ward's responsibility to prove that he was not living on their immoral earnings, either wholly or in part. In 1960 the two girls had gone to live in a flat in Comeragh Road. 'There they were frequently visited by the defendant, he bringing on a number of occasions his men friends to see them. Indeed he paid for half the rent on one occasion with a cheque he had received from Lord Astor,' Griffith-Jones said.

In June 1961 Christine went to live with Ward, he went on. She had brought men to the flat – Profumo and Ivanov among them – for intercourse. In the case of some of the men she was paid money. Keeler would say that over a period she must have paid to Ward about half of what her earnings were from this. Sometimes Ward would ask Keeler to ring one of the men up and go round to see him, earn her money and then bring it back. Sometimes the man would go to the flat and Ward would be there throughout, although not actually near by. On one occasion he told her to go out and see

'Charles' [Clore]. She did so and was paid £50. 'When she came back she paid some of that money to Ward by way of repaying him money he had lent her,' Griffith-Jones said.

He then turned to Mandy Rice-Davies. When she moved to Ward's flat he introduced her to an Indian doctor [Emil Savundra]. The defendant told her that the doctor wanted to rent her room in order to bring girls there. Later, after Rice-Davies and the doctor had had coffee together the defendant had said something like, 'Why let outsiders in? Why don't you be the person who goes to bed with him?' Rice-Davies agreed and thereafter when the doctor left between £15 and £25 on the dressing table, she paid Ward some £2 or £3 a time.'

The third count concerned two prostitutes, Ronna Ricardo and Vickie Barrett. Griffith-Jones concentrated on Barrett. Ward had picked her up in Oxford Street and had driven her to his flat in Bryanston Mews, he said. Ward told her that he would get her clients and look after her money for her. 'The defendant told her that there was already a man in the bedroom. He gave her a contraceptive and sent her into the bedroom where she had intercourse with the man.' When they came out, said Griffith-Jones, Ward gave them coffee and when she asked for payment he said he would save the money for her.

'Thereafter for the next two and a half months, according to the girl some two or three times a week, the same thing would happen. That is, in ordinary language, just brothel keeping. Finally the girl left but she never received a penny of the money which she had earned and which had been paid to the defendant to save for her.'

As for the procuring charges, Griffith-Jones told the jury two stories, one about Sally Norie and another about a Miss R. Ward and Keeler were in a restaurant when Ward noticed Norie and her boyfriend at another table. Ward persuaded Keeler to approach the pair to 'try to do something'. The upshot was that Keeler went off with the boyfriend thus allowing Ward to get to know Sally Norie. He invited her to Cliveden and in due time she went to bed with him and 'was introduced to other men'.

Griffith-Jones said that Ward had seen Miss R. through a shop window. He sent Keeler in to talk to her. This girl was respectable and did not want to go to bed with anyone. But in the end she did in fact go to bed with Ward. This was all Griffith-Jones had to say about Miss R. and the jurors must have been left wondering if they were being asked to consider this a criminal offence.

They must have been puzzled, too, by Griffith-Jones's long story about a two-way mirror in the Bryanston Mews flat. This allowed people in the sitting room to look into the bedroom; no one in the bedroom knew that they were being watched. Mandy Rice-Davies had broken it while she was there but when Ward moved in 'it was proposed to have it put in order again'. Griffith-Jones said that Ward had met Miss X, an 18-year-old, at a respectable party. He later called on her for afternoon tea. 'Ward said to Miss X that he had a new flat. He told her that the flat had a two-way mirror through which you could see from the lounge into the bedroom and he said he thought he could make a little money there from people who would pay to watch through the two-way mirror people performing on the bed,' Griffith-Jones said. Miss X, he went on, said that she was not the least interested in watching anything like that, whereupon Ward said, 'I don't want you to *watch*. I want you to *perform*.' Lest the jury think that this whole story was an example of Ward's sense of humour, Griffith-Jones concluded: 'This is not a case of a boy trying to take up a girl perhaps hoping to go to bed with her. You may think there are matters far more sinister.'

This last remark sums up the tenor of Griffith-Jones's opening speech. Without making any specific allegation he invited the jurors to draw the worst possible conclusion from evidence they were yet to hear. For 90 minutes he did his best to blacken Ward's character by innuendo, allusion, extravagant language, moral posturing, and by implying he would not have done this unless he had powerful evidence to support it. By the time Griffith-Jones had finished, the outlook for Ward was very black indeed.

The prosecution's first witness was Christine Keeler. She wore a mustard-coloured suit and had allowed her long, copper-coloured hair to fall freely to her shoulders. She was nervous in the witness box and ill-at-ease with Griffith-Jones, especially when he showed signs of impatience. These signs became more frequent as Keeler's evidence progressed and it became clear that matters were not as Griffith-Jones had earlier stated. Griffith-Jones's version of what had happened when the girls were living in the Comeragh Road flat was that 'Ward was paying for the girls' accommodation and bringing men around to see them'.

Keeler's version was that Ward had indeed brought men around and that she had had intercourse with one or two of them – she had difficulty in remembering. But when it came to the crunch question: 'Were you paid for it?' Christine replied firmly, 'No.' So Griffith-Jones tried another approach. 'Did you receive money from anybody while you were living at Comeragh Road?' Christine said yes, she met 'Mr Eylan' at that time and was having intercourse with him and receiving money from him. 'And who introduced him to you?' Again he was disappointed. 'I met him myself,' she replied.

So Griffith-Jones moved on to the first count on the indictment, that Ward had lived off Christine and Mandy's prostitution at Wimpole Mews. Griffith-Jones's contention was that Ward would sometimes be short of cash, and that he would tell Christine to telephone one of the men who was seeing her regularly and who was paying her £20 a time. Christine said that the only man paying her this sort of money was Eylan, so to substantiate what he had said, Griffith-Jones now asked Christine: 'Did Dr Ward ever say anything to you about going to Mr Eylan?' And Christine replied : 'No.'

'What about Charles?' asked Griffith-Jones. 'How did you come to have intercourse with Charles?' Christine said that Ward had suggested that if she went to Charles he would give her money. She did, and Charles had given her £50. What had she done with it? 'I repaid *a loan* with some of it to Dr Ward.' This was obviously not quite the answer that Griffith-Jones expected because he returned to it. 'Can you tell the jury,' he said, 'what proportion, roughly speaking, of the money you received from men you gave to the defendant while you were at Wimpole Mews?' The answer he wanted was 'one half' – the proportion he had given in his opening speech. But Keeler's reply was significantly different: 'Well, I usually owed him more than I ever made; I only gave him half of *that* [i.e. what she owed him].'

Griffith-Jones had more success with Christine Keeler on the charges against Ward to do with procuring. She confirmed Griffith-Jones's account of how Ward had got her to approach Miss R., the shop assistant, and Sally Norie in the restaurant. And he managed to imply that these were not isolated instances. 'You are telling us that it became the understood thing that you find girls for him?' he asked Keeler. 'Yes,' she replied. In case the jury began to wonder why Keeler had therefore not also been charged with procuring, the judge explained that the prosecution had given an undertaking not to take action against her.

Ward's counsel, James Burge, then rose to cross-examine Keeler. His approach was very much to the point. 'You know the prosecution are endeavouring to prove that Ward had been living on the earnings of prostitution?' Keeler said she did. 'When you were living at 17 Wimpole Mews, is it right to say that you were frequently hard up for money?' Keeler replied, 'Yes.' Burge went on to elicit from Keeler that she was living rent-free at Ward's flat, and had the use of telephone, lights and hot water. However, when she had money she sometimes made small payments to Ward. 'But you never returned to the accused as much as you got from him?' Burge asked. Keeler's answer was firm. 'No,' she said.

There remained the problem of 'Charles' [Clore]. Burge asked Christine Keeler, 'Are you really saying it's true that the accused asked you to go and get fifty pounds from . . . ' Keeler interrupted him. 'He never *asked* me. He *suggested* that I could get some money from Charles because I was hard up.' – a very different version from that of the prosecution. The judge then pressed Keeler to tell the court exactly who Charles was. 'You have remembered Charles. And you have remembered he lived in a house off Park Lane and you have told me that you did know his name. Take your time. What was his name?' But Christine, for whatever reason, wanted to protect Clore and replied immediately, 'I really can't remember what it was.'

Christine Keeler was the prosecution's principal witness. At the end of her evidence, how did the case against Ward stand? At this stage of the trial a reasonable assessment would be: Christine Keeler had been living in part on Ward's earnings, rather than the other way around. He had, however, used her to help him pick up girls, some of whom subsequently went to bed with him.

One of these girls took the witness stand the next day. Sally Norie, a quiet, attractive girl in a black dress, gave her evidence in a soft, educated whisper. She had met Ward in a restaurant and had gone out with him a number of times. She had grown to like him, their affair developed and eventually she was intimate with him. It was not the first affair she had had or the last. And to Burge's question in cross-examination: 'I don't suppose you thought that you were participating in criminal activities during this time?' She replied, as would almost anyone, 'No, I didn't.'

So Sally Norie's evidence confirmed the account outlined by the prosecution (and largely repeated by Christine Keeler) except in one important aspect. Griffith-Jones in his opening speech had said that Sally Norie had gone to bed with Ward and '*was introduced to other men*', with the implication that this was for sexual intercourse. Yet there had not been even the slightest suggestion in Norie's evidence that Ward had done this. Griffith-Jones simply failed to substantiate the earlier charge.

Miss R.'s evidence was of even less use to the prosecution. She was an Austrian 22-year-old, rather heavily built, pretty, and dressed in a blue skirt and white sweater. She agreed that Ward had come to know her through Christine who was a customer in the shop where she worked. He had taken her out several times and eventually she had gone to bed with him on a visit to the Cliveden cottage. She agreed with Burge that this was not the first time she had been to bed with a man and that she had had affairs before she came to England.

The two-way mirror episode came up next. Miss X, aged nineteen, a tall brunette in a pink dress, told the court how she had been introduced to Ward, had gone out with him, and had met him by appointment on the afternoon they had the conversation about the two-way mirror. She confirmed the facts as earlier outlined by the prosecution – that Ward had said he did not want her to watch through the two-way mirror but to perform on the other side. But she was sufficiently honest to negate the whole legal importance of the story with her answers to just two questions posed in cross-examination by James Burge. 'The question I put to you,' said Burge, 'is that the proposition about your performing was a bad joke in bad taste?' Miss X replied, 'I thought it was.' Burge then asked, 'It was not a serious proposal at all? Miss X said, 'No.'

Mandy Rice-Davies's evidence was another matter. She appeared in the witness box in a simple grey dress and a little petalled hat, a saucy-looking 18-year-old, very confident and unabashed by her surroundings. From the beginning the names came tumbling out. 'Who paid the rent of the flat at Comeragh Road?' – 'Lord Astor.' 'Who introduced you to Lord Astor?' – 'Stephen, the defendant.' 'Did you have intercourse with him?' – 'Not when he paid the money. Two years later.' 'Were you having intercourse with any man or men at Comeragh Road?' – 'Peter Rachman. Douglas Fairbanks. A boyfriend of mine.' 'Were you paid by anyone?' – 'No. Except Peter Rachman. He kept me. I had a weekly allowance.'

Next, Griffith-Jones drew from Mandy a story which, if true, did establish that Ward intended to benefit from Mandy's immoral earnings. She said that Ward had been behind with his rent so he had asked her if she could borrow £250 for him from a man named Billy Ropner. She said that she did not fancy Ropner, did not go to bed with him, and did not ask him for the loan. But Griffith-Jones got from her the point he wanted to make. 'I only want to know what the idea was. Was the idea that you should go to bed with him and then borrow the £250?' Mandy said it was.

The prosecution next moved on to the Indian doctor, Emil Savundra. (He was referred to only as 'the Indian doctor' throughout the trial.) Rice-Davies said she had first met him with Ward in a coffee bar in Marylebone High Street. Later Ward asked if she liked him. She said she had and Ward had then said, 'He is a very rich man and wants to have your room because he has got a girlfriend and it is very difficult for him to take her anywhere . . . If you like the doctor, why let his girlfriend go out with him? Why don't you go out with him?'

Mandy said she would like to see Savundra again and he came round to the flat the next day. She had intercourse with him. He began to come to the flat every second or third day. The smallest amount he gave her after intercourse was £15 and the largest £25. She had given Ward, in all, about £25 and in addition she had paid for the food. Then came what would, in retrospect, turn out to be a very important question. Griffith-Jones asked Mandy, 'Apart from the £20 or so from modelling and what the Indian doctor was paying you and what I gather Mr Ropner gave you, had you any other money coming in?' Mandy Rice-Davies replied, 'What Stephen gave me.'

The Defence Counsel, James Burge, set out in cross-examination to show that Mandy Rice-Davies had been under police pressure to say what they wanted her to say; that she was not averse to telling lies; that she resented the fact that Ward had taken over her old flat in Bryanston Mews, and that she hoped to make big money out of the case. He was only partially successful. He persuaded Mandy to tell the court about the motoring charges, her spell in prison, the visit there from Herbert and Burrows, and the theft charge over the television set. And then he said, 'In those circumstances you have given this account of the Indian doctor?' To this Mandy replied, 'Yes, sir.'

Burge got her to admit that at West London Magistrate's Court, the magistrate, Seymour Collins, said of her that if she wanted to get something and get it by a lie then she would lie. Burge got her to agree that she thought the Bryanston Mews flat should be hers by right because of her relationship with Rachman and that she did not like Ward being there. And she said that it was true that she had been negotiating with a number of newspapers to sell her story and was still under contract to a daily paper. When Burge asked if she realised that, because of British libel laws, her story would not have the same value if Ward was acquitted, Mandy replied, 'I hope he is acquitted.'

But Burge failed to budge Mandy on the most damaging part of her evidence – that she had been to bed with the Indian doctor in Ward's flat in Wimpole Mews and had given Ward some of the money that the doctor had given her. For Ward's defence on this point was inhibited by his desire to keep his friends out of the case. His defence, in a nutshell, was that Mandy's assignations with the Indian doctor took place after she had left Wimpole Mews and had gone to live with Christine Keeler in a flat in Great Cumberland Place, in which case the prosecution's case virtually collapsed. The only way that Burge could raise this, was by a direct question to Mandy on these lines. As might be expected, since to say otherwise would prove her earlier evidence was lies, she denied it. It would be 'quite wrong' to say that, she replied.

But Burge did manage to show that Griffith-Jones's accusation that Ward had persuaded Mandy to sleep with Savundra by saying 'Why let outsiders in?' was a distortion of an entirely innocent remark by Ward. Burge got Mandy to agree that she had asked Ward to let the room in his flat to her. Ward had replied that he was thinking of letting it to an Indian doctor. Burge then said, 'Did he say he would sooner have you whom he knew rather than an outsider coming in?' Mandy replied, 'Yes, sir.'

Margaret (Ronna) Ricardo was the prostitute who had been approached by the police to give evidence against Ward. Herbert and Burrows, as we have seen, threatened to have her sister and Ronna's own daughter taken into care unless she co-operated. At first Ricardo agreed. At the Magistrate's Court hearing her evidence had been damning. She had said that Ward had invited her to his Bryanston Mews flat and on each occasion she had been asked to stay behind to meet somebody. Men had arrived and she had gone to bed with them. On another occasion she had gone with Ward to a flat in Grosvenor Square. 'He introduced me to a man but I can't remember his name. I had sex with this man in the flat. He gave me a pony.'

But after having given this evidence, Ricardo had gone both to Scotland Yard and to the *People* newspaper and had made statements taking back most of what she had previously said. The truth was that she had been to Ward's Bryanston Mews flat only once. The only person she had had intercourse with had been her boyfriend. Ward had never introduced her to men with whom she had slept for money. Her statement to Scotland Yard concluded: 'The statements which I have made to the police were untrue. I made them because I did not want my young sister to go to a remand home or my baby taken away from me. Mr Herbert told me they would take my sister away and take my baby if I didn't make the statements . . . I believed what Mr Herbert said and so I made the statements – three or four of them – and gave my evidence. I don't want to give false evidence again, particularly at the Old Bailey. I told my solicitor about this and he advised me to tell someone about it. This afternoon I went to the office of the *People* newspaper and made a statement to them. That is my signature on it. I just want everyone to know why I committed perjury.'

There was a long bout of questioning by Griffith-Jones aimed at getting Ronna Ricardo to admit that she had originally told the truth and had then changed her evidence in order to sell her story to the *People*. When he failed to shake Ricardo, Griffith-Jones, helped occasionally by the judge, then pressed her to explain why, if she had indeed been leaned on by the police, she had not complained to anyone. 'Who could I complain to?' she said. Her other explanations for making statements to the police were in keeping with this answer – 'I thought if I helped them, they'd help me . . . At the police station I was kept so long I was ready to sign anything . . . I was told I would not have to give evidence.'

But, courageous though Ricardo's turn-about was, that part of her evidence which she agreed was true must have harmed Ward in the eyes of the jury. It did not reveal any criminal behaviour but helped highlight the prosecution's picture of Ward's moral character – that of a sexual reprobate. On the one occasion she went to Ward's flat, Ricardo said, she was there with her boyfriend, her girlfriend and Ward. She had intercourse with her boyfriend, and her girlfriend had intercourse with Ward. Then Griffith-Jones, helped by shocked interventions from the judge, dragged the details out of her. 'In the same room?' – No answer. 'All four of you together?' – Ricardo nodded. 'Were you all taking part together?' – Ricardo nodded again. The judge took over. 'I want to know what happened in that room, the four of you together. Was there anything *beyond* sexual intercourse?' Ricardo must have been puzzled by this question, but she shook her head and the judge accepted this as an answer. Griffith-Jones left it at that. He had made his point that Ward was a man who went in for sexual foursomes.

The next witness was Vickie Barrett. She was the prostitute the police had arrested for soliciting and in whose diary they had discovered Ward's telephone number. They had told her that if she did not give evidence against Ward, 'You'll never be able to show your face in Notting Hill again.'

Barrett turned out to be a small, elf-like blonde. She wore a green raincoat and a white neckscarf and seemed terrified of the court and its officers. The writer Rebecca West later described her as looking like a photograph for a famine relief appeal. Yet, frightened and alone, she was to play a dramatic part in this case. Griffith-Jones took her slowly through the sordid details of her story. It was largely as he had outlined in his opening speech. But then came a variation. On one occasion Ward did not give her a contraceptive. Instead, when she went into the bedroom there was a cane on the bed. At the man's request she used the cane on him, wearing only her underwear and high-heeled shoes. On other occasions she used a horsewhip to beat two or three men. The men were middle-aged or elderly. The market price for these beatings was £1 a stroke. For sexual intercourse the price was £5. Ward had never given her any of this money, although he had bought her some clothes.

Ward's reply to all this emerged during cross-examination by his counsel, James Burge. He had picked up Vickie Barrett near Oxford Street and had twice paid her for her services – that was all. Indeed, Burge quickly established that Barrett was a liar. He asked her if she knew a man called Douglas Burns, a photographic agent. Barrett said she did; she had last seen him either three weeks earlier, or the previous week – she was not certain; she had not come to court with him that morning. But Burge was later shown a photograph of Barrett arriving at the Old Bailey with Burns. When Burge taxed her with this she agreed that she had lied because 'I thought I might get him [Burns] into trouble'. She also admitted that she had lied about her business relationship with Burns – there was an agreement being negotiated for Burns to sell photographs of Barrett to the Press.

Detective Chief Inspector Samuel Herbert gave his evidence in the voice that all policemen use in court – clear, flat and expressionless. A heavily-built man in a brown–green suit, he brushed aside all suggestions that the police had put improper pressure on Ronna Ricardo or any other witness. He agreed that he had approached Mandy Rice-Davies on two occasions to give evidence about Ward – in Holloway Prison and at West London Court before she was due to appear there. But he denied that to approach her at such vulnerable moments could be construed as putting pressure on her. He agreed that he had gone personally to London Airport to detain Mandy over the case of the television set. Burge asked him: 'Are you really saying that a Chief Inspector went down to London Airport because you felt that a woman was leaving the country because she had stolen an £82 television set?' Herbert replied, 'Yes.'

It was left to the judge to save Herbert from the ridicule this reply would have brought. He asked, 'If you by legal rights had certain powers that you could exercise would you hesitate to exercise them in order to keep a witness in this country?' Herbert said no. 'Would you have been doing your duty if you had failed to prevent her going abroad in certain circumstances?' Herbert said, 'I think, Sir, I would have been failing in my duty.' The law at the time was that the police could not stop someone from leaving the country unless there was a specific charge. The police used this to allow Keeler to leave the country before the Edgecombe trial, but, although Mandy was restrained from leaving, she was never formally charged.

Herbert spent some time in the witness box trying to explain why he had not taken a statement from Ward after he had arrested him on 8 June and had taken him to Marylebone Lane Police Station. Although he and Burrows had questioned Ward for an hour and a half, he said, 'it did not strike me to ask the defendant to make a written statement'. He said that Ward was frequently cautioned and therefore should have realised that what he said might be used in evidence.

So instead of a written statement by Ward, the court had only Herbert's statement (later backed by Burrows) of what he alleged Ward had told him. There were only two passages which seemed damaging to Ward. According to Herbert he asked Ward, 'Where did Mandy get her money?' and Ward replied, 'She seemed to have plenty of boyfriends. I cannot help it if they gave her money.' Herbert said he had also asked Ward, 'Did you know she had sexual intercourse with different men at your flat and received money?' To this Herbert said Ward replied, 'I thought she might have done, but it was nothing to do with me. I was not always there.'

Ward's counsel challenged Herbert's account of Ward's verbal statements in the police station, but largely on minor points. On the whole, Herbert's evidence (and that of the other police officers Burrows, Eustace and Glasse) was accepted as being true as far as it went. There was a simple reason for this, one which Arthur Eustace put very succinctly 22 years after the trial. In 1985 he told us, 'There was nothing for the police to lie about when all the witnesses were lying.'

Burge had shown that Vickie Barrett was not averse to telling lies when it suited her. He now recalled that Christine Keeler did the same. To counter Christine's evidence that Ward had introduced her to marijuana, he had earlier asked her whether, on the contrary, Ward was so concerned about her use of it that he had taken her to Scotland Yard for counselling by officers of the narcotics squad. Keeler had denied that such a visit had ever taken place. Now Burge confronted her with a statement from the narcotics officer who had advised her, confirming the visit. Trapped in the lie, Keeler reluctantly admitted the truth.

That ended the prosecution case. How strong was it? Griffith-Jones had succeeded in establishing that Christine Keeler and Mandy Rice-Davies took money for sex. He had shown that both girls gave money to Ward. Even though, given that in law the dividing line between living *with* a prostitute and living *on* a prostitute is very thin, the prosecution's weak point was that both girls owed Ward – one way or another – far more money than they ever paid him. In his opening speech Griffith-Jones had said of Ward, 'Whatever the extent of his earnings for this period may have been, from the evidence you will hear, and indeed from what he has told the police, they were quite obviously not sufficient for what he was spending.' Yet no evidence had been brought to show this at all; in fact the police admitted that they had been unable to find out what Ward's earnings were. Ronna Ricardo had gone back on her evidence given in the Magistrate's Court and Vickie Barrett's evidence was somewhat suspect because she had been shown as willing to lie if she felt it necessary. The two procuring charges had been exposed as ludicrous. Ward must have been feeling cautiously optimistic as his counsel, James Burge, rose to open the case for the defence.

# 34 | *A Spirited Defence*

Ward had decided to retain Burge's services for his Old Bailey trial – even though Burge was not a Queen's Counsel – because he had been impressed with the way he had handled the hearing in the Magistrate's Court. Some of his friends thought that this was a mistake. Burge, a large jovial man, always ready with a smile, was witty and intelligent. But he had spent most of his time at the Bar doing licensing cases and defending motorists on drunken driving charges. His best days at the Bar were behind him and as he says himself he began with a handicap – he was convinced Ward was innocent. 'It's much more difficult to defend someone you are one hundred per cent sure is innocent because of the strain and anxiety of having to prove it,' he told us. On top of that, Marshall placed the burden of proof on the defence to prove Ward innocent, rather than on the prosecution to prove him guilty and then directed the jury accordingly.

Moreover, it appeared to those in court that the judge did not like Burge. He employed some of the tricks that small-minded judges use in British courts to put down counsel they do not care for; in this instance Sir Archie Marshall would, when addressing Burge, allow a long pause between the title and the surname: 'Mister . . . Burge.' This gave the jury the impression that Burge was so unimportant that the judge had difficulty in remembering who he was.

The acoustics of the courtroom were not the best and Burge had frequently to ask a witness to repeat the answer to his question. On these occasions the judge would sometimes intervene and repeat the answer himself (he was closer to the witness box than Burge). When he did this the judge would raise his voice, speak slowly, and enunciate each syllable as if Burge were a 5-year-old child. But Burge was a fighter, and, as he launched into Ward's defence, he was not about to give up.

Burge made three important points: the effort the police had put into the case was out of all proportion to the offence; Ward's case had been prejudiced by the widespread publicity which followed the Magistrate's Court hearing; and the prosecution's case was based more on moral outrage than on evidence. 'For months on end following the declaration in the House of Commons on 22 March, the police have combed the country in a frenzy in order to find evidence implicating the accused,' Burge said. 'After the earlier publicity, before he ever had a trial, before any evidence was offered, quite obviously it was thought that [Ward] *was* a procurer and a man who lived upon the earnings of prostitution . . . Although public opinion has obviously been horrified by the scandal that was raised through no fault of this man, and therefore demands expiation, some speedy sacrifice so that the matter can be established and disposed of and forgotten, that is not a consideration that will affect you in deciding the issue here.'

The first witness for the defence was Ward himself. He gave his evidence in a firm, clear voice that impressed many in the court with its power and personality. The juror we interviewed recalled, 'They were two of a kind – Griffith-Jones and Ward. We were impressed by their military bearing, the way they spoke and behaved. We were captivated by both of them. We wouldn't have noticed if there had been no one else in the courtroom.'

Ward had simple explanations for most events that the prosecution had cast in a criminal light. Describing the matter of the rent for the Comeragh Road flat, Ward, still protecting Astor, said, 'I had seen that the two girls were broke. They were contemplating doing a moonlight flit and were anxious about it. I happened to mention it to Lord Astor in conversation one day. He said he would give me a cheque and I could pay him back later. It was a personal loan to me and, in fact, I gave it direct to the landlord. It didn't seem to have any sinister implication.'

Ward dealt with the financial arrangements between him and Christine Keeler and Mandy Rice-Davies. Christine had been living rent-free and during the time she was at Wimpole Mews he had given her £70–80. She had repaid some of it. Mandy had paid £6 a week rent, even though the room was worth far more. Her total payments for herself and her parents when they had come to stay at the flat after her attempted suicide would have come to about £24 for the two-month period plus £5 or £6 for the telephone.

Ward made a telling point about Christine Keeler, and about Vickie Barrett's evidence. He said that during the very time he had been accused of living off Christine Keeler's immoral earnings he believed his flat was under observation by MI5 officers because he had told them about Keeler's relationship with Profumo. Would he really have lived on the earnings of prostitution at that address at a time it was being watched by law officers? And during the period that

Vickie Barrett claimed that she was visiting Ward's flat to have intercourse with some men and to whip and cane others, not only was his flat besieged by journalists, but he had a house guest, a girl called Sylvia Parker, sleeping on the sofa in the living room. (Parker, a friend of Tom Corbally, repaid Ward's hospitality by coming from Rome at her own expense to give evidence confirming this, saying she had seen nothing of Vickie Barrett.) Ward agreed that he knew Vickie Barrett. He said he had picked her up in Tottenham Court Road and had taken her back to his flat where he sketched her, had intercourse with her, and paid her £2. The rest of her story was lies, he said. 'If this girl is telling the truth, then I am guilty. My case must depend on saying this girl is lying, and why she is lying we must find out.'

Griffith-Jones devoted much of his cross-examination to attacking Ward's morals. 'So we start this story, do we, with a man of forty-eight or forty-nine chasing two girls of sixteen.' – 'Quite so, Sir.' 'With nothing in common except sex.' – 'I wouldn't have said that, Sir.' 'Let's just get the picture. Here are two thoroughly promiscuous girls set up in a flat for which you are arranging to pay the rent and introducing them to men much older than themselves, with some of whom they appear to have gone to bed?' – 'It is a false picture.'

Ward returned to this point later, arguing that by compressing incidents into a short space of time, Griffith-Jones was giving a false picture of his lifestyle at Wimpole Mews. 'Most of the time I was playing bridge or drawing.' When Griffith-Jones made a catalogue of Mandy's lovers Ward said, 'During the whole of that three and a half year period she was in my flat for six weeks only and you are making me responsible for all the relationships during that period . . . I met her half a dozen times in Comeragh Road and for the next year barely at all . . . She was a pretty girl and she was taken out by people. There wasn't a question of living off her. *If anything, she was living off me.*'

Griffith-Jones summed up Ward's evidence with a series of loaded questions. If he was telling the truth then Keeler was lying, even though he had helped her from the beginning, tried to stop her smoking marijuana, tried to get her out of Rachman's hands? Ward said yes, Christine was lying. 'It may be a variety of things which caused her to do this. She has committed certain stories [to] the papers . . . ' Griffith-Jones said that Ward would have it that Mandy Rice-Davies was lying too, even though he had helped her with the rent, had her parents to stay and had done a lot for her. Ward said yes, Mandy was lying. 'We have her own admission that it was malice . . . After she came back from Rachman her character had changed and I told her parents, and she turned viciously against me.'

Ricardo was originally lying? Griffith-Jones asked. Vickie Barrett was lying? 'Yes,' Ward said with great emphasis, hitting the side of the witness box with his hand. 'This is the bottom of the bucket. If they question 150 or 160 people it is easy to find at least half a dozen willing to come forward through some motive – malice, cupidity – who will make some statements against a person who has some sort of irregularities in life such as I have and who lays himself open to this type of representation.'

Burge's re-examination was brief. His main questions, highly relevant to the charges of living on immoral earnings, were to do with Ward's income. Ward said he was earning about £4,000 from his practice and another £1,500 or so from his drawings – a total of between £5,000 and £6,000 a year. (In today's values about £50,000.) 'If the prosecution's picture of a man procuring, and the picture of people in high places and very wealthy men was true, would you have needed to carry on your practice and work as an osteopath?' Burge asked. 'If that were true, evidently not,' Ward replied.

Ward had given a good account of himself. But the jury was less influenced by his carefully-worded replies than by two damaging questions put to him, one by Griffith-Jones and one by the judge. In the middle of Ward's admission that he had picked up a prostitute, Griffith-Jones suddenly said, 'Are your sexual desires absolutely *insatiable*?' Ward answered carefully, 'I don't think I have more sexual relationships than any other people of my age, but possibly the variety is greater.'

Then, just as Ward was about to leave the witness box, the judge said, 'Dr Ward, when do you say a woman is a prostitute?' Ward thought for a moment and then replied, 'It is a very difficult question to answer, but I would say when there is no element in the relationship between the man and the woman except a desire on the part of the woman to make money, when it is separated from any attachment and indeed is just a sale of her body.' The Judge pressed Ward further. 'If anyone does receive a payment when the basis is sexual is she not in your view a prostitute?' he asked. Ward said that when sentiment or other factors entered into the relationship, it became a more permanent relationship, like a kept woman. 'You cannot possibly refer to such a woman as a prostitute,' he said.

The significance of this exchange was not lost on the jurors. The judge's questions had made it clear that in his view a kept woman was as much a prostitute as a woman who plied the streets, whereas Ward's view was that kept women were no more prostitutes than women who married for money. In the judge's view, therefore, both Christine and Mandy were prostitutes. And since Ward was living *with* them, the onus was on him to prove that he was not living *off* them. In Ward's view the girls were not prostitutes. The jurors would have to decide which view they would accept.

The court adjourned until Monday. Ward was staying in the flat of a friend, Noel Howard-Jones, the former law student whose rent he had once paid when Howard-Jones was a waiter at the Brush and Palette Restaurant. But Ward and his latest girlfriend, Julie Gulliver, 22, did not want to spend the weekend in London, so they went off to the country. The *News of the World* had an article on Christine Keeler's life in the flat of her friend Paula Hamilton-Marshall. The others had brief reports on the trial. It was clear that the case would end sometime during the following week. They were waiting until then.

The last witness for the defence was Noel Howard-Jones. He said he frequently visited Stephen Ward. 'I knew perfectly well that Ward had a number of girlfriends and I knew perfectly well that he was a moral man. I found him extremely kind and entertaining. I never had the slightest suspicion that he was doing anything of the sort with which he is charged.' He added that he would not have brought his wife around if he had known Keeler was taking men there for sex.

But, as we have seen, Howard-Jones and Keeler were lovers and the prosecution knew this because Keeler had told the police. So now Griffith-Jones hit Howard-Jones with a sudden question: 'Did you have intercourse with Miss Keeler?' – 'Yes, Sir.' 'On how many occasions?' – 'Two or three occasions I believe, Sir.' 'At the flat?' – 'Yes.' Griffith-Jones let the answer hang heavily for several seconds. Howard-Jones hurried to add, 'May I say that this was before my marriage, when I met Miss Keeler.' But the damage had been done. The young man who had said he would not have taken his wife to a flat if he had thought anything immoral went on there had behaved immorally there himself. Another defence witness had been partly discredited.

Burge now made his closing speech for the defence. He began by reminding the jury what the case was *not* about. 'If this trial was concerned with establishing that Ward led a thoroughly immoral life, a demoralised and undisciplined life, your task would be a simple one. No one has thought to disguise that fact from you. If you wanted to make sure that the public conscience was shamed by a major scandal and should be appeased, and the penalty should be paid, you would hardly find a more suitable subject for expiation than Ward, who has admitted he is a loose liver and whose conduct is such as to deprive him of any sympathy from any quarter.'

But the case was about whether Ward was living off prostitutes' earnings, Burge said. If Ward had been living off Christine Keeler's earnings one would have expected her to be loaded with money and not have to borrow off him. Keeler was not to be trusted to tell the truth, he said. The Lucky Gordon appeal would show that. There were many reasons why Christine might be lying. 'Indeed, after all the interviews she had with the police and the Press she might, quite genuinely by now, be unable to distinguish between truth and fiction,' Burge said. As for Mandy Rice-Davies, the £6 a week which Mandy paid Ward for the bedroom at Wimpole Mews was a reasonable rent. 'Just as a lawyer or a greengrocer who receives a reasonable remuneration for services they are giving to a prostitute – not *as* a prostitute but as an ordinary person – is not guilty of living on her immoral earnings, so, in my submission Ward was *not* living on her immoral earnings *if* she was a prostitute.'

Burge said that for the prosecution to make its case, Keeler and Rice-Davies's evidence required corroboration. Ricardo's original evidence had done that but she had retracted it. Then, conveniently, Vickie Barrett had come on the scene. 'She turned up, did she not, at a very opportune moment for the prosecution. She comes out of the blue, just when she is wanted, on the very day of Ward's committal. She tells the story of an absolutely conventional ponce, which is entirely different to anything else in this case. A key witness emerges for the prosecution because there were great difficulties about the case of Miss Keeler and Miss Rice-Davies. What a turn-up for the book. I suggest to you it is too good to be true.' Burge reminded the jury of the evidence of Frances Brown, a prostitute who had volunteered to give evidence for Ward after reading about Barrett's testimony in the newspapers. Brown had said that she had been soliciting with Barrett nearly every night and would have known if Barrett had been going regularly to Ward's flat.

What, then, had been the role of the police in this matter? Burge was too experienced in courtroom tactics to accuse the police outright of framing Ward. But he managed to convey to the jurors that the police, too, had been under pressure during the Ward investigation. 'An important element in this case is that at the time the investigations started, public indignation had mounted following certain scandals. It was quite clear that something had to be done. Obviously the highest authorities were concerned with this investigation. It was a situation in which the police officers can either make their names or sink into oblivion. It is obviously a matter which they could go into with the knowledge of what was behind it and the knowledge that they have to do their very best to provide a case,' Burge said.

'A man would be clearly not human if he were not influenced in the enthusiasm of his inquiry by these considerations. [The police officers] have allowed their enthusiasm and the fear of the possibilities of failure, to spur on their investigation of the various witnesses and to colour their evidence in the interpretation of facts that are alleged to have been said on June 8 [the interview with Ward].'

Burge had one last point to make, the one he considered to be the key to the case. 'Was this life of Ward's led for fun or for profit?' he asked. 'Was he conducting a business, living as a parasite on the earnings of prostitution? It is a very, very wide gap and a big step between a man with an artistic temperament and obviously with high sexual proclivities leading a dissolute life, and saying he has committed the offence of living on the earnings of prostitution. On a fair and impartial view I will ask you to say that these charges have not been made out and find him not guilty.'

The prosecution in the criminal case in England has the advantage of the first and the last word. We have seen how Griffith-Jones took full advantage of his opening speech to blacken Ward's character. He now used this second chance to twist the knife. His closing address was not so much a review of the evidence as a story, a vividly told, cleverly constructed account of the life of Stephen Ward and his relationship with the women in the case. He used phrases and expressions more appropriate to a soap opera and he delivered them with an actor's skill. Stephen Ward became 'this filthy fellow'; Christine and Mandy became 'two girls of sixteen, recently in London from their homes in the country'; when Christine left Wimpole Mews and Mandy moved in, Ward was 'changing mounts'. The flavour of Griffith-Jones's act can be caught in this extract from his speech:

Having got the Comeragh Road flat and their rent paid for them, Ward pays them frequent visits, as he has admitted and he introduces a number of his friends, Astor and Fairbanks and certainly two others . . . Where are we getting to, members of the jury? Do you think if this is just brotherly interest and kindness he is going to take his friends round to those two girls in the flat? . . . Those two penniless, promiscuous little girls, setting up as they were, and then this West End osteopath, Dr Stephen Ward, trotting around there with his middle-aged friends . . . The evil of this, members of the jury, and it is evil, you may think, goes very deep. You may remember after his first meeting at the club, when he is trying to get his hands on her, this respectable Dr Ward not only rings Christine up but goes and sees her little people down at Staines. What for, unless to deceive?

Certainly we have come from the very depths of lechery and depravity in this case – prostitution, promiscuity, perversion and getting girls to go out and borrow money by giving their bodies for it. But you won't convict the defendant just because he was at the centre of all this and just because his homes at Wimpole Mews or Bryanston Mews were the pivot on which all this turned. While you will not convict for that reason alone, you may think that the fact that he was at the centre of it in itself lends the strongest inference that these charges which are now laid against him are true bills – that in fact he was taking money from these various women, money earned by prostitution. If you think that is proved, members of the jury, you may think *it is in the highest public interest* [emphasis added] to do your duty and return a verdict of guilty on this indictment.

It was a masterly performance and it is interesting to consider how it must have appeared to the jurors. The whole panoply of the State had brought them to the Old Bailey, surely not for nothing? The prosecutor, a man appointed by the State, had now told them that Ward was an evil, wicked, filthy fellow, and it was *in the highest public interest* that they should do their duty and convict him. It is understandable, therefore, that they missed the legal significance of an event that occurred in the closing stages of Griffith-Jones's speech. Appropriately it concerned that bane of Christine Keeler's life, Lucky Gordon.

# 35

# *An Unprecedented Intervention*

Herbert and Burrows, the leaders of the police investigating team, had set up Lucky Gordon at a time when they thought they might need him as a witness at Ward's trial, and also as a *quid pro quo* favour to Christine Keeler, to help her get rid of Gordon. They charged him with having assaulted Christine on 17 April at Paula Hamilton-Marshall's flat in Devonshire Street. As we have seen, Christine's injuries had actually been caused in a scuffle with Paula's brother John. Unknown to the police, two other West Indians, Fenton and Camacchio were at the flat when Gordon arrived and could, if necessary, give evidence that Gordon had *not* assaulted Keeler.

In the event, Herbert and Burrows decided not to put Gordon forward as a witness in the Ward trial, but by that time the fake assault charge against him had gone too far to be stopped. Christine was forced to go through with her false evidence and lie in the witness box, swearing that it was Gordon who had injured her. The police, too, were embarrassed because Gordon demanded that Fenton and Camacchio be produced as defence witnesses, and the police had to lie and say that they did not know where they were. In fact the police knew exactly where they were – Camacchio was actually on remand at the time.

Without his main witnesses, Gordon was convicted on 7 June and sentenced to three years' imprisonment. But then a series of rapid-fire events changed everything. A freelance journalist, Alastair Revie, had been engaged by Keeler's manager, Robin Drury, to ghost Keeler's story, working from Drury's 12-hour taped interview with her. When Revie heard what Keeler had to say on this tape, he wrote immediately to George Wigg, explaining: 'I believe the verbatim account I have sent contains vital new evidence in the Lucky Gordon case.' We can easily deduce what this evidence would have been – Christine's confession that she had helped the police to frame Gordon. Meanwhile Christine, realising how foolish she had been, made desperate efforts to shut up Fenton and Camacchio, first offering them money and then complaining to the police that Camacchio was blackmailing her.

But she was too late. Wigg had passed Revie's letter to the Attorney-General, Sir John Hobson, who acted quickly. The police suddenly managed to find Camacchio and Fenton. Camacchio made a statement exonerating Gordon and, by implication, accusing Keeler of lying. Robin Drury and Alastair Revie made statements about what Keeler had confessed about Gordon in her tape-recordings, and Paul Mann told the police what Fenton had revealed to him about the frame-up. John Hamilton-Marshall also made a statement agreeing that *he* had inflicted Keeler's injuries. (Ward offered to make a statement but was told it was not needed.) On application from Gordon's lawyer, the Lord Chief Justice, Lord Parker, gave Gordon leave to appeal against his conviction and ordered Drury to hand the Keeler tape to the police.

On Tuesday, 30 July, with Griffith-Jones at the Old Bailey about to launch into his closing speech, farther west, at the Court of Criminal Appeal in the Strand, three judges sitting an hour earlier than usual, took just nine minutes to quash Gordon's conviction. Lord Parker said simply that further statements had been taken by the police since Gordon's trial and that if this evidence had been before the jury at the time they might have felt a reasonable doubt about his guilt. Lord Parker said that 'for obvious reasons' it was inadvisable that the persons from whom the statements had been obtained should give any evidence to this court.

But where, then, did this put Christine Keeler? She had sworn on oath that Gordon *had* assaulted her. Two witnesses – Camacchio and John Hamilton-Marshall – and three people who knew about the frame-up – Drury, Revie and Mann – had now sworn that this was untrue. As a result, the Court of Criminal Appeal had been obliged to quash Gordon's conviction. By any rational interpretation, this meant that Keeler had been lying, and, indeed, the Court of Appeal ordered that the papers on the case should go to the Director of Public Prosecutions to see whether any action should be taken against her for perjury.

The importance of this cannot be emphasised too strongly, because during the Ward trial, Christine Keeler had been asked about her evidence in the Gordon case.

Burge: Did you take the oath on a previous occasion when you attended the trial of a man called Gordon? – Yes.
Did you tell the whole truth about that? –

Yes, I did.

Did you say that your injuries were caused by Gordon? – Yes, and they were.

And that he might wish to call two witnesses, one called Fenton and a man called Camacchio? – Yes.

And did you say that those two men were not present at the time of the incident? – Yes. I said that they were not present because they were not present.

So if Keeler had lied at the Gordon trial, then she had also lied at the Ward trial, and all her evidence there would have to be considered worthless. To appreciate the full significance of what now happened, we need to jump ahead to December that same year. For the Director of Public Prosecutions decided that indeed action should be taken against Keeler for perjury in the Gordon case. She was tried, convicted, and sentenced to nine months' imprisonment.

Yet Lord Parker went out of his way in announcing the Court of Appeal's decision, to say that the court was *not* holding that the evidence of Christine Keeler was untruthful and, in fact, she might well have been speaking the truth. Gordon's appeal had been allowed solely because the evidence from new witnesses might have raised a doubt in the jury's mind. As soon as the Lord Chief Justice had given his decision, it was immediately transcribed by the court shorthand writers, given to Lord Parker to check and revise, and then sent by special court messenger down The Strand to the Old Bailey.

So it was that Griffith-Jones, in the very middle of discussing Christine Keeler's truthfulness, had to try to explain to the Ward trial jurors the Court of Appeal's apparently contradictory ruling. 'Gordon's appeal has been upheld,' he announced. 'That does not of course mean to say that the Court of Criminal Appeal have found that Miss Keeler is lying. As I understand it from the note I have, the Lord Chief Justice said it might be that Miss Keeler's evidence was completely truthful, but in view of the fact that there were witnesses now available who were not available at the trial, it was felt that the court could not necessarily say that the jury in that case would have returned the same verdict as they did if those two witnesses had been called. That is all it amounts to.' Anyway, Griffith-Jones concluded, if the jury decided to convict in the Ward case, and should there later turn out to be anything relevant from the Gordon hearing, then Ward would be able to appeal, and no injustice would have been done.

But consider the circumstances. James Burge had raised the question of Christine Keeler's truthfulness by linking her evidence at the Ward trial with her evidence at the Gordon trial. In his closing speech he had invited the jury to treat her as a liar: Gordon's appeal was about to be upheld; Keeler would be marked as a perjurer; they could not possibly convict on her evidence. In these circumstances it was no accident that the Court of Criminal Appeal then sat early, rushed to release its decision, and then sent that decision post-haste to the Old Bailey.

We believe the purpose was to undermine Ward's defence. This is a serious accusation to make about the Lord Chief Justice and his fellow judges. But it is a view shared by eminent lawyers. Sir David Tudor-Price, one-time Common Serjeant at the Old Bailey who crowned a long and distinguished legal career by becoming a High Court judge, was junior counsel to James Burge at the Ward trial. Speaking of the affair 22 years later he was still angry.

'This was a matter that still rankles with me. It has left a burning sense of injustice. The only possible purpose of the Lord Chief Justice's action was to cut away the foundations of what James Burge had been saying to the Ward jury. The Court of Criminal Appeal said that it thought that Gordon's conviction was unsatisfactory, but it was not saying that Christine Keeler was a perjurer. Words to that effect were read out by Archie Marshall to the Ward jury in his summing up, for the very purpose of discrediting, or rather taking away, the value of the point made by James Burge. And that's something that I've never known done before or since. The Ward case was easily the most celebrated case in my whole career. I suppose I was young and impressionable, but I was left with an unpleasant taste in the mouth; that this really had not been just.'

There was one way in which the Court of Criminal Appeal could have justified its action. The Lord Chief Justice could have argued: Keeler's veracity is at issue in the Ward trial; Ward's counsel has raised the Gordon appeal as a test of that veracity; it is important, therefore, that in the interests of justice we indicate what bearing Keeler's truthfulness had on our decision to quash Gordon's conviction.

But this argument collapses for one simple reason. The Lord Chief Justice and his fellow judges made their decision on Gordon's appeal without *hearing* the evidence of the witnesses who accused Keeler of lying. The judges *read* the statements and then made their decision without revealing what the statements said. Thus the public was deprived of the chance to learn in open court what the evidence was that revealed Keeler as a liar – evidence so strong that Keeler, as we have seen, later went to jail for perjury.

There can have been only one reason why the judges in the Court

of Criminal Appeal decided to conceal from the public the evidence
the three witnesses had given about Keeler's truthfulness: if the court
had revealed the evidence and the Lord Chief Justice had then said
that Christine might have well been speaking the truth, there would
have been laughter from one end of London to the other.

The fact that the evidence was *not* made public negates any claim
that the Court of Criminal Appeal was interested only in justice at the
Ward trial. For if the Ward trial jurors had been able to assess the
evidence that Keeler had lied at Gordon's trial – and had therefore
lied on oath again at the Ward trial, when Burge had asked her about
it – then they could never have reached the verdict they did. Our
conclusion is that Lord Chief Justice Parker and the Court of
Criminal Appeal acted the way they did so as deliberately to
undermine Ward's defence.

# 36

# The Need for a
## Sacrifice

Ignorant of the Court of Criminal Appeal's ruling, the Ward jury
spent the rest of Tuesday afternoon listening to the judge's summing
up. To read today what Mr Justice Marshall had to say is to read a
carefully-balanced précis of the case with a clear explanation of the
legal definitions and interpretations. This is not how those in court
remember it.

The French, who have an ear for these things, solved the paradox.
'However impartial he tried to appear,' the *France Soir* reporter
wrote, 'M. Marshall was betrayed by his voice. M. Marshall is a
Puritan, and Ward, the debauched libertine, the cynic, horrified him.
True, the judge's summing up was completely impartial if one were
content only to read it; the arguments for the defence get the same
prominence as those for the prosecution. But each time M. Justice
Marshall explained to the jury the questions they would have to
answer, his voice revealed all – M. Marshall did not like Ward, the
man who had brought scandal down on England.'

Ludovic Kennedy, in court throughout for his book, *The Trial of
Stephen Ward*, agreed. 'It was not that the Judge had omitted what
was favourable to Ward – the record belied that. It was, simply, a
question of emphasis. When the Judge was pointing out to the jury
those things in Ward's favour, he then did so in a matter-of-fact
voice. He appeared so uninterested in what he was saying that one
could not be interested oneself: the mind automatically shut off from
him. Yet when he came to matters which told against Ward, his tone
changed: his voice and bearing became brighter, livelier; he held the
attention whereas elsewhere he had lost it. It was this that made the
summing up seem so one-sided . . . All the people I talked to who
were in court that day agreed that we had heard a "hanging" summing
up.'

Ward himself certainly thought so. Throughout the trial he had
been his cheerful self. He was sufficiently intelligent, however, to
realise the danger he was in. 'It's an extraordinary predicament. There
must have been motives that started the police inquiry other than just

an interest in my sex life. I think that primarily the thing was that I knew and liked a Russian. It may sound rather far-fetched to say that this is in the nature of a McCarthyist witch hunt, but I have no doubt at all.

'One of my great perils is that at least half a dozen of the people [witnesses] are lying and their motives vary from malice to cupidity and fear . . . In the case of both Christine Keeler and Mandy Rice-Davies there is absolutely no doubt that they are committed to stories which are already sold or could be sold to newspapers and that my conviction would free these newspapers to print stories which they would otherwise be quite unable to print [for libel reasons].

'Therefore, not only do these two witnesses have a vested interest in doing what they are doing, but it's also quite clear from their behaviour that they are being primed to do so. Christine Keeler has already admitted in court that she was using the words of her ghost writer. There is a strong vested interest because their stories will be valuable only in the event of my conviction. This is a grave peril. One can see how easy it is in the atmosphere prevailing at this time, almost an atmosphere that might make the witnesses feel that they were doing a public duty in getting me convicted.'

But despite this astonishingly accurate summary of what was happening, Ward remained confident. He kept busy during the hearings, passing a stream of notes to his solicitor, Jack Wheatley, and to his counsel, James Burge, or sketching those taking part. He seemed supremely confident. At the end of each day's events, when he was allowed to leave the dock, he would chat briefly with his lawyers, wait for his bail to be renewed, and then leave quickly by taxi.

He had remained certain of acquittal almost to the last. He told his counsel, Burge and Tudor-Price, 'I've got absolute faith in British justice. I'm not guilty of these matters, and I've got great faith in British justice.' Burge, who knew more about the vagaries of British justice than Ward, had tried to warn him. 'Well, you know, you're going to have a very hostile summing up from this Judge. Marshall is dead against you and he's going to give you a loaded summing up.' Ward had smiled and repeated his expressions of confidence and faith.

But on that last day of his life Ward suffered two bitter humiliations that must have finally brought realisation that what he had considered unthinkable was about to occur – he would be convicted, he would be sent to jail, his life and reputation would be forever ruined, and his faith in British justice had been cruelly misplaced. The first blow was delivered with casual arrogance by

Griffith-Jones. In full flood in his closing speech he so misrepresented the evidence that Ward, in a rare loss of control, shouted 'No' from the dock. The judge warned him, and Ward apologised, saying, 'I am sorry, my Lord. It's a great strain.' Griffith-Jones jumped in. 'Of course it's a great strain,' he said, slowly and with deliberation, 'for a guilty man to hear the truth at last.'

Ward was still recovering from this public humiliation when the judge struck at him in an even more wounding manner. Ward, he said, had been abandoned by his friends. He made this point not only once, but twice, each time with a clear implication that only a guilty man would be left alone in this way. 'There may be many reasons why Ward has been abandoned in his extremity. You must not guess at them, but this is clear: if Stephen Ward was telling the truth in the witness box, there are in this city many witnesses of high estate and low who could have come and testified in support of his evidence.' Later the judge returned to this point. 'Many witnesses who could have been called have not been called in connection with the defence. They could have enormously strengthened the case concerning the earnings of prostitution.'

This last remark was debatable, but its effect on Ward had nothing to do with its validity in legal terms. It was a painful reminder that his English friends were prepared to allow him to go under so as to save their own reputations. (Three of his American friends had each independently sent him $1,000 to help with his legal costs.) Vasco Lazzolo and Noel Howard-Jones might be prepared to be cross-examined by Griffith-Jones on their sexual partners and preferences, but older, closer friends were not. This, and the fact that the jury were not to be allowed to assess Keeler's evidence in the light of the Appeal Court's decision in the Lucky Gordon case, and the whole tenor of the judge's summing up, made Ward give up hope. At the end of the day's hearing, Burge and Tudor-Price went to speak to him, to try to offer some comfort, but Ward was too upset even to discuss the case. Tudor-Price remembers, 'We wanted to talk about the Court of Appeal thing. But when we saw how desperately upset he was, all we could say was "You've still got the jury. Have faith in the jury even though the judge is hostile."'

Suppressing his distress, Ward left the court smiling as usual – 'I never saw a man put such a brave face on things,' wrote Ludovic Kennedy. But before he took a taxi to Howard-Jones's flat in Chelsea, he spoke briefly to Tom Mangold, a friend who was reporting the trial for the Daily Express, and he told him his real feelings. 'This is a political revenge trial,' he said. 'Someone had to be sacrificed and that someone was me.'

# 37 | To Disappoint the Vultures

Stephen Ward spent most of the evening writing letters. He gave them to Howard-Jones and told him that they were to be delivered only if he was convicted and sent to prison. He made one telephone call – to Tom Critchley, Denning's assistant – and tried to explain to him his true role in the whole affair. (Critchley could not have been impressed because the call was not mentioned in Denning's report.) At 9 p.m. he cooked a meal for himself and Julie Gulliver and at about 11 p.m. he drove her back to her flat in Bayswater. As he left her on her doorstep she said, 'Good luck for tomorrow, darling.' Howard-Jones vaguely remembers hearing Ward return about midnight, so perhaps in that last hour he drove his white, drop-head Jaguar around the streets of the West End, his neighbourhood for so many years.

He was no doubt thinking not only of the case but about a scathing review of his exhibition of sketches, currently at a Bloomsbury art gallery. That very day, a BBC radio art critic savaged the exhibition in a most personal manner, calling Ward 'a man of tiny talent'. Ward had realised that, no matter what the outcome of the trial, he had lost his friends and his practice. He had consoled himself with the thought that he might be able to start life all over again as an artist. Now this hope, too, was shattered.

Back at the Chelsea flat, Stephen Ward went to the kitchen, got a glass of water, and swallowed enough Nembutal tablets to kill a horse. He had persuaded his friend, Dr Teddy Sugden, to give them to him, saying, according to Sugden, that he had difficulty in sleeping. But Sugden's motives in providing the Nembutal are open to question. The police had warned Ward that even if he were acquitted at this trial, he would still have to face the more serious charge of helping to procure an abortion. The main evidence here was that Ward had given a pregnant girl Sugden's name as someone who could help her. So there was every possibility that if the second lot of charges against Ward had gone ahead, Sugden, the society abortionist, would have found himself in the dock too.

After taking the tablets, Ward sat down at the table and began his last letter. It was to Noel Howard-Jones, his friend and host, to whom he left his car. It is a dignified and logical explanation of what compelled him to take his own life:

Dear Noel,

I am sorry I had to do this here! It is really more than I can stand – the horror, day after day at the court and in the streets.

It is not only fear, it is a wish not to let them get me. I would rather get myself. I do hope I have not let people down too much. I tried to do my stuff but after Marshall's summing-up, I've given up all hope. The car needs oil in the gear-box, by the way. Be happy in it. Incidentally, it was surprisingly easy and required no guts.

I am sorry to disappoint the vultures. I only hope this has done the job. Delay resuscitation as long as possible.

The last line tailed off, as the drug began to take effect and the act of writing grew more difficult. When the cigarette he was smoking fell from his hand, Ward managed to reach a mattress on the floor which had been his bed. He then lost consciousness.

At 8.30 a.m. Noel Howard-Jones was awakened by the ringing of the telephone. It was Vasco Lazzolo's wife, Leila, calling, as she had done every day of the trial, to wish Ward luck. Since the telephone was in the lounge alongside Ward's bed Howard-Jones waited for Ward to answer it. When it went on ringing he got up to take the call himself. He saw Ward and knew immediately what had happened. 'His face was purple and he was foaming at the mouth, breathing only once every thirty seconds or so. I shouted his name and slapped his face but he didn't stir. I thought it was probably already too late, but I phoned 999 and waited for the ambulance. When they had taken him away I had a running fight all the way up the stairs to slam the door before the photographers could get in. They were bastards. They were waiting for us every day when we went to court.'

At the Old Bailey, the judge had barely taken his seat when Griffith-Jones rose and said, 'Ward is apparently ill. It is said that he has taken an overdose and is at the moment in St Stephen's Hospital. I have a certificate from a doctor which reads: "This man has been admitted to this hospital this morning. He will be unfit to attend court today."' Ward's solicitors had made further inquiries, Griffith-Jones added. 'They have told me that the hospital authorities say Ward will certainly not be well enough to attend here this week. With the Bank Holiday intervening, Tuesday would be the earliest day he could possibly attend.'

There followed a discussion between the judge and the two counsel on whether the trial could continue in Ward's absence. The judge decided that it could. Then, a little late, he said, 'I give instructions that the defendant shall immediately be put under surveillance. I shall give instructions for bail to be withdrawn from now on and normal steps to be taken for greater security.' It remains a mystery why the judge had not done this the previous day. It is the normal procedure in criminal trials to withdraw bail when the judge begins his summing up – so as to prevent just such an occurrence. If the custom had been followed in Ward's case it might well have saved his life.

From that moment on the trial was an anticlimax. The judge continued with his summing up and concluded by telling the jury, 'You now have to discharge your own responsible duty. The ball is in your court.' The jury, eleven men and one woman – took four and a half hours to bring in a verdict. They threw out the two charges of procuring. They dismissed the charge of living on Vickie Barrett's immoral earnings, but found Ward guilty of living on the immoral earnings of Christine Keeler and Mandy Rice-Davies. It is instructive to learn how they reached their decision. The juror we traced remembers:

'Most of us had already made up our minds when we heard about all the perversions and sex. You've got to remember that we weren't as liberal-minded as we are today. It was all very disgusting to us. But some of us found it odd because Stephen Ward didn't look like what he was supposed to have done. It was all a bit beyond our comprehension, these two-way mirrors and whippings and things. And to some of us even the charges at first meant very little. I didn't understand what it was to be living on immoral earnings. What swayed most of us was the prosecution lawyer, Griffith-Jones. He had such an air of utter supremacy that when the poor young man went into the dock he was already done for before he opened his mouth. By the time Griffith-Jones had finished his summing up most of us had already made up our minds. We were told that Ward was guilty by Griffith-Jones and the judge guided us towards the fact that he was indeed guilty.'

When the verdict was announced, the judge thanked the jury for their work and said he would wait until Ward was physically ready to appear in court. He would then come back and deal with him. The two charges concerning abortion would stand over until the next session. (This meant that no matter how the judge 'dealt' with Ward – and the sentence could have been anything from 5 to 14 years in prison – Ward would still have the abortion charges hanging over him.) The judge made a little joke with the jury; excusing them from further jury service for twenty years, he added, 'That may let some of you out altogether.' Finally he directed that the verdict be communicated to Stephen Ward.

Ward was in no state to receive it. He was dying. The hospital had placed him on a life-support system. He had suffered brain damage; he could not breathe without assistance; he had developed bronchial pneumonia and his heart was failing. On the morning of Saturday, 3 August, the hospital began to use respiratory stimulants offered by drug manufacturers, even though some were still in the very early experimental stage. For example, a drug manufactured by the U.S.-based pharmaceutical company, A. H. Robins, later known as Doxapram but then called only 619, was administered to Ward even though the company was still experimenting with the correct dosage in 1973, ten years later. It was all to no avail. Ward died at 3.50 p.m. without regaining consciousness. His bed was surrounded with bunches of flowers sent by well-wishers, all but one (from Susan Ward, no relation) anonymous!

The news reached Ward's counsel, James Burge, as he was strolling with his wife along the beach at Brighton where he lived at the time. He was overcome with emotion and wept. Christine Keeler heard a few hours later. She broke down completely and her doctor put her under sedation and refused to allow anyone to see her. That same night Charles Stainsby, the editor of *Today* magazine, who had followed the scandal from the beginning, was at a party and saw Mandy Rice-Davies there drinking champagne. 'She showed no visible signs of remorse or regret,' he says. 'I remember thinking at the time what a tough little bitch.'

The funeral service six days later was at Mortlake Crematorium. The six mourners, all men, included Ward's younger brother and his solicitor, Jack Wheatley. Apart from the wreath of roses from Ward's family, there was only one other wreath. It contained one hundred white carnations. It was from Kenneth Tynan, the playwright and critic; John Osborne, who had written *Look Back in Anger*; Annie Ross, the jazz singer; Dominick Elwes, who had stood bail for Ward; playwrights Arnold Wesker and Joe Orton; and Penelope Gilliatt, the critic. Their card said it all:

To Stephen Ward
Victim of Hypocrisy.

# 38 | *Mystery, Whitewash and Retribution*

The end of the trial and Ward's dramatic suicide swept the Profumo scandal off the British scene. It was as if one moment the newspapers had been full of only that and the next moment there was nothing. There had already been some tidying up of loose ends. Over the weekend of 27/28 July a well-dressed man had walked into the Bloomsbury art gallery which was selling Ward's drawings. (It sold 123 for a total of £11,517, which at that time meant that Ward would have been financially quite comfortable.)

The man selected every drawing of the Royal Family on show – including those of Prince Philip, Princess Margaret, the Duchess of Gloucester and the Duke of Kent – declined to give his name, paid with a bank draft for £5,000 and took the drawings away immediately. Frederick Read, who had arranged the exhibition, told some people that he had reason to believe that the money came from the Canadian newspaper magnate, Roy Thomson, who was elevated to the peerage a few months later. Another version was that the buyer was the Keeper of the Queen's pictures, Anthony Blunt.

Then there was the mystery of Ward's letter to the Home Secretary, Henry Brooke. On the night he killed himself Ward had a brief meeting with his journalist friend Tom Mangold, and the *Daily Express* photographer, Bryan Wharton. Wharton took some shots of Ward writing letters. One of the shots was looking over Ward's shoulder. Wharton remembers, 'As I focussed, I saw that the letter was addressed to Henry Brooke and that it contained a lot of names. I took the film in to the *Express* for processing that night. Next day, when I learnt that Ward was in hospital, I went straight to the *Express* to see the negatives. They had all disappeared.'

In retrospect we can see how the nation's focus of attention had moved during those last weeks from Profumo to Ward. What had at first appeared to be a national scandal had been turned into one man's wickedness. As might be expected in this atmosphere, the last burst of venom was reserved for the victim. Peter Earle wrote a profile of Ward in the *News of the World* the day after his death. He described

Ward as 'a cornered rat', an 'utterly depraved man' with 'a fiendish smile' and 'dirty hands now with ugly little marks on them.' He said that Ward had been 'a central figure of evil' and that 'quite literally my flesh crawled sometimes in his presence.' Earle concluded, 'By the end he was in a dour cuckoo-land of delusion, phoney innocence and snake-like cunning. Now that he is dead I am not surprised. I had known for a long time that he was a coward.'

There was some disquiet. George Gale wrote in the *Daily Express*: 'When the jury returned its verdict at 7.09 pm yesterday Stephen Ward was half guilty, half innocent, half dead, half alive, in the most deeply disturbing trial I have ever had the misfortune to witness.' But, in general any attempt to counter the picture of Ward as a sexually dissolute monster met with strong opposition.

Ward's art dealer, Hugh Leggatt, wrote a letter to *The Times* saying that dozens of men had pestered him to persuade Ward to sketch their wives or girlfriends. None had ever suggested that Ward had been guilty of the slightest impropriety. (This is corroborated by all those patients and fellow osteopaths of Ward's we have interviewed.) Leggatt said he was amazed that none of those men who had pestered him had come forward at the trial to say this on Ward's behalf. *The Times* refused to print the letter. (It eventually appeared in the *Daily Telegraph* and the *Evening News*.)

Harold Macmillan appeared on television while Ward was dying, to be interviewed by Kenneth Harris in what was described as the first step in his 'comeback'. Looking buoyant and confident he said some recent events had wounded him and pained him, and although political life as Prime Minister was sometimes hard and cruel it was 'a wonderful job'. Harris asked him if Lord Denning's report on the Profumo affair would be published, and the Prime Minister said, 'Oh yes. It will be published as a Command Paper.'

It was. Issued in September that year, it turned out to be a whitewash. The problem was in the nature of the inquiry. The Government had decided to use none of the established methods, Royal Commission or Judicial Inquiry, to establish the truth. Denning was required only to produce a personal report to Mr Macmillan, which many lawyers said was the worst possible use of a judge. As Denning himself complained, 'I have to be detective, inquisitor, advocate and judge.'

Ward was Denning's only villain. He attacked his politics and his personality. 'Ward', he said, 'admired the Soviet régime and sympathised with the communists. He advocated their cause in conversation with his patients, so much so that several became suspicious of him. He became very friendly with a Russian, Captain

Eugene Ivanov.' Since Denning published no notes, there is no way
of knowing on what evidence these accusations are based. Ward was
'utterly immoral'. He 'catered for those of his friends who had
perverted tastes.' He was 'ready to arrange for whipping and
other sadistic performances.' He 'kept collections of pornographic
photographs', and 'he introduced [Keeler] to the drug Indian hemp
and she became addicted to it.'

Again, there is no way of knowing what evidence Denning had for
these statements except this: Ludovic Kennedy reveals that he
telephoned one of the officials who had assisted Lord Denning and
that this official had told him that most of the allegations against
Ward had been provided by Christine Keeler, Mandy Rice-Davies
and other prosecution witnesses, including Vickie Barrett. But had
Denning not read the defence's answer to these allegations? According
to Kennedy, the official replied, 'Well, I dare say we were a bit unfair
to Ward there. We were under a lot of pressure, as I expect you
know, and we really didn't have time to read the report of the trial in
detail.'

So Denning had to rely largely on the witnesses he called. The
majority of these were against Ward. Some of Ward's friends who
wanted to speak up for him, like Stungo and Lazzolo, volunteered to
give evidence to Denning but were rejected. Friends who were
allowed to give evidence on Ward's behalf were disappointed to find
that what they had said was not included in Denning's report. This
was not all that Denning omitted. There is also an indication that MI5
told him of Ward's true role in the Ivanov 'honey-trap' operation but
Denning decided not to mention it. This comes in the statement of an
MI5 officer – 'Nowhere in the Denning Report does it say that Ward
was acting under our instructions. That is indeed unfortunate' –
which carries the clear implication that MI5 expected Denning to
mention this but that he chose not to do so.

In short, Denning is open to the criticism that he showed more
interest in the sex and rumour part of the affair than in security,
which was his brief. Many of the witnesses said that he quizzed them
on salacious and irrelevant details ('Mr Kennedy, can you tell me
what fellatio is?' . . . 'Mr Wigg, what do you know about the Duchess
of Argyll's affairs?' 'Mr Roth, do you know of any other politicians
involved in this affair?'), sending the official stenographer out of the
room when he thought that she might be embarrassed by the
evidence. He called Commander Michael Parker, Prince Philip's
equerry, to check out rumours of Ward's links to Buckingham
Palace.

More than 20 years later Lord Denning stands firm behind his conclusions. He told us that Ward was 'a really wicked chap' whereas Profumo was 'a man who was foolish; who was in a scrape, entwined with these monkeys, trying to prevent it coming out.' Some of the evidence about Ward was 'so filthy that I sent the shorthand writers out . . . one wouldn't do it nowadays, but all these perversions and so on!'

Lord Denning said, 'My impression of Ward then, whatever he may say himself, was that he really was utterly immoral. He did really get these girls out of nightclubs and then introduced them to his rich friends and patients. And the way he ran his establishment – all these two-way windows and all that sort of thing. I still think that it was a very wicked, corrupt, immoral set-up. He was using these girls quite wrongly, and he was the centre of immorality and vice.'

If the purpose of the Denning report was to end the Profumo affair for ever, it did not succeed. A sense of unease began to spread. Could *everything* have been Ward's fault? Could he really have been as filthy and corrupt as had been suggested? Was his trial a fair one? Ludovic Kennedy's book, *The Trial of Stephen Ward* revealed that the Lord Chief Justice, Lord Parker, had personally ruled that the transcript of Ward's trial should not be released. What was there to hide? Ward had always maintained that the main problem of mounting an effective defence to the charges made against him was that he would have to say that nearly all the prosecution witnesses were lying and that a jury would find this hard to accept. It now began to appear that Ward's accusation about the witnesses was right. One of the letters he had written on the last night of his life was to Vickie Barrett. 'I don't know what it was or who it was that made you do what you did,' he wrote, 'but if you have any decency left, you should tell the truth like Ronna Ricardo. You owe this not to me but to everyone who may be treated like me or like you in future.'

About half an hour after Ward's death, R. Barry O'Brien, a *Daily Telegraph* journalist who had given evidence on Ward's behalf, took a copy of this letter to Vickie Barrett's flat in Notting Hill Gate. He told Barrett that Ward was dead and then showed her the letter. Barrett began to cry, but kept repeating that her evidence was true. Then, after a few minutes she began sobbing violently and said, 'It was all lies. But I never thought he would die. I didn't want him to die. It was not *all* lies. I did go to the flat but it was only to do business with Stephen Ward. It was not true I went with other men.'

Barrett then told Barry O'Brien how Herbert suggested what evidence she should give and had threatened that if she did not do what he wanted she would never be able to show her face in Notting Hill again. O'Brien repeatedly asked her if she was telling the truth and now she insisted that she was. He said it was a very wicked thing to have lied at Ward's trial and Barrett replied, 'Yes, and I did it.' O'Brien said that he wanted her to come with him to Ward's solicitor Jack Wheatley and tell him the whole story. Barrett agreed to do so.

But when she went to repair her make-up, Barrett's landlady came to see her and persuaded her not to go. She further persuaded her to call Herbert and told O'Brien that Herbert was coming round. On Wheatley's advice O'Brien then went to Scotland Yard where he made a statement to the police about his conversation with Barrett. Barrett was scared of the police, like most prostitutes, and later retracted her admission to O'Brien and insisted that what she had said at the Old Bailey was true. But her emotional outburst on learning of Ward's death and the reasons she gave for lying – especially in the light of Ronna Ricardo's similar experience with the police – remain a much more likely account of what occurred than her subsequent frightened retraction.

In December of that year Christine Keeler pleaded guilty at the Old Bailey to perjury and was sent to jail for nine months. (She served six.) Of the three principal witnesses against Ward that left only the testimony of Mandy Rice-Davies still intact. But not for long. In January 1964 her memoirs were published by Confidential Publications Ltd under the title of *The Mandy Report*. In the book she revealed the pressure she had been under from the police to give the evidence she had. Now, at last, she told the truth about her relationship with Stephen Ward.

> Frankly, I thought the whole business [of the trial] was a farce. No one would deny that Stephen was a depraved and immoral man. But to suggest he made a living out of it is nonsense. Much was made of the fact that I was paying him a few pounds a week whilst I was living in Wimpole Mews. But I said before and I say it again – Stephen never did anything for nothing and we agreed on the rent the day I arrived. *He most certainly never influenced me to sleep with anyone, nor ever asked me to do so.* (Emphasis added.)

So Mandy's evidence at the trial that had resulted in Ward's conviction for living on her immoral earnings – her story that Ward had suggested she sleep with Dr Emil Savundra and with Ropner – turns out to have been untrue. Also untrue was the evidence she gave about her income during that period. Asked by Griffith-Jones what money she had coming in apart from Savundra's gifts and a little money from modelling, she had replied, 'What Stephen gave me.'

But now, in her book, Mandy revealed that while she was at

Wimpole Mews, Rachman, even though she was no longer sleeping with him, had continued to pay her an allowance of £100 a week. If this had emerged in evidence then it would have been very difficult for the jury to have convicted Ward of living on Mandy's immoral earnings because the £100 had not been earned immorally.

One other confession was to come, but it took a long while. The Ward jury was left with the impression that Ward's account of having worked for MI5 was one of his fantasies. If he had indeed been helping MI5 set a trap for Ivanov and had told his case officer, Mr Woods, about the Keeler–Profumo affair, then this would have greatly improved his standing in the eyes of the jury, and would have made it impossible later for Denning to accuse him of being a crypto-communist. But instead the jury was left wondering why, if Ward's account of his MI5 service was true, the defence had not called Mr Woods as a witness to confirm it. Ward's solicitor, Jack Wheatley, had indeed made attempts to locate Woods, but, of course, Woods was a cover name, and the War Office simply denied that anyone of that name worked for it.

Then in 1982, Nigel West, in his history of MI5, *A Matter of Trust*, revealed the 'honey-trap' operation and Ward's role in it. West wrote of MI5's embarrassment at Ward's evidence of his contacts with the service and how relieved MI5 was that efforts to trace Mr Woods had failed.

The *Sunday Times* now managed to find Mr Woods, who had since retired. His real name is ——.* He confirmed to them, and later to us, Ward's story in detail, and told how MI5 had recruited Ward as an agent and how Ward had done his best to help the service in its entrapment operation. 'I felt rather sorry for the poor chap at the end of the day,' he said. Another, more senior MI5 officer involved in the operation said it was a pity that Ward's true role had not been revealed at the time of his trial. 'I think that everyone involved did feel very sorry about Ward and the final outcome,' he said. 'Nowhere in the Denning report does it say that Ward was acting under our instructions. That is very unfortunate.' The officer said Ward would have been encouraged to see himself as a patriot working for his country. MI5 had no idea that the operation would end in the manner it did 'and we were going to burn our fingers in this way'. But could not MI5 have found some way to have confirmed that Ward was working for the service? 'Yes,' the officer admitted. 'Ward might have been alive today if that had happened. But we didn't expect the final outcome and we were very cut up when we learned he was dead.'

*We have been officially asked not to give the name.

As for the police, Sam Herbert was promoted to Superintendent, John Burrows became a Detective Inspector and the two 'hunters', Arthur Eustace and Mike Glasse, were invited to sit their examinations for promotion. (They declined.) All the officers had been told before Ward's trial that if the prosecution was successful they would receive promotions – 'but not immediately, because it would not look good'.

Sam Herbert died of a heart attack on 16 April 1966, only three years after Ward, and aged only 48. In his will he left only £300, commensurate with the rather meagre police salaries at that time. But his bank account was discovered to contain no less than £30,000 (£300,000 by today's values). There was an internal police investigation to discover the source of this money but if it came to any conclusion it was never announced.

(By coincidence, in the tape recordings which Christine Keeler made with her manager, Robin Drury, Keeler says that John Lewis, Ward's bitter enemy, had offered her £30,000 for information leading to Ward's conviction and the bringing down of the Conservative Government.)

John Burrows left the Metropolitan Police soon after the Ward trial 'under a cloud'. His colleagues say variously that he was found drunk on duty, or that he had decided to emigrate to Australia and neglected his work. His trail vanishes in 1966.

The views of the junior police officers, Eustace and Glasse, who have both retired, are very relevant. Glasse now says that he never believed that Ward had lived on the immoral earnings of any of the girls but that he was technically guilty of procuring girls under 21 for his friends. Eustace agrees about the immoral earnings charges. 'Ward was neither a pimp nor a ponce,' he says. 'At worst he was a "recruiting agent". He procured girls to maintain his social position.' He agreed that the police never obtained any evidence against Ward on either charges during their seven months' surveillance. 'If we had relied on the direct evidence of the police,' he said, 'then there was nothing to it and there would not have been a case.' Asked for his final comment on Ward, Eustace said, 'I felt sorry for the man.'

The lawyers appear to have been haunted by the trial. James Burge left Britain and went to live in Spain. He is now 80, in poor health, and, until we approached him, had never spoken of Ward – 'because it upsets me too much'. He told us, 'Ward's case was rigged. It was a political trial because of Profumo. Judge Marshall murdered Stephen Ward. It's as simple as that.' Burge's junior, Tudor-Price, told us, 'There must have been great pressure for a conviction. The Lucky Gordon appeal coinciding with Ward's trial and coming to the conclusion it did was totally reprehensible.'

Many other lawyers at the time felt strongly about what had happened. Lord Goodman remembers, 'There were many individual members, particularly in the judiciary, who were affronted by the case. Ward's trial was an injustice which took place in full view of everybody, clear to the world at large.'

Even the prosecuting counsel, Griffith-Jones and the judge, Mr Justice Marshall, showed signs of being upset. Ward had written letters to both of them before he killed himself. Neither ever revealed what the letters contained. Griffith-Jones's colleagues said he was shaken to receive his, and when the journalist Barry O'Brien delivered the judge's letter, he remembers the judge reading it, turning white, and then repeating, 'But he was guilty, you know. He was guilty.' A few weeks later, by chance, a colleague of O'Brien's found himself in the same train compartment as Marshall and brought up the trial. Again Marshall began repeating, 'But he was guilty, you know. He was guilty.'

Marshall's distress and Tudor-Price's suggestion of pressure tend to confirm a story we heard from a lawyer who impressed us as reliable: 'In the final days of the trial Judge Marshall had a telephone call from a person very high up in the judiciary. Someone was accidentally able to overhear part of the conversation. This high-ranking person said to Marshall, "Are you certain that you'll be able to get him?" And Marshall replied, "Don't worry, I'll get him on the immoral earnings charge."'

Some may have thought Ward was innocent, but Lord Denning was not among them. In September 1984, 21 years after the publication of his report, his book *Landmarks in the Law* was published. He referred to the Profumo affair in a chapter headed 'My Most Important Case'. Appearing on television to publicise the book, Lord Denning made it clear that his view of Ward had not changed. He referred to him as 'the most evil man I have ever met.'

Yet he remains reluctant to produce the evidence for this assertion. In 1977 he told the House of Lords that the only remaining copy of the evidence he had gathered for his report had been destroyed. The then Prime Minister, James Callaghan, denied this and said that the evidence was locked away in the Cabinet Office. Denning apologised for misleading his fellow peers but then suggested that the 30-year period during which documents are kept secret should, 'in this particular case', be extended to 50 years.

As for the others, Christine Keeler went rapidly downhill after Ward's death. By the time of her trial for perjury she had lost most of her friends. Mandy had dropped out of her life and Robin Drury, Paul Mann, John Hamilton-Marshall, Lucky Gordon, Michael

Eddowes, John Lewis, and even Peter Earle had all turned against her. Earle wrote about her in the *News of the World*. 'You took advantage of your closest friends. You traded on their generosity and sympathy only to throw it in their faces . . . We always thought you were scruffy and grubby. We saw you in your tatty underwear, a cigarette burning itself out in the dressing table ashtray. Are you crying this morning, Christine? . . . We'd like you to cry a little — for yourself and the many others you have sullied and who have sullied you.'

Six months later Christine emerged from Holloway Prison, chastened but not broken. She told a journalist, 'I stepped outside the gates of Holloway Prison truly afraid to lift my eyes from the dust at my feet, imagining Stephen's body clinging to my very soles.' She soon met Freddy, a young relative of the Kray brothers, the East End gangsters. A stormy relationship developed which ended when he found Christine in bed with a pop star.

Next she married Jim Levermore, a labourer, and quickly became pregnant. Within a year they were divorced. Christine joined Release, a drug addicts' rehabilitation group and then married Antony Platt, a wealthy businessman. Within a year she gave birth to a second son, Seymour. But she was not happy. Three months after Seymour was born Christine walked out. She found marriage suffocating and she missed the excitement of London.

Before going to prison she had given power of attorney to her lawyer, Seymour Lyons, only to discover on her release that he had taken nearly 80 per cent of her earnings in such a way that she was never able to recover it. The alimony she received from Platt was barely sufficient. She also found she had very few friends. 'I came back to London with nothing but Seymour. During the seventies I was not living, I was surviving.'

At the time of writing Christine Keeler lives in a council flat in a tower block at World's End, Chelsea, and collects Social Security. In 1984 she contributed to a book called *Sex Scandals*. In it she said that most of what she had said or written about Ward before was lies. She said that Ward was 'no kind of a sex pervert' and that he had never made her do anything she did not want to do. When the playwright and barrister John Mortimer asked her what she thought of the affair in hindsight, her reply was, 'It probably wasn't anyone's fault. It was silly, wasn't it? Silly Profumo, silly Stephen, silly me. I don't think about it a lot.'

John Profumo probably does. He never got back into politics, but instead devoted his life to charity work in the poorer parts of the East End of London. He was awarded the CBE for this work in 1975. He and Valerie Hobson are still married.

Harold Macmillan resigned as Prime Minister in October 1963 and retired from Parliament in September 1964, just one month before the Conservatives were defeated in the general election. He felt bitter about the affair. David Astor, then editor of the *Observer*, recalls, 'I think Macmillan blamed us, the Astors. He blamed my brother Bill and somewhere he associated me with it too, because from then on he refused to answer my letters or to speak to me. He obviously felt that Bill had done him an injury by allowing dubious figures to mix with his Cabinet while he, the Prime Minister, was trying to uphold the affairs of state.' Macmillan later accepted a peerage and, as Lord Stockton, became the grand old man of the Conservative Party. He died in 1986, aged 92.

Mandy Rice-Davies split up with Christine and began a new life as a singer in Eve's Bar in Munich in 1964. She told reporters, 'I'm nervous. Because of my name, I've got to start at the top.' She went on to tour the world as a nightclub singer. In 1966 she married an Israeli, divorced him in 1977 and married again. In Israel she made a new career for herself as a nightclub owner, also making the occasional film. She had a small part in the film *Absolute Beginners*. She currently lives in London, and has recently published a novel.

Lord Astor went to pieces after Ward's death and within months was confined to a wheelchair. As with Ward, all Astor's friends abandoned him. His wife, Bronwen, remembers, 'It was like living a nightmare. There was an awful silence. All your friends don't know what to say and you're not invited to anything. I remember we would turn up at functions and people would literally turn their backs and walk away from us. They didn't want to know. People don't want to line themselves up with losers and Bill turned out to be a loser in that sense.'

Astor's health declined to such an extent that his wife decided to have Cliveden exorcised and asked the well-known Roman Catholic exorcist Dom Robert Petitpierre to perform the ceremony. A few weeks later Dom Robert returned to exorcise Ward's cottage – the new tenant had committed suicide by drowning himself in the kitchen sink. Bronwen remembers, 'Dom Robert wouldn't let me near the cottage otherwise I would have been knocked sideways. Even he could hardly walk through the door.' According to Dom Robert's own account, 'the evil powers emanating from the cottage were some of the strongest I've ever experienced.'

Astor died, friendless and broken in spirit, in January 1966. That spring, Bronwen left Cliveden for good. The house was handed over to Stanford University on a 21-year lease, with the purpose of promoting Anglo-American relations. The lease expired recently and

Cliveden has been turned into a 28-bedroom luxury hotel and restaurant. Christine Keeler attended the opening night party.

George Wigg was rewarded for his role in exposing Profumo. When Harold Wilson became Prime Minister in 1964 he made Wigg the Paymaster General for the new Labour Government. Wigg was given an office in 10 Downing Street and spent his time checking security matters for Wilson. He was known around Westminster as the 'Spymaster General', 'Wilson's early warning system' and 'ear-Wigg'. In 1967 he became Baron Wigg of Dudley. His behaviour became increasingly eccentric and in 1976 the police arrested him for kerb-crawling – trying to pick up prostitutes from his car.

The police alleged in court that they had seen Wigg on previous occasions trying to pick up prostitutes, and on the night mentioned in the charge they had followed him around Mayfair and had seen him try to solicit eight women. Wigg was acquitted but the judge warned him to stay away from the area. He died in 1983.

Mariella Novotny began writing novels and published the first, *King's Road*, in 1971. The story, she said, was 'an attack on upper-class young layabouts . . . I blast their hypocrisy and shallowness.' She followed this in 1974 with a series of articles in the magazine *Club International* in which she described her affairs with the British double agent Eddie Chapman, Black Power leader Malcolm X, Brian Jones of the Rolling Stones, British business magnate Judah Binstock, and many others.

In 1978 she announced that she had started her autobiography. She said it would include details of her work for MI5 – how as agent 'Henry' she had given the service information about the private lives of people in high places. This provoked a woman doctor, Caroline Olsson, to admit a three-year relationship with Mariella. She said that Mariella had dominated her totally – 'she wanted me to be her slave, both mentally and physically'. Mariella's claims about MI5 brought a denial from Scotland Yard which said that she was just a police informer.

In November 1980, just before publication of her memoirs, Mariella told the Press that she would be 'naming names'. She was, she said, 'part of a plot to discredit Jack Kennedy.' She said that she had had affairs with both the Kennedy brothers during her visit to the United States and added, 'I kept a diary of all my appointments in the UN building. Believe me, it's dynamite. It's now in the hands of the CIA.' This was Mariella's last fantasy. Less than a year later she died of asphyxiation, choking to death on jelly while under the influence of drugs. In her more lucid moments she admitted that most of what she had said and written at the time of the Profumo affair had been lies: although she knew Stephen Ward, he had had nothing to do with her trip to the United States; she had never met Christine Keeler or Mandy Rice-Davies; they had never been to her house; they had never attended any of her parties.

Lucky Gordon still lives in Notting Hill, just round the corner from Ronna Ricardo. They see each other occasionally. In the mid-1960s Gordon worked for a time with Chris Blackwell who founded the very successful Island Records. At the time of writing he is a cook with Sarm Studios West, in Notting Hill. He never sees Christine Keeler.

John Lewis died in 1968, marrying his housekeeper of eight years just before his death. His company had collapsed and his political career never revived. Michael Eddowes has spent much of his life trying to link Stephen Ward with the Kennedy assassination. His most recent move was to have Lee Harvey Oswald's body exhumed in an effort to show that it is actually that of a Soviet impostor.

Sir Colin Coote, the man who introduced Ward to Ivanov, quickly distanced himself from Ward's posthumous reputation. In his autobiography published in 1966 he wrote that Ward was childish and inane and that they had little in common except that Ward was his osteopath. Coote died in 1979.

Intrigued by the stories of Rachman's property business which had emerged during the trial, the *Sunday Times* Insight team went back on his trail and wrote the story of his years of exploiting London's housing shortage. But no one picked up the story of the 'Indian doctor', Dr Emil Savundra, who, mysteriously, had been so protected during the trial. Had they done so, they might have saved the thousands of motorists who lost their money when Savundra's company, Fire Auto and Marine, went spectacularly bust in 1966. Two years later Savundra was sentenced to eight years' imprisonment and fined £50,000 for various offences concerned with the running of his company. He died in 1979.

Noel Howard-Jones left Britain for good soon after Ward's death, and now lives in Belgium. When he was putting Ward up during the trial, his wife decided to leave, saying that she could not stand the constant ringing of the telephone and the hordes of reporters besieging the flat. They were later divorced. Ward's conviction sickened Howard-Jones. He says that he had been brought up in a middle class family that believed firmly in British justice and the integrity of the Government, the police and the judiciary. 'What happened to Stephen shattered all that,' he says, 'and I couldn't wait to leave it all behind.'

Peter Earle retired from the *News of the World* in December 1986

after a 50-year career in Fleet Street. He speaks as he writes. He refers
to Ward as 'that diabolical devil', and that 'malevolent manipulator'.
He told the police that he did not know of anything that Ward had
done that was criminal in law but he explains this now by saying,
'Ward's crimes could never be dealt with by any earthly court.'

Finally, it is intriguing to contrast the treatment Ward received
from the authorities with that accorded to Jeremy Thorpe, MP, later
leader of the Liberal Party. During exactly the same period as the
Profumo affair was developing, Thorpe was having a homosexual
relationship with a stable boy called Norman Scott. Scott told his
landlady who in turn told the police. At the same time as the
Marylebone police were enthusiastically investigating Ward, saying
that they were doing so because of an anonymous tip-off that he was
a procurer, Chelsea police were taking a statement from Scott about
his affair with Thorpe. Scott also handed them two letters from
Thorpe indicating that the affair had started when Scott was a minor.
Yet Thorpe was never interviewed about this and the letters and
Scott's statement were locked away in the Assistant Commissioner's
safe at Scotland Yard for the next seventeen years.

At Ward's trial the judge implied that the evidence of prostitutes
was perfectly acceptable, as was the evidence of witnesses who had
sold their stories to newspapers and had an interest in seeing Ward
convicted. But when Thorpe eventually appeared at the Old Bailey in
1979 charged with having conspired to murder Scott, the judge
warned the jury to be wary of accepting the evidence of Scott,
because of what he was, and of other witnesses because they had sold
their stories to newspapers and therefore had an interest in the
outcome of the trial – an indication of how times had changed, and
perhaps, that the courts had at least learnt something from the Ward
case.

It is nearly a quarter of a century since Ward's trial and death.
Although for many he was a devil incarnate – 10,000 holiday-makers
a day queued at the chamber of horrors of Louis Tussaud's Waxworks
in Blackpool to see his effigy – his place in British history is as a
victim of the establishment. As he himself said, society needed a
sacrifice. Ward's way of life and the fact that he was an outsider –
despite his establishment friends – made him an obvious choice.
Once he had realised this, he had the courage to deny his enemies an
easy victim. He became the only player to leave the stage with dignity.

We give the last word to Lord Goodman: 'Stephen Ward was the
historic victim of an historic injustice.'

# SELECT BIBLIOGRAPHY

The books on the Profumo affair break down into three categories: the scandal as a whole, the trial itself, and the recollections of the principal characters.

The three outstanding books in the first group are *Scandal '63* by Clive Irving, Ron Hall and Jeremy Wallington (Heinemann, 1963), *The Profumo Affair* by Iain Crawford (White Lodge Books, 1963), and *The Profumo Affair: Aspects of Conservatism* by Wayland Young (Penguin, 1964). *Stephen Ward Speaks: The Profumo Affair*, by Warwick Charlton and Judge Gerald Sparrow (*Today Magazine*, 1963) is not as analytical as the other three but does have the advantage of Charlton's account of his conversations with Ward. A useful sidelight is provided by *Rachman*, by Shirley Green (Michael Joseph, 1979).

*The Trial of Stephen Ward* by Ludovic Kennedy (Victor Gollancz, 1964) is not only a thorough account of the court proceedings but a brilliant dissection of the strengths and weaknesses of the evidence.

Christine Keeler (with Sandy Fawkes) tells her version of events in *Nothing But* . . . (New English Library, 1983) as does Mandy Rice-Davies in *The Mandy Report* (Confidential Publications, 1964) and, later, with Shirley Flack, in *Mandy* (Michael Joseph, 1980).

*A Matter of Trust, MI5 1945–72*, by Nigel West (Weidenfeld & Nicolson, 1982), a history of the security service, has a section devoted to Ward's relationship with the service, and Profumo's meetings with MI5.

*The Denning Report* (HMSO, 1963) presents Lord Denning's very personalised view of the affair.

# INDEX

Abortion, 54; Ward trial
charges, 1, 216, 244, 246
Adams, Paul, 41, 50
Alexandra, Princess, 49
Argyll, Duchess of, 250
Armstrong-Jones, Anthony
(Lord Snowdon), 50, 65
Arran, Earl of, 83, 110–11,
191
Aspinall, John: Clermont
Club, 126
Asquith, Martin, 193
Astor, Bridget, 11, 12
Astor, Bronwen (Bronwen
Pugh), 30, 209, 257
Astor, David, 31, 210, 257
Astor, Nancy, Lady, 2, 30–1,
49, 81
Astor, Lady Philippa, 32, 46
Astor, William (Lord Astor),
34; FO letter, 90; house
burgled, 151; naval
intelligence, 31, 75; police
interview, 168, 172, 175;
Profumo affair, 84–6, 132,
133, 137, 257; relationships
with: Ivanov, 106, 108,
109; Keeler, 85, 159–60,
167, 172, 175, 179; Rice-
Davies, 172, 175, 214, loan,
81; Ward, 30–2, 49, 132,
139, 175–6, 209, declines to
give evidence, 209–10;
loans, 160, 176, 229; trial:
references, 216, 221, 234;
social ostracism, 257; see
also Cliveden
Athenaeum Club, 209

Baddeley, Hermione, 23
Bailey, Eunice, 23, 26, 28
Baines, Patricia, 26, 28–9, 203
Ball, Dr Dorothy, 18
Ball Dr Samuel, 19
Baroda, Maharaja of, 2, 16, 18
Barrett, Vickie, 173–4, 216,

217; Ward trial, 224–7,
229, 230–1, 233, 246, 250,
251–2
Bates, Charles W., 199, 200,
201
Beauchamp, Anthony, 23, 39
Beecham, Sir Thomas, 2
Belcher, John, 181
Belmont, A.H., 202
'Berlin crisis', 91, 108
Betjeman, Sir John, 2
Bikel, Theodore, 23
Birch, Nigel, 195
Black, Gerald, 136
Blackpool, Louis Tussaud's
Waxworks, 260
Blackwell, Chris, 259
Bligh, Sir Timothy, 141–2,
186; Ward meeting, 177–8
Blom-Cooper, Louis, 215
Blunt, Anthony, 248
Bossom, Clive, 205
Boyle, Katie, 212
Brien, Alan, 48
Brook, Sir Norman, 88
Brooke, Burnham, 14–15
Brooke, Henry, 116, 162–4,
177, 185–6; Ward letters,
178–9, 248
Brothels, 15–16; Ward and, 1,
172, 217
Brown, Frances, 233
Brown, George, 147
Brown, Margaret, 47–9, 51–2,
203
Bruce, David, 157, 158, 181,
197, 201, 204, 205
Brush and Palette, 61
Bryanston Mews flat, 59–60,
82, 138, 170, 174, 216–18,
222, 223, 235
Bulow, Claus von, 210
Bundy, McGeorge, 203, 206
Burdett, William C., 201
Burge, James: Ward trial, 242,
247, 254; cross-

examination, 213, 219–23,
225–6; defence summary,
227–8, 231–4, 237–9
Burns, Douglas, 225
Burrows, Det.-Sgt John,
138–40, 165, 166–7,
169–75, 211, 225–6, 236,
254
Butler, Rab, 63

Caccia, Sir Harold, 91, 108,
110
Callaghan, James, 255
Call girl rings: KGB, 199;
UN, 99, 198, 205; Ward, 7,
45, 164, 188, 191, 198
Camacchio, Clarence
Raymond, 170, 191, 236–7,
238
Canford School, 11–12
Capes, Stella, see Novotny,
Mariella
Carney, Kalita, 14–15, 16
Carpenter, Paul, 70–1
Carrington, Lord, 144
Carroll, General Joseph, 201,
202, 205
Carroll, Madeleine, 15
Cartland, Barbara, 83
Castle, Barbara, 5, 146, 153–4,
155
Chapman, Henrietta, see
Novotny, Mariella
Charlton, Warwick, 43, 166,
171, 174, 175, 180
Christian, Prince, of
Hanover, 2
Christiansen, Arthur, 45
Christine Keeler Company
Ltd, 9, 190
*Christine Keeler Story*, 191
Churchill, Sarah, 3
Churchill, Winston, 2, 17,
20–1
CIA, 8, 107, 199, 202, 205,
258

Cliveden, 258; exorcism, 257; parties, 3, 49–51, 81, 86–7, 111; Set, 106; swimming episode, 84–5, 115, 133, 142, 158, 179, 189; Ward's cottage, 46–9, 51, 58, 139, 173, 217, 220, ransacked, 151, vacated, 174–5, 211

Clogg, Derek, 134, 135, 146, 154

Clore, Charles, 167, 173, 217, 219, 220

Collins, Joan and Jackie, 25

Collins, Seymour, 222

Comeragh Road flat, 80–2, 218, 230, 234; Astor rent, 172, 175, 216, 221, 229

Contempt law, 6, 130

Cooch Behar, Maharaja of, 2, 39–41, 50

Coote, Sir Colin, 3, 68–70, 72, 106, 208, 259; SIS work, 75

Corbally, Thomas J., 71, 157–8, 197, 200, 205, 230

Cordet, Helen, 70

Corkery, Michael, 213

Court of Criminal Appeal, 237, 238–40, 243

Critchley, Thomas, 244

Crossman, Richard, 5, 146–7, 153, 155, 158

Cuban missile crisis, 105–14, 122, 126, 139, 161, 182, 190, 204

Cunningham, Sir Charles, 163

*Daily Express*, 45, 148, 159, 243, 248, 249

*Daily Mail*, 151

*Daily Mirror*, 9

*Daily Sketch*, 150, 158, 203

*Daily Telegraph*, 68–70, 72, 95, 249, 251

Dartmouth, Lord and Lady, 49

Day, Frances, 23, 24, 35

Deedes, William, 155

Denning, Lord: *Landmarks in the Law*, 255; Report, 9, 76, 128, 132, 133, 137, 140, 142, 150, 178, 244, 249–51, Keeler disappearance, 149, 159–60, MI5, 112, 250, 253

Derby, Lord, 49

Dibben, Horace, 97, 98, 200

Diefenbaker, John, 64

Dilhorne, Lord, 210; Inquiry, 183, 185, 190

Dors, Diana, 82

Douglas-Home, Robin, 4

Doxapram (619), drug, 247

Drury, Robin, 123, 184, 191, 236, 237, 255

Dudley, Earl of, 208

Dufferin and Ava, Lady, 212

Dymengeot, Mylène, 64

Earle, Peter, 8, 99, 130–1, 132, 142, 192–3, 259–60; on Keeler, 256; Ward profile, 248–9

Eddowes, Michael H.B., 122–3, 131, 164, 191, 200, 202, 256; and Kennedy assassination, 259

Ede, Chuter, 179, 184, 185

Eden, Sir Anthony, 2

Edgecombe, Johnny, 117, 129; Keeler as trial witness, 3–7, 121–2, 130, 132, 133, 142, 148–50, 158–60; silence attempt, 136–7, 148; shooting incident, 3–6, 121–2; trial, 148, 150, 225

Edmonds, Joyce, 37, 41

Ednam, Lady (Maureen Swanson), 3, 72, 127

Ednam, Lord, 72, 127

Eichmann, Adolph: trial sketches, 69

Ellis, Ruth, 38

Elwes, Dominick, 191, 247

EMI: Russian music, 71

Espionage, 74–5, 76–7, 107–8, 112; Anglo-Soviet, 68, 96; defectors, 74; Ivanov: 'agents of influence', 105, 106, intelligence gathering, 66–7, 73–5, 128, 197, 200, MI5 entrapment, 75–7, 87–9, 126–7, 133, 141, 250, 253, MI5 surveillance, 74, 114, 161, nuclear secrets, 77, 87, 123, 191, Soviet spokesman, 90–2, 108–12, 113, 161, 182; Keeler references, 7, 123, 124, 131–2, 139, 146, 162, 163, 166, 182, 191, 202, 204; naval attachés, 68; UN, 99, 198, 205, 258; Ward: call girls, 164, 199–200, nuclear warheads, 77, 123, 124, 131–2, 139, 146, 162, 163, 166, 191, 195

Eustace, Sergeant Arthur, 165, 171, 172, 226, 254

Evans. C.A., 206–7

Everard, Sir Lindsay, 34

Eversleigh Club, Chicago, 15–16

Eylan, Major James, 81, 218

Fairbanks, Daphne, 3, 49–51

Fairbanks, Douglas, Jnr, 2, 64, 200, 214, 221, 234

FBI, 8, 98–9, 104, 158, 199; interest in Profumo, 198, 201, 203–6

'Fedora', 198–9

Felton, Earl, 200

Fenton, Rudolph 'Truello', 170, 191, 236, 237, 238

Ferrer, Mel, 21

Ferrier, Arthur, 22–3

Ferrier, Freda, 22–4, 41

Fire Auto and Marine, insurance company, 119, 259

Fisz, Benjamin, 126

Flagellation, 8, 97, 101, 102, 138, 174, 224, 250

Floyd, David, 70

Foreign Office: Ward approaches, 90–2, 106, 108–9, 110, 182, 209

Foster, Reginald, 144, 150, 151

*France Soir*, 241

Fraser, Hugh, 95, 205

Furstova, Madame, 72

Gadd, Nina, 130

Gagarin, Yuri, 70, 72

Gaitskell, Hugh, 2, 63

Galbraith, Thomas, 125, 144, 147

Gale, George, 249

Gandhi Mahatma, 2, 16–17, 20

Gardner, Ava, 2, 21

Getty, Paul, 2, 63, 72–3, 106, 210

Gilliatt, Penelope, 247

Gladwyn, Lord, 49

Glasse, Sergeant Michael, 165, 174, 203, 226, 254

Gloucester, Duke and Duchess of, 2, 65, 248

Glover, Mary, 28

Godfrey, Cardinal, 64

Goldsmith, James, 126

Goodman, Lord, 147, 255, 260

Gordon, Aloysius (Lucky), 3, 102, 129, 130, 138, 235, 255, 259; appeal, 233, 238–41, 243, 254; Keeler 'assault', 7, 103, 117, 121, 170; Keeler perjury, 236–40; knife fight, 117–18, 150; meets Keeler, 100–1; and police, 171, 236–7; trial, 7, 191, 236–9; Ward trial, 236–8, 243
Gourlay, Logan, 127
Government: Ministerial scandals, 115–16, 125, 132–3, 135, 143, 144, 164, 189ff, 250
Gradwell, Leo, 3, 214
Griffith-Jones, Mervyn, 172, 255; Ward trial, 213–26, 230–2, 234–5, 238, 243, 245; personality 213, 229, 246
GRU (Soviet military intelligence), 67, 68, 74, 106, 107, 108, 127, 198
Gulbenkian, Nubar, 2, 63, 84, 106
Gulliver, Julie, 232, 244
Gwynne Jones, (Alun) Arthur (Lord Chalfont), 151

Hailsham, Lord, 8, 35, 49, 194, 210
Haley, Sir William, 151
Hamilton, Denis, 82
Hamilton-Marshall, John, 170, 236, 237, 255
Hamilton-Marshall, Paula, 170, 232, 236
Hammond, Charles, 204
Hanson, James, 126
Harper, Kenneth, 39, 42
Harriman, Averell, 2, 19
Harrington, Lord, 72, 73
Harvey, Laurence, 23
Hawkins, Jack, 2
Herbert, Sir Alan (A.P.), 2, 3, 64, 66
Herbert, Chief Insp. Samuel, 165, 166–7, 169–75, 210, 211, 223, 236, 251–2; bank balance, 254; Ward trial, 225–6
Hitchcock, Billy Mellon, 157
Hitchcock, Center, 118, 157
Hoare, Sir Frederick, 212
Hobson, Valerie, see Profumo, Mrs John

Hobson, Sir John, 133, 137, 146, 154, 237; confronts Profumo, 134, 135, 149, 155
Hollis, Sir Roger, 76, 87, 88–9, 133, 135, 141, 142–3, 163, 165, 182
Holloway Prison, 169, 225, 256
Home, Lord, 91, 116; Cuban crisis, 109, 110
Homosexuality, 27, 83, 116
Hoover, J. Edgar, 99, 104, 202; Profumo scandal, 198–202, 205ff
Howard-Jones, Noel, 61, 62, 71, 84, 88, 128, 211, 259; Ward trial, 232, 243, 244, 245
Hylton, Jack, 2, 70

Il Tempo, 158
Illustrated London News, 64
India, 16–18
Inland Revenue, 32, 45
Ivanov, Yevgeny M. (Eugene), 9, 161; atomic bomb threat, 202; bridge-playing, 71, 128; 'double agent', 133; family, 67; political arguments, 70–1, 114, 122; recall, 128; relationships with: Keeler, 4, 6, 7, 85, 89, 114–16, 122–3, 131, 134, 139, 141, 145, 181, first meeting, 73, non-sexual, 86–7, 89, 189; Rice-Davies, 73, 114, 189; Ward, 69–77, 84, 89, 90–2, 113–14, 128, 242, 249–50, domination, 111–12, 122, 127, espionage awareness, 73; 'Stalinist', 114; see also Espionage

Jaipur, Maharaja of, 2, 40, 50
Journal American, 9, 202, 205
Journalism, investigative, 151, 152–3

Kanu, Ahmed, 58
Kaye, Danny, 2, 22
Keeler, Christine: cabaret offer, 191; champagne bath, 102; club showgirl, 57, 79, 191; 'Confessions', serial, 7, 189, 190; death threats, 184, 208; disappearance, 4, 5, 148–50, 152ff, 158–60; Dolphin Square flat, 101–3;

drugs, 100, 124, 133, 140, 211, 226, 250, 256; family, 53–4, 58–9, 60, 88, 130, 150; film, 191; finances, 78, 81, 101, 103–4, 128–31, 136–7, 149, 160; marriages, 256; 'memoirs', Press, 129–37, 148, 149, 162, 184, 200, 206, 236, 242; men, attitude to, 82; perjury: imprisonment, 238, 252, 256; personality, 57, 62, 124–5, 129, 166; photographs, 53, 142, 150, 159, 189; portrait, 2; prostitution, 81, 101, 102, 167, 172, 184, 195, 202, 216, 218–19, 226, 231–2; relationships: Rice-Davies: flat-share, 80–2, 172, 175, 216, 218, 221, 222, first meeting, 79–80; Ward, 58–60, 80, 88, 100–1, 166, 189, 230, 'blackmail', 136–7, break-up, 129, 138, desertion, 211, flat-share, 59, 60, 82, 88, 89, 219, 229, legal actions, 132, 135–7, non-sexual, 59, Ward's death, 247; sex appeal, 54, 57; sex life, 54, 56, 60, 62, 78, 86ff, 100–1, 117, 170, 189, 206, 218; sons, 54, 256; subsequent life, 255–6; tape recordings, 184–5, 206, 236, 237; USA: model career, 130, 150, visit, 103–4, 203, 204, 206
Kempson, Trevor, 151
Kennedy, John, 66, 70–1, 101–2, 250
Kennedy, President John F., 8, 105, 107, 111, 112, 258; assassination, 198, 259; Hoover obsessed with, 99, 104, 202, 206–7; and Keeler, 206; Profumo, reactions to, 196–8; visits Britain, 196, 202
Kennedy, Joseph, 2
Kennedy, Ludovic, 250; Trial of Stephen Ward, 215, 241, 243, 251
Kennedy, Robert, 202, 206–7, 258
Kent, Duchess of, 2, 49, 65
Kent, Duke of, 65, 248
Kenya Coffee House, 25, 59, 110, 113

Kerby, Henry, 145
KGB, 74, 77, 107, 141, 164, 190, 198, 199
Khan, Ayub, President, 7, 49, 84, 86, 106
Khrushchev, Nikita, 69, 90, 105–7, 111, 112
Kirksville College of Osteopathy and Surgery, 13
Kray brothers, 256
Kuwait, 94–5

Labour Party, 146–7, 153, 154, 183–4
*Lady Chatterley's Lover*, 83; trial, 213–14
Laithwaite, Sir Gilbert, 84, 208
Lambton, Michael, 78, 80, 103
Lazzolo, Leila, 208, 245
Lazzolo, Vasco, 39, 41, 208, 245, 250; Ward trial, 210, 243
Leggatt, Hugh, 63, 64, 249
Levermore, Jim, 256
Lewis, John, 37, 96, 162, 256, 259; hostile to Ward, 42–5; Keeler meeting, 124–5, 146; £30,000 offer, 185, 254
Lewis, Joy, 42–4
Libel laws, 6, 130
Littman, Mark, 137
Lloyd, Selwyn, 63
Loginov, N.A., 109, 110
Longford, Lord, 49, 111
Lord, Cyril, 2
Loren, Sophia, 2, 64
Lovell, Sir Bernard, 64
Luard, Nicholas, 191
Lynch, Admiral R.B., 197, 200
Lyons, Seymour, 256

McClurg, William, 14
McCone, John, 202, 205
Macleod, Iain, 115, 155
Macmillan, Harold (Lord Stockton), 35, 48, 84, 108–11, 177; leadership questioned, 194, 195–6; political scandals, 116, 125, 144; Profumo: awareness of, 142–5, 154, 157, 158, 162, 165, 195, cartoon, 192, conference, 186, political backlash, 189–90, 193–6, 200, 249, reluctance to act, 181–3, resignation

acceptance, 187, supports Profumo, 157, 178, 182–3, 184, 185, 'that tart', 194; resignation, 196, 257; Ward, sketch, 2, 63
McNamara, Robert, 201, 202–3, 205
Makarios, Archbishop, 2, 64
Mangold, Tom, 243, 248
Mann, Paul, 124, 130, 149, 159, 162, 184, 237, 255
Manu (Iranian student), 82
Margaret, Princess, 2, 49, 65, 248
Marina, Princess, 2, 65
Marshall, Sir Archie Pellow, 212–13, 255, anti-Burge, 228, 239, hostile summing up, 240–1, 242, 254
Martin, Mary, 2, 21, 22, 23
Martin, Vickie (Valerie Mewes), 37–42, 52, 59, 129, 167; film, 39
Marylebone Magistrate's Court: Ward committal, 1, 3, 171, 213, 214, 223, 229
'Masked man', 8, 192–3
Massereene and Ferrard, Lord, 83
Mathew, Sir Theobald, 212, 237, 238
Mewes, Valerie, *see* Martin, Vickie
MI5, D-Branch, 67, 74–5, 114, 116, 125, 258; Mrs Profumo, 163; Profumo case: criticism fear, 143, 'harassment', 163–4, interviews, 88, 89, 133–4, 178, Ivanov meeting, 87, 106, security appraisal, 141–3, 182, 183, 195, Ward disclosures, 87, 134, 162, 178–9, 182, 188, 229, 253; Ward, links, 75–7, 92, 112, 140–2, 148, 162, 176, 250, prosecution talk, 163, 165, surveillance, 122–3, 126–7, 229
MI6, 67–8, 74
Midgets, 21
Milford Haven, David, 2
Minton, David, 43
Mirror, two-way, 82, 217–18, 221, 246, 251
Mitchell, Graham, 141–2, 143
Mitchell, William, 210
Moore, Beecher, 175
Moore, Sir Henry, 2

More, Kenneth, 2
Mortimer, John, 256
Mountbatten, Lord, 84, 106, 210
Mulholland, Brendan, 144, 150, 151
Mullally, Frederic, 38, 39, 43, 44–5
Murphy, Captain Thomas W., 9, 197–8
Murray, Alex, 184
Murray, Percival, 55–7, 58, 114
Murray's Cabaret Club, 55–7, 78–9, 114–15, 124
Myers, Harry, 72

Nahum, Baron, 2, 23, 39
NATO, 196, 202
*News of the World*, 7, 8, 99, 130, 142, 145, 151, 159, 192, 193, 232, 249, 256, 259; 'Confessions of Christine', 189, 191
*Newsweek*, 9
Nicholson, Sir Godfrey, 68, 91, 106, 108–9, 179, 208
Norie, Sally, 86, 216, 217, 219; evidence, 220
Novotny, Mariella (aka Capes, Chapman), 8, 192–3; marriage, 97; police informer, 258; prostitution, 98–9, 200, 205; publications, 258; Ward, 259
Nuclear missiles, 192; Cuba, 105–11; West Germany, 77, 87, 123, 124, 131, 139, 146, 162, 163, 166, 182, 191, 196

O'Brien, R. Barry, 251–2, 255
*Observer*, 190
O'Connor, Maureen, 55
Office of Special Investigation (OSI), 205
Official Secrets Act, 163, 165, 166, 182
Olsson, Caroline, 258
Osborne, Sir Cyril, 191
Osborne, John, 247
Osteopathic Association Clinic, 19
Osteopathy, 2, 13–14, 21

Paget, Reginald, 153, 154
*Paris Match*, 158

Parker, Lady, 212
Parker, Lord Chief Justice, 51; Gordon appeal, 237–40, 251
Parker, Sylvia, 230
Parkin, Ben, 152, 179, 183
Penkovsky, Colonel Oleg V., 74–7, 107–8, 112
Pennington, Commander Frederick C., 165
*People*, 223
Pertwee, Jon, 23–4, 42
Pertwee, Michael, 26, 55
Peter, King, of Yugoslavia, 2, 21
Petitpierre, Dom Robert, 257
Philby, H.A.R. ('Kim'), 190
Philip, Prince, 23–4, 26, 250; portrait, 2, 64–5, 210, 248
Photographs, stolen, 86, 140, 162, 248
Pimping (immoral earnings): Ward, 199, CID investigation, 139–40, 167, 169, 172–5, 254, trial charges, 1, 216–24, 226, 229–36, 252
Platt, Antony, 256
Plunket, Lady, 212
Police, CID: interview Keeler, 138–40, 166–73; interview Rice-Davies, 138–9, 168–70, 172–3, 222, 252; investigate Ward, 163, 164–80, 183–5, 188, 203, 223–5, phone tap, 171, under pressure, 165, 228–9, 233–4, 254, verbal statement, 225–6, witnesses, 208
Pornography, 171–2, 210, 250
*Private Eye*: Trog cartoon, 192
Proby, Jocelyn, 13, 26
Procuring: Ward, 45, 163, 167, 172–3, 204, 210, CID investigation, 7, 139–40, 172–3, 254, trial charges, 1, 216ff, 227, 246
Profumo, John: aviation interest, 34, 36; charity work, 256; Cliveden party, 85–6, 133; Edgecombe gun, 122; Keeler affair: 4, 5–7, 85–9, 116, 131, 133–4, 139, 141–2, 167, 184, 205, 251, receives blackmail letters, 164, Cliveden meeting, 85, 115,

Commons statement, 4–6, 154–7, 158, 177, 178–9, 183, 186, 195, confession, 186, Government interrogations, 134–5, 155, holiday return, 185–6, impropriety denials, 134–5, 182, 185, Keeler disappearance, 148–9, 153–4, 159–60, her memoirs: legal moves, 135–7, Parliamentary debate, 152–3, public knowledge, 126, 144–6, 152, revelations, 123–4; letters, 89, 124, 130, 133, 134, 135, 137, 139, 145, 157, 162, 179, 189; libel moves, 7, 133, 134, 135, 146, 156, 158, 195; marriage, 33, 36; MI5 recruitment, 88; nuclear secrets, 87, 123, 131, 146, 162, 163, 166, 182, 191; political career, 33, 34–6, 84; resignation, 148, 151, 186–7, 194; Secretary of State for War, 93–5, 106; security risk, 5, 88, 89, 96, 115–16, 133, 141–3, 152–3, 161, 167; war service, 33, 35; Ward, support from, 159, 160, 161–2, 176, 178–9
Profumo, Valerie (Hobson), 6, 32, 84, 85, 154, 156, 189, 256; anonymous letters to, 163, 164
'Profumo Affair': national outrage, 9–10, 194, 229, 232, 233; political repercussions, 9, 144–5, 189ff, 200; Press reaction, 8–9, 130–2, 144–6, 151, 152, 158, 179, 180, 189–90, 193–4, 248; public frenzy, 7–8, 189, 191–2, 202; US interest, 158, 196–9
Prostitution, 1, 12, 15–16, 26, 27, 29, 98, 173–4, 258; definition of, 231–2

*Queen*, 4, 126, 131

'R, Miss', 216, 217, 219; trial evidence, 220–1
Rachman, Audrey, 118–19, 138
Rachman, Peter, 80, 103, 164, 169, 170, 230; death, 118; Keeler affair, 59–60; Rice-

Davies, mistress, 82, 103, 118–19, 221, 253; slum racket, 259
Radcliffe Tribunal, 143
Ravensdale, Baroness, 83
Rawlinson, Sir Peter, 132–3, 134, 154
Raymond, Paul, 83
Read, Frederick, 248
Redmayne, Martin, 116, 134–5, 144, 146, 154, 155, 184, 190; Profumo confession, 186
Rees-Davies, William, 132, 135–7, 149, 208–9
Renton, Sir David, 93
Revie, Alastair, 236–7
Ricardo, Margaret (Ronna), 174, 216, 217, 251, 252, 259; trial evidence, 223–4, 225, 227, 230, 233
Rice-Davies, Marilyn (Mandy), 3, 6, 9, 117–18; criminal charges, 7, 168–70, 222–3; early career, 78–9; film: *Absolute Beginners*, 257; finances, 81, 82, 120, 222, 226, 252–3; jail, 169, 222, 225; love life, 82, 118–19, 214; *Mandy Report*, 252; memoirs, Press, 150, 192–3, 222, 242; 'orgies', account, 8, 192; prostitution, 81, 172, 216, 222, 226, 231–2; relationships with: Keeler, 79–80, 257, Ward: flatshare, 119–20, 221–3, 229–30, 233, 252, marriage offer, 119, sex, 80–1, death, 247; subsequent career, 257; suicide attempt, 119, 229; USA visit, 103–4, 203, 206; 'Well, he would, wouldn't he?', 214
Richards, Morley, 45
Robertson, Terence, 41
Robins, A.H. Ltd, 247
Robinson, Sugar Ray, 9
Roosevelt, Archie, Jnr, 206
Ropner, William, 221, 222, 252
Rositzke, Harry, 105
Ross, Annie, 247
Roth, Andrew, 145, 250
Rothenstein, Sir John, 64
Rothermere, Lord, 2
Roxburgh, Duchess of, 49
Royal Armoured Corps, 17

Royal Army Medical Corps, 17
Royal Family, 8, 9–10, 23–4, 26, 106; Ward portraits, 2, 49, 64–5, 248
Rusk, Dean, 201
Russia: alternative information channels, 90–2, 106–12; diplomacy, 105; intelligence operations, 67, 74–5, 77, 105; Kremlin 'doves', 106–7, 112; Politburo, portraits, 69– 70, 72
Russian Embassy, London, 67, 108, 109; KGB/GRU officers, 74
Rutland, Duchess of, 49

St John, Betta, 23
Sandys, Diana, 20
Sandys, Duncan, 20, 49
Sargent, Sir Malcolm, 2, 48
Savundra, Emil, 119–20, 173, 217, 221–3, 252, 259
Scott, Norman, 260
Secret Intelligence Service (SIS), 74–5
Security, national, 88, 115–16, 183, 190, 203
Sellers, Peter, 2
Sessler, Siegi, 22, 39
Sexual morality, British, 8–9, 82–3
Sexual Offences Act (1956), 1
Shackleton, Lord, 49
Shaw, Robert Gould, 30, 31
Shawcross, Lord, 2, 64
Shepherd, William, 113, 122, 144, 161; MI5 connections, 114, 116
Sherwood, Robert, 81
Simpson, Sir Joseph, 163, 165, 186
Sinatra, Frank, 2
Soames, Christopher, 126
Soskice, Sir Frank, 162
Special Branch, 139–40, 165, 191
Spencer, Stanley, 64, 66
Stainsby, Charles, 247
Steele, Tommy, 48–9, 66
Stephenson, Sir Harold, 109
Stockwood, Dr Mervyn, 191
Street Offences Act (1959), 1, 83
Stungo, Ellis, 18, 25–6, 30, 211, 250
Sugden, Dr Edward, 54–5, 244

Sullivan, William C., 201
Summit conference: proposal (1962), 108–9, 112
Sunday Mirror, 189, 190, 193
Sunday Pictorial, 116. 125; Keeler memoirs, 130–9, 144, 145, 149, 160, 179
Sunday Telegraph, 160
Sunday Times, 190, 253, 259
Swank, Emory, 201

Taylor, Elizabeth, 2, 3, 50
Taylor, Maxie, 22–4
Taylor, Robert, 2
Tessiers, Madame Mary, 73
The Times, 249; leaders, 150–1, 193–4
Theodore Goddard and Co., 134, 186
Thomas, Terry-, 2, 79
Thomson, Lord (Roy), 248
Thorpe, Jeremy, 191, 260
Tit-Bits, 53
Today, 166, 180, 247
Todd, Mike, 2, 3, 50
Topolski, Feliks, 2, 26
Torquay, 11, 12–13, 17, 18
Towers, Harry Alan, 98–9, 200
Tudor-Price, Sir David, 239, 242, 243, 254, 255
Tynan, Kenneth, 247

United Nations, 99, 198, 205, 258
United States, 13–16, 98–9, 103–4, 150; Air Force base, Ruislip, 202; Air Force personnel, 204; Embassy, London, 158, 197, 201, 204; Government: Profumo scandal, 201–7; State Department, 158, 200, 201, 204

Vassall, William, 96, 116, 125, 143, 147; Tribunal, 144, 151–3
Vigors, Edward, 13

Wakefield, Sir Wavell, 179
Walker, Mark Chapman, 142
War Office, 75, 94, 139, 253
Ward, Reverend Arthur (father), 11
Ward, Bridget (sister), 12
Ward, Eileen (mother), 11
Ward, George, 208
Ward, Stephen Thomas: army

service, 16–18; arrests, 7, 14, 15, 188, 209, 225; art: portraits, 2, 20, 61, 63, 173, 231, 249; exhibition, 244, 248; Royal Family, 2, 49, 64–5, 248, Soviet leaders, 69–70, 72; boyhood, 11–12; communism, 112, 113, 175, 249, 253; consulting rooms, 21, 32; early career, 12–13; education, 12–14; enemies, 36, 44–5, 95, 124, 146; establishment victim, 260; family, 11; finances, 25, 29, 32, 45, 50, 52, 63, 196, 231; friends, desertion by, 208–11, 243; funeral, 247; girlfriends, 23, 28, 31, 38ff, 47ff, 232; gossip-monger, 65, 89, 197; homes, 25, 32, 47ff, 59, 60, 138; imprisonment, 211; India posting, 16–18; intellect, 18, 48; letters, 179, 244, 251, 255; lifestyle, 21–3, 26, 47–9, 51, 168, 175, 180; litigation, 44–5; marriage, 28–30, 119; medical college, 13–14, 16; moral character, 138–9, 167, 213, 215, 216, 218, 224, 230, 232, 234–5, 249–51; osteopathic practice, 2, 13–14, 17ff, 25, 30, 32, 62, 129, 197, 231, ruin of, 175, 178, 180; patients, 2, 17, 19–21, 30, 62, 68, 209, 249; personality, 19, 21, 59, 252, 260; political intermediary, 77, 90–2, 105–6, 108–12, 126, 161, 182, 204; prostitutes, 15–16, 27, 29, 173; Russian visa, 69; sexuality, 14, 18, 27, 29, 59, 62, 100, 173–4, 231, group sex, 224; silencing operation, 164–80; social attitudes, 11–12, 13, 16, 26–7, 39; suicide, 244–5, 247; USA visit, 13–16; wax effigy, 260; women, attraction for, 13, 25–7, 30, 42
Ward, Susan, 247
Ward Trial (Old Bailey): committal proceedings, 214; defence witnesses,

Ward Trial (*cont'd*)
208–11, 230, 232, 233,
243; jurors, 214, 215, 216,
229, 246; justice under-
mined, 239–40; Keeler,
216–17, evidence, 218–19,
233, Gordon case, 237ff,
veracity, 226, 230,
238–40; moral outrage,
229, 232, 233; newspaper
contracts, 222, 230, 242,
260; 'political revenge',
243, 254; prejudicial, 213,
214–16, 228–9;
prosecution witnesses lie,
222, 225–6, 230–1, 233,
237–40, 242, 251–2, 256;
Rice-Davies, 80–1, 216,
217, evidence, 221–2,
230; transcript
suppressed, 251; verdict,
'public interest', 235,
246–7; Ward at, 171, 172,
212, bail, 215, 247,
charges, 1, 216, 246,
evidence, 229–31
Warner, Suzanne, 43
*Washington News*, 202

*Washington Post*, 8, 194
*Washington Star*, 8, 192
Weedman, Gerry, 84
Wells, Alfred, 126, 157–8,
204–5
Wesker, Arnold, 247
West, Nigel: *Matter of
Trust*, 76, 253
West, Rebecca, 224
West London Magistrate's
Court, 222, 225
*Westminster Confidential*,
145–6
Wharton, Bryan, 248
Wheatley, Jack, 242, 247,
252, 253
White, Gordon, 126
Wigg, George (Lord Wigg
of Dudley), 236, 237,
250, 258; army interests,
93–5; Profumo's
'betrayal', 95, exposé
dossier, 4, 5, 146–7, 151,
158, 161, 181, 182, 183,
196, parliamentary
questions, 152–3, 160,
184, report, 162, 164;
Ward, meeting, 161, 194

Wilcox, Desmond, 187–8
Wilson, Alexandra, 62
Wilson, Harold, 42, 146–7,
258; exchanges with
Macmillan, 181–3;
parliamentary attack,
194; Ward letters, 126,
161, 162, 179, 181
Wimpole Mews: Ward flat,
60, 133, 148, 216, 219,
222, 229, 230, 233, 234,
235, 252, 253; shooting
incident, 3, 120–1
Windmill Theatre chorus,
26
'Woods' (MI5 officer), 75–7,
87, 123, 127, 134, 141,
142–3, 253
Wraysbury, 53–5, 58, 60,
130
Wyndham, John, 142

'X, Miss', trial evidence,
218, 221

Zieger, John, 86, 128
Zulueta, Philip de, 48